SHARING
the TABLE
at GARLAND'S
LODGE

Recipes and recipe text by AMANDA STINE

General text by MARY GARLAND

PAULA JANSEN
Photography

CAROL HARALSON
Art direction, design, editing, and production

GARLAND'S LODGE
8067 North Highway 89A, Sedona, Arizona 86336
www.garlandslodge.com
info@garlandslodge.com
928.282.3343

ISBN 0-9773349-0-2

First printing 2005
Second printing 2006

Printed in Canada

TO BILL AND GEORGIANA GARLAND,
WITH GRATITUDE FOR THEIR EQUANIMITY,
WISDOM, AND LOVE

{ Contents }

The LODGE

TODDS LODGE
OAK CREEK CANYON, FLAGSTAFF ARIZ.

I t is said that a retrospective look at one's life sometimes reveals a marvelous design. Serendiptous encounters and events tie people and places together. Maybe it is the storyteller in us that perceives the pattern, the grand design that seems almost intended if not predestined. Garland's Lodge has such a story.

The first claimholder of the land now occupied by the Lodge arrived in the early 1900s, when the Homestead Act of 1862 was bringing many settlers to the West. He was nicknamed "Crookneck." He never built a homestead, but left his name behind; the property became known as Crookneck Flat. Flat fertile places were a rarity in the Canyon, and thus worth naming.

In 1908 Jesse J. Howard, son of the famous local hunter "Bear" Howard, took possession of Crookneck Flat and built the original log cabin that would later expand into our kitchen and dining room. The cabin was built with local stone and hand-hewn Ponderosas from the hills above the creek, so from its very beginning the Lodge

had a special relationship to the land. Howard lived in it until his death in 1923, when the place passed to a man named James Lamport, who would sell it a few years later to Frank and Catherine Todd.

The Todds had moved to Flagstaff from Colorado in 1924, their six-year-old son, Bill, in tow. Catherine Todd had tuberculosis, and they were seeking a place where she could heal. In those days there was no effective treatment for "the wasting disease," and many sufferers migrated to the Southwest in hopes of a natural cure. In Catherine's case, it seems to have worked. Bill Todd remembered his mother feeling instantly better and hiking to the top of Sunset Crater after only three weeks in the new climate.

While working at Arizona Lumber in Flagstaff, Frank Todd met Charles Isham, a local banker (and Georgiana Garland's father). Through Mr. Isham, Frank learned of a caretaking job at the old Howard place in Oak Creek Canyon. The Todds packed a picnic and drove their Model T down the one-lane road from Flagstaff to see the place,

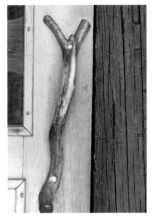

and Catherine fell in love. She persuaded her husband to take the job, and not long later the Todds bought the property. Charles Isham was a notary on the 1928 deed of sale.

The Todds lived in the original log cabin for ten years. They kept cows and chickens, farmed apples and peaches, and picked wild berries. Catherine raised chrysanthemums by the hundreds, which she sold to the Northern Arizona State Teacher's College. Bill Todd attended the Oak Creek grammar school at Slide Rock, in

Long before "vortexes" and "feng shui" became buzzwords in Sedona, the Todds' good instincts guided the layout of beautiful lawns and gardens surrounding their quaint cabins. Facing page, early black-and-white postcard of Todd's Lodge. At right, guests gather around the fire in the new Lodge dining room, added in 1943. (The date was confirmed by the discovery of a buffalo nickel embedded in the foundation.)

summer fly fishing for native trout (the daily limit was twenty-five!) When it was time to attend high school, he moved to a rooming house in Flagstaff, where he met Georgiana Isham and her brother, Phil.

In the early 30s, Jerome was the largest city in the state, its copper mines going gangbusters. Miners from Jerome who fished Oak Creek were always in need of a meal, and the Todd cabin became a friendly stop. Flagstaff natives including the Babbitts, Riordans, and Georgiana Isham and her parents were also regular guests at the Todd table, driving down the canyon for dinners that featured all the fried chicken you could eat plus apple pie or homegrown peaches with cream for dessert.

According to Georgiana, the Todds' friend Ray Babbitt suggested that they build him a little cabin because the drive home was just too long after eating all that food. It seemed a good idea. When Bill Todd graduated from high school, he took a year off and helped his dad build a few cabins with logs from Mexican Pocket at the top of the switchbacks.

And so Todd's Lodge began, opening at Easter and closing after Thanksgiving. Catherine Todd was in charge of the kitchen, and everything served to guests was grown on the premises. Cream and milk came from the family's Jersey cows. The old stone chicken shed housed an

Relics of Todd's Lodge now adorn the tool shed. At right, with customary thrift and ingenuity, the old restroom became employee lodging in the lower orchard when more modern amenities were added onto the Lodge in 1955.

estimated 3,000 hens over a year's time. Succulent dinners were prepared in cast-iron skillets on a pair of wood-fired stoves. Catherine's brother, John McIlwee, became the cook and gardener. F. A. (Frank) Todd, sometimes referred to as the Sage of Oak Creek, was a gracious host until he passed away in 1952.

Bill married Evelyn Murray, a talented pianist who taught for several years on the Navajo Indian Reservation before making her home in Oak Creek. Bill and Evelyn built a quaint knotty pine house in the upper orchard where they raised four daughters. Family was staff; occasional hired hands became family. It was a pattern that would continue throughout the Lodge's history. Cabins were added over time, two by two; a beautiful new dining room was constructed in 1943. Time-worn leather bound guest books bear testimony to decades of appreciative guests.

By the early 70s, the Todds' four daughters had grown up and married; Bill and his wife had parted ways. Catherine Todd and her brother were not so young as they'd been. When Bill's new friend Abe Miller made an offer on the Lodge, the Todds accepted. Abe could see the potential of the place, but he was at the time engaged in building a large, walled "village" of shops and galleries in Sedona called Tlaquepaque. It was an enormous endeavor and its planning and construction had become all-consuming. For a year Miller's pilot and his wife ran the place, but by 1972 Abe was thinking of selling the Lodge. And thus began the "Garland chapter."

Georgiana Isham Garland was raised in Flagstaff but remembers summers in Oak Creek Canyon near Pine Flats in a simple cabin lit by lanterns, with drinking water hauled from Oak Creek. After high school, she earned a teaching certificate from the University of Arizona and began teaching in Phoenix. She met Bill Garland at a boarding house there before she left with the Red Cross for India during World War II. Bill had moved to Phoenix from Seattle to learn the steel business but was also caught up in the war. While flying B-17s, he was shot down over Czechoslovakia and spent nine months in a German prison camp. In 1945, he returned to Phoenix to marry Georgiana.

The Garlands raised three children, Gary, Susan, and Dan, as Phoenix boomed around them and Bill's steel company flourished. Summers were

Bill and Georgiana Garland (far left and right) flank Mary and Phil Isham. On the bench are Gary and Susan Garland, Judy and Chuck Isham. Pine Flats, ca. 1951.

spent fishing, hiking, and swimming at the family's Pine Flats cabin in Oak Creek. As the kids were finishing college, Bill sold Garland Steel and began to explore other projects. In the summer of 1972, Susan Garland heard that Abe Miller was preparing to sell Todd's Lodge. In love with the Lodge and the idea of running it, she made a beeline to her dad with the news.

The family took on the project with gusto; everyone had a designated role. Bill, of course, provided business expertise. Georgiana, an excellent cook, lent recipes for pies, pancakes, and waffles still served today. Susan became head chef and vegetable gardener. Gary, a recent graduate of the University of Arizona School of Engineering, was slotted for construction and renovation projects. As Gary's new wife, I joined in as kitchen assistant and waitress. Dan Garland was to be the resident horticulturist. When he married Tricia, she was groomed to be bookkeeper. It was a very egalitarian endeavor. Everyone took turns doing various jobs, including the dishes and maid work.

Sedona was not the tourist mecca it is today. In 1972 its 2,500 inhabitants still frequented the Oak Creek Tavern for gossip and fun. The Oak Creek Owl, The Turtle, Silver Spruce, Grey Shadows, and a smaller version of Poco Diablo were the town's only restaurants. There was no stoplight at the Y, and 89A in West Sedona was a two-lane road through Grasshopper Flats. Biddles Nursery & Flower Shop housed the Montgomery Ward Catalog operation; other retail options included Yellow Front, The Village Dress Shop, and the Grasshopper Shopper. King's Ransom, Canyon Portal, and the Matterhorn were the main hotels. Newcomers Joanne Goldwater and Carol Steele had really stuck their necks out building the trendy La Pasada shops in West Sedona, as it was not at all clear that the west side of town would ever take off.

There were no guarantees that the Lodge would take off either. Business was slow in the beginning. Bill Garland laboriously wrote to everyone in the old Todd's Lodge guest books to let them know the place was open again, but reservations were patchy. Family members joined

Staff and family, 1970s. Standing left to right: Carol Putnam, Gary Garland, Amanda and Morgan Stine, Almond Sherbert, Debbie Lane, Scott Martin, Hope Geller, Michael Urciuoli. Seated: Patty Sperling, Lynn Anderson, Will Garland, Marianne Higbee, Ted and Mary Garland, Rainy Lautze, Nora Daley, and John Schaefer. At right, the first Garland's Lodge brochure, 1972.

The crew in 2005. Back row: Yesenia Torazon, Antonio Delgado, Jerry Dobrota, Pam Ing-Dobrota, Geoffrey Worssam, Mario Valeruz, Stabo (Steve Hosmer), Laura Garnica. Middle row: Pablo Delgado, Christopher, Oren and Akasha Lane, Denise Wright, Gary Garland, Amanda Stine, Mary and Ted Garland. Front row: Teela the dog, Donald Zealand, Forest Hunter, Bill Huber, Lindsey Riibe. At left, Mary Garland.

the guests in the dining room to pad the numbers, with Bill entertaining everyone with stories after dinner. Slowly but surely the word got around, and by the late 1970s annual reservations had become a coveted commodity.

In the fall of 1976, Bill and Georgie and newlyweds Dan and Tricia started Garland's Navajo Rugs, buying homes in "Sedona proper" shortly afterwards. That same year Susan took off for Paris to attend La Varenne cooking school. She returned to wow the guests with French cuisine, firmly establishing the Lodge's reputation for excellent food. In 1980 she married Alan Grodzinsky and moved to the Big Island of Hawaii.

On a lucky day in 1980, Gary and I met Amanda Neveau at the wedding of mutual friends. Amanda had always wanted to live in Sedona. When she was invited to become head chef at the Lodge, she left her catering job in Scottsdale and moved to Oak Creek in April, 1981.

Some years ago Amanda was hospitalized with life-threatening pneumonia. Without her as hub, the kitchen somehow wobbled along, but it was a

bent wheel. We missed her and we were acutely concerned for her. As she emerged from a three-week coma, I leaned toward her, listening for a request. Her words were emphatic. "Don't give my job away! It's what I love to do!" Amanda recovered and returned to the Lodge, to everyone's delight. Through the experience of those difficult months, we resolved to do what we had talked about off and on for so long—to honor her presence at the heart of the Lodge with this book.

Amanda and her marvleous food are woven inseparably into a pattern of people and events that began when a pioneer homesteader set up camp along Oak Creek—and continues today as Garland's Lodge. Crucial all along has been the reciprocal part of the pattern—our guests. The people who rock on the stone porches of our cabins and lift a glass at the candlelit tables of our dining room, making friends with the Canyon and with each other, and often becoming our enduring friends as well. For decades, new and returning guests have begged to know "the secrets of Amanda's kitchen." Well, here, at last, they are.

MARY GARLAND, 2005

ABOUT AMANDA

As so often happens, Amanda's love of good food began at home. Her mother, Ginger Renner, haled from Louisiana and New Mexico, passing on the savory comforts of Southern and Mexican cooking and a love of the West to her daughter. Ginger's lifelong involvement in the art world exposed Amanda to catered events and excellent cuisine. Amanda's first restaurant job was at Blackie's Fish Creek Inn, while a "ski bum" in Jackson Hole, Wyoming. A life-altering mountain-climbing accident in the Tetons brought her back to Scottsdale for a year of recuperation. Our paths crossed serendipitously at a local wedding in 1980; Amanda remembers telling Gary and Georgiana that she would like to work at the Lodge. The rest is history.

When she was invited to become chef, she left her catering job in Scottsdale and came to Sedona. Later that year she met Morgan Stine; they were married at the Lodge the following April. (Somehow she managed to cook for her own wedding and still make a radiant bride.) They have lived in the old Todd house in the upper orchard ever since, raising two children while Amanda honed her craft.

She is largely a self-taught "foodie." Countless cookbooks line the groaning shelves of her knotty

pine kitchen. Closets harbor orderly stacks of culinary magazines, through which she stays current while living in the country. Trends come and go; Amanda's cuisine has always reflected a love of simple cuisine made from excellent ingredients.

I learned from Amanda that it is possible to cook and be well-groomed, and that work areas could, in fact, *must*, remain clean and organized throughout the cooking process. In Amanda's kitchen there is a place for everything and everything is in its place. A stress-free restaurant is an oxymoron, but her focus and time management create that illusion—no small feat when trying to please fifty diners each night with a single menu! Guests depart each year marveling that the food was even better than the year before.

Amanda and her small kitchen staff are very "hands on." Days are full and don't leave a lot of time for documenting and imparting the details of each meal. Amanda has avoided the limelight all these years, keeping her focus on the task at hand rather than the "front of the house." So it is a special delight to see this book take form, as a celebration of Amanda and all her hard-won knowledge from twenty-five years in this kitchen. She has been an integral part of the success of the Lodge, for which we are deeply grateful.

Seasons

{ It's a blessing to have a life so in sync with the seasons. }

Most of March is dedicated to spit-shining the cabins, painting projects, the inevitable plumbing fixes, and coaxing old heaters back to life. A heads-down season, during which you can wear the same pair of Levis for days in a row, rationalizing that you're just going to get dirty anyway. Walls and floors are scrubbed and polished, mattresses flipped, curtains cleaned. The orchard is patiently pruned by hand while the trees are dormant. Sticks are stacked, then chipped into huge piles. Cleaning out the chicken coop provides a heady but handy source of nitrogen, the start of next season's compost.

Appointments with job applicants can be complicated when the creek is swollen with snowmelt and the only way across is a swaying footbridge. Interviews take place in a winter-chilled office. We assure our applicants that really, honestly, everything will be organized and beautiful in just a couple of weeks! It is an exercise in trust that quickly weeds out the faint of heart. The crew reassembles after the winter break with stories to share and reminiscences of faraway trips. Novices meet the returning staff at the preseason wine tasting. . . always a lively affair.

And then as promised, spring arrives and the beauty begins. Crocus and violets waste their talents long before guests arrive. Almonds, plums and cherry trees put on a scented show, strewing the lawns with a shower of delicate petals. A blazing yellow forsythia, an exquisite tulip magnolia, swathes of daffodils and tulips herald our first arrivals. Pink blossomed peach trees are soon upstaged by the apples, with early varieties leading the way. When the bloom is at its peak, orderly rows of trees resemble ballerinas festooned in white tulle.

All the while, daily high and low temps are monitored with fingers crossed that newly set fruit will not be frozen. The orchard crew, Rob, Robert, and Mario, watch for bees to pollinate the trees, applying garlic and fish oil sprays at the first appearance of thrip, which makes the orchard smell like a giant caesar salad. Rainfall is a special gift this time of year.

The first weekend guests are a hearty and flexible group—neither rain, nor sleet, nor snow daunts this bunch who return every year for our opening. On the occasional year that it is not glorious and warm, they happily don parkas and snow boots. This is a time for hot Banjo Bills (our house drink made with Garland's apple cider and spiced rum) around a roaring fire. Whatever the weather, these veterans are thrilled to be back,

SEASON'S GREETINGS
from
THE GARLANDS

Christmas Eve at
Garland's Oak Creek Lodge

to see one another, and to discover changes wrought by winter projects.

In the coming weeks, the front lawn greens up and the weather settles down. May is a time for beautiful hikes and bird watching as the trees sprout out in shades of chartreuse and lime. The shrill call of the black-tailed hawk announces his return, canyon wrens and hummingbirds rebuild exactly where they nested last year. The chatter of birds begins at 4 A.M., is raucous for almost an hour, then quiets down, an avian version of the morning news. One recent spring guest was thrilled to report sighting thirty different birds in thirty minutes! The days grow longer. Rows of tender seedlings are moved from the greenhouse out into the garden. Guests start to congregate around picnic tables for tea and cocktails.

In summer the Lodge is an oasis of green. Against a dense backdrop of native walnuts and elms, the flower garden pops. Peonies, columbine, and lilies are engulfed in a sea of white daisies. Kids cavort with the dogs, play croquet and Ping-Pong, while older folks relax with books on chaise lounges in the long shadows of towering fir trees.

Unique to this area and to the summer season is the annual return of the monsoons. Cool mornings give way to humid afternoons. Huge cumulus clouds build and darken. Gentle breezes become gusts of wind. A crack of thunder opens the sky and huge raindrops plop, here, then there, soon a drenching downpour that sends sunbathers scurrying with towels overhead, retreating to cabins for afternoon naps, safe and secure, hypnotized by the rain pelting on metal roofs overhead.

Fall is a kaleidoscope of changing light and color. The cooler air is crisp and clear, bringing new energy to harvest the apples and press the

cider. Tomatoes, peppers, squash, and basil abound in the garden. Anything not needed in the kitchen is sold at local farmer's markets or frozen for the winter ahead. Apples are dried, chilies are roasted, jams are jarred, and pesto puréed before the first frost. Clumps of magenta, gold, and rust chrysanthemums and marigolds mark the garden's last hurrah. Garden hoses are wound and stowed away. It is time to button things up and take a welcome rest. What a blessing to have a life so in sync with the seasons! —MG

Oak Creek

{ As you ford the narrow crossing, cool water streams past . . . }

Crossing the creek is the initiation into Garland's Lodge. Diverting off the highway, the driveway beckons the guests up the hill and around the bend, into an enchanted little place on this earth, a place of comfort and peace, where things stay mostly the same. Cell phones are put to rest; it's time to relax and revel in the Nature's sights, sounds and sensations.

Artesian springs all along Oak Creek make up the stream that meanders around huge boulders, forming trout ponds and swimming holes along the way. Crystal clear drinking water comes from our unfaltering Banjo Bill spring. Lawns and gardens and apple orchards draw their lifeblood from water diverted off the creek. A mile-long irrigation ditch, patched and repaired each spring, remains the key to this oasis in the high desert.

Water has always been the draw here. Native Yavapai Indians raised beans and squash on the banks of Oak Creek until General Crook's scouts relocated them to the nearby Rio Verde Reservation. In 1871, J. J. Thompson was the first white settler to "discover" the remnants of their gardens while hunting in Oak Creek and was the first of many homesteaders to make the Canyon his home.

These days it is tourists who come to explore. On hot summer days, picnickers flock to the shade and water and cooler temperatures of the canyon. Locals remind visitors to respect this pristine resource. Then after Labor Day, temperatures drop and the crowds thin out. Oak Creek becomes a collage of color under brilliant blue skies. Trails beckon hikers and photographers into side canyons where red maples hide. Giant yellow sycamore leaves and sprigs of sumac are treasures collected along the way.

In the off season, the creek belongs to us again. The only visitors at our crossing are a family of Mallard ducks and a few resolute fly fisherman in thick waders and wool caps. Intermittent snowstorms hush the Canyon. Icy waters turn milky and sea green.

When snowpacks thaw, washes run high and waterfalls cascade from the top of the sandstone cliffs. Sometimes the creek swells into a thunderous, brown torrent. We watch the water rise and know when we can cross and when we can't. Sometimes we do as we're told and just stay home. —MG

COOKING AT GARLAND'S

{ Tips and notes on tools & techniques }

Finally! After many, many years of saying "Well, we're workin' on it" and lots of patient support and encouragement, we've pulled many of the best recipes from the last thirty years of Lodge meals out of our heads and off our prep cards and collected them in this book. I believe that all of these recipes can be prepared easily by good home cooks and many are good for beginning cooks as well. We offer some suggestions within many of the recipes themselves about what to pair with what—which soups and salads, for example, nicely complement entrées and the appropriate sides. We've also included a small selection of menus that we serve throughout a season so you can take some ideas from there. Of course, many of you who have been our guests for years will already be familiar with these—we hope your favorites will be here!

Some basic tips to using the recipes in this book and a few notes about tools and such that we like in our kitchen:

Please read the recipe through completely before beginning your preparation.

All eggs are graded large.

All butter is unsalted.

All juices are freshly squeezed.

We use only pure vanilla, almond, lemon, orange and other flavoring extracts. These extracts plus orange flower water and rosewater are available at natural food grocery stores. They are worth the price.

We use extra virgin olive oil, pure olive oil, canola oil and pure walnut and hazelnut oils. We like olive oil for higher heat sautéing and extra virgin in dressings and seasoning where heat is not a factor. We use canola primarily for breakfast, and the flavorful nut oils in dressings.

The Lodge uses a specific bread flour from northern California in all its breads, but I tested the recipes for this book with "Better for Bread" by Gold Medal and King Arthur flour, both available nationally. Our all-purpose flour is called Red Rose unbleached, from Cortez Mills in Colorado, but any good quality unbleached flour will do. The King Arthur brands, from Vermont but sold more and more across the country, are of excellent quality and King Arthur is a great company to boot. The company is owned by its 200 employees.

Sugar is a vital ingredient in our kitchen. I say that because many, many of our recipes have at least a pinch of sugar. It's often the very touch that exactly finishes the sauce or dressing just the way it needs to be.

We use dry measures for dry ingredients, following the dip and sweep method. Brown sugar is always packed to the rim. We use liquid measuring cups for all liquids, syrups and honey.

A most important ingredient and a key to

achieving full flavor is good quality salt, and the second is fresh-cracked pepper. In fact, I think it's *the* most important in the kitchen. At home I have an assortment of salts that I like to use for different things, like basic kosher for general cooking, fine sea salt for baking, Maldon sea salt for steaks, chops and veggies before grilling, fleur de sel for finish seasoning. Our friends from the Hell's Backbone Grill in Boulder, Utah, turned us on to a local product called RealSalt, a beautiful pale pink salt that has become a favorite. It's available at most natural food stores. Please try some of the great salts available now.

Kosher salt is used in all the recipes that follow, except baked goods. I use kosher salt in all yeasted breads, but plain salt can be used in most other baked goods.

Remember to add salt bit by bit throughout the cooking process so the flavors will be fully layered and developed. Salt also acts on the food itself, breaking it down some to meld with other seasonings. If salt and pepper are added only at the end they just kind of sit on top and taste salty.

A few tools we love: Food processors, both standard sized and the mini. Cuisinart and Kitchen Aid are the standards. A hand-held immersion blender, also known as "the Joy Stick," which is a wonder for quick blend/purée jobs.

A standard blender. A hand-held mixer.

A stand mixer with paddle and dough hooks—really, it is the best thing for properly creaming ingredients, mixing heavy doughs and whipping egg whites. A hand-held mixer can be used instead, but not generally for bread.

A mandoline. We use one for all fine slicing and julienne. Models run from $40 to $150.

Microplane graters. These offshoots of the woodworking tool are great for quickly grating Parmesan, chocolate and citrus. We use a citrus stripper/zester, or a stick-type zester when long fine strips of zest are desired.

Spice grinders (really coffee grinders.) We have a few, one for sweet spices and one for hot spices and herbs. Of course, one for coffee, too.

A bench knife/scraper—use it for dividing and gathering dough, transferring prepped ingredients to your pan, and cleaning off your work surface.

Sheet pans (12- x 17- x 1-inch jelly roll pans), an essential. Parchment paper, to line your sheet pans.

Heavy weight stainless steel saucepans, sauté pans and stockpots. Heavy nonstick frying pans (8-inch and 10-inch) for eggs and omelets.

A large rectangular griddle with handles that fits across two burners, for an instant extra cooking space.

Small and large whisks.

Small and large heat resistant spatulas.

Wooden spoons, maple or other hard wood.

A citrus juicer.

One item that I use at home a lot is a cast iron skillet. I have two, a 10-inch and 12-inch, and find that they're just the best for quick-searing steaks, chops, chicken and fish. I've had mine a long time and have a good season on them but Lodge Cookware now makes them pre-seasoned. They are very reasonably priced, available everywhere, and, with care, will last a really long time.

All of these items are available in several price ranges and in many stores across the country. The catalogs that cram our mailboxes are also filled with them. It's likely that you already have most or all of this equipment, because the truth is we keep it pretty basic here.

We all really love what we do here, and we try to have a few laughs every day (often at ourselves). Have fun in the kitchen, keep your workspace clean and orderly, honor and respect the food you prepare and don't manipulate it too much; keep it simple and it will be delicious!

AMANDA STINE, 2005

BREAKFAST

Some say our breakfasts are "like mother used to make"... maybe Gary's mother, certainly not mine! According to Gary Garland, there is "not much to cooking breakfast other than technique. The critical elements are organization, the best fresh ingredients, everything made from scratch, and every plate cooked to order."

The food operation at the Lodge didn't go into full swing until the spring of '73. Prior to that, guests enjoyed a simple continental breakfast of coffee, juice and the finest Danish pastries that Flagstaff had to offer. That first snowy winter we ate communally in the Lodge, taking turns "practicing" cooking, expanding home recipes to feed a group. Breakfast menus included family favorites such as stewed prunes, lofty buttermilk pancakes, and pan-fried trout with corn fritters, now classics in our repertoire.

In the early days, we invented and named breakfast dishes for our neighbors. Tom Pendley would often wander up his irrigation ditch from Slide Rock to check out the new kids on the block, bum a smoke (Tom always hid his smokes in his back pocket before arriving) and a cup of coffee. Besides being tight with cigarettes, Tom never seemed to have the tool he needed. So each trip up the ditch he would ask to borrow this or that tool, which was never seen again. Every Christmas, Gary would go down and pay Tom a visit, bum a smoke back, and pick up the tools Tom had borrowed over the season.

Tom's comeuppance came one evening at the Oak Creek Tavern when Bill Todd saw Pendley's truck out front, a fresh pack of smokes on the dash. Apparently this "borrowing game" had gone on before our time. Bill snatched the pack and offered cigarettes to everyone in the Tavern. Pendley happily indulged in his old neighbor's generosity until somebody let it slip that these were his very own precious smokes being passed around. He stomped out of the bar, incensed, and didn't speak to anyone for months. In his honor we created "Eggs Pendley," poached eggs on English muffins, ladled with a cream sauce containing bits of ham, onions, green pepper, and mushrooms. A hearty country dish for a good ol' country boy.

{ everything made from scratch, and every plate cooked to order... }

Most often seen wandering the grounds in faded 501s and a gnarly sweatshirt, ruggedly handsome Gary is often mistaken for the handyman. Gary clearly prefers the "back of the house." Quiet and capable, strong and steady, Gary has been the bulwark and foundation of the Lodge in so many areas.

He is the father-figure, difficult to know, feared by some, but ultimately respected by all. He has quietly and thoughtfully guided the Lodge's unobtrusive and graceful growth. His numerous projects have been carefully chosen and impeccably executed. Gary's degree in civil engineering began a lifelong education in how things work and how things are made. He apprenticed at Garland's Steel under master welders, building steel water tanks in the hinterlands of Arizona. He has always had a rapport with and respect for hard workers and an appreciation of a job well done.

The guests positively swoon when Gary has time to spend a few minutes chatting. These "special occasions" usually occur around a plugged-up sink or a blaring smoke alarm. During infrequent spring floods, Gary is especially present, shuttling guests across the creek, with bags and gear loaded in the back of the Lodge Suburban. Veteran guests remark how great it was to finally meet Gary after all these years!

After observing several cooks attempt breakfast with very mixed results, he set his mind to mastering the technique and now prides himself on the many cooks he has trained.

at Garland's Lodge   27

Mary's Irish mother was of the generation that explored every new convenience in a box, from Swanson's fish sticks to Van De Camp's enchiladas. What her mom lacked in culinary skills, she more than made up for with her gift of gab and her curiosity about the people at her table. From her German dad Mary learned a strong work ethic, the value of a positive bottom line, and a belief that people are good.

A fortuitous friendship with Susan Garland in college resulted in a blind date with Susan's brother. And so it happened that Susan "set her up for life"! Smitten, Mary moved from San Francisco to Sedona in her red Ford Mustang in 1972, with all her belongings in tow. Various odd jobs in Sedona acquainted her with the town that would become her home. She and Gary were married just after the purchase of the Lodge and have lived there ever since.

A self-professed shy violet in the beginning, Mary emerged as the forward face of the Lodge, working evenings in the dining room while Gary cooked breakfast. . .ships passing in the night as they handed off the responsiblility of raising their two children. Out of necessity, Mary became the Lodge chameleon, filling in where the gaps in staffing emerged. Sometimes waitress, cook, or flower gardener, sometimes queen and sometimes worker bee. Lodge guests have called her "a magnolia with a steel back" and "the glue that holds the Lodge together."

Our other neighbor to the north, Tommy Anderson, got wind of this distinctive honor and asked why we didn't name a dish for him. Well, that was easy. Tommy was neat as a pin, with a shaved head, always dressed in a navy blue jumpsuit, one of those soft-hearted guys with a gruff exterior. So Eggs Anderson was devised: two soft-boiled eggs on a white plate.

Like Pendley's smokes, some of our favorite breakfast dishes were "borrowed" as well. . . Eggs Blackstone from Perry's Restaurant on Union Street in San Francisco, Mary's hangout before coming to Oak Creek. Huevos Borrachos from City Grille in Santa Monica. The basic granola recipe from Macy's Coffeehouse in Flagstaff. Our most recent delight is Jen's Black Powder Biscuits from Hell's Backbone Grill in Boulder, Utah.

Over the years we have seen many fad diets come and go. While at the Lodge, we ask our guests to put aside their "diet du jour," to relax and enjoy our classic recipes. Our food philosophy is simple. Eat fresh food of the best quality. Eat what you enjoy. And push your plate away when you have had enough.

Sour Cream Muffins

ONE DOZEN

Serving muffins with breakfast was an easy solution to limits of space and time in the morning. Muffins can be prepared ahead, spooned into tins, then cooked in batches and served "hot off the presses" in cloth-lined baskets by the wait staff. Our basic recipe is tried and true, yummy with homemade jams or honey.

2 + 1/2 cups all purpose unbleached flour

1 tablespoon baking powder

1/4 teaspoon salt

1/4 cup sugar

1 egg

1/4 cup canola oil

1 +1/2 cups sour cream

Preheat the oven to 400°. In a medium bowl, sift together the flour, salt, and baking powder and set aside. In another bowl, beat the egg and oil together. Stir in most of the sour cream.

Make a well in the dry ingredients and mix in the wet ingredients until the batter coheres. The consistency should be closer to that of biscuit dough than batter. Be careful not to overmix.

Fold in any additional ingredients gently. Spoon into muffin tins that have been sprayed well with vegetable oil. Bake 20 to 25 minutes or until golden brown.

Possible variations are endless—some of our favorites are given below. If you use dried fruit, soak it in warm water or orange juice for 15 to 20 minutes to plump. Drain well before adding to the muffin mixture.

MAPLE BRAN MUFFINS: Add 1/2 cup bran flakes and substitute 1/2 cup maple syrup for the sugar.

CORN MUFFINS: Add to the basic recipe 2/3 cup cornmeal, 1/3 cup frozen corn kernels, 1/3 cup sugar, 1/4 cup additional sour cream.

LEMON BLUEBERRY MUFFINS: Add 1 cup blueberries and 1 to 2 teaspoons grated lemon rind.

SOUR CREAM PEACH OR APRICOT MUFFINS: Add 1 cup chopped fresh or drained canned fruit, plus a dash of nutmeg if desired.

CRANBERRY MUFFINS: Add 1 cup dried cranberries (plumped in orange juice, then drained well), 1 teaspoon grated orange rind, and 1 cup chopped walnuts.

Festive Fruit with Flair

In addition to fresh juices, we always offer a couple of fruit options to precede the entrée. This list was compiled by Mitchell Foudray, a cheerful early riser with an artistic bent, who was the breakfast waiter and flower gardener for years. Use the freshest seasonal fruits, pay attention to color combinations, as well as flavor and texture, then add a pretty garnish. Mint and lemon balm grow wild here, so we use those, or edible flowers (wonderful too) . . . pansies, violets, johnny jump-ups, nasturtiums, marigolds, calendulas.

pineapple wedges, cored and sliced,
    tops trimmed and left on

raspberries, blueberries, strawberries,
    perhaps in combination with yogurt

cantalope and honeydew slices

honeydew and seedless red grapes

sliced strawberries and bananas with kiwi wedges

fresh pineapple chunks and kiwi

sliced pears and strawberries

garden ripe melon balls

casaba with kiwi or red seedless grapes

mixed melon with red grapefruit sections

mixed fruit compote of melon balls or chunks,
    pineapple, berries, red grapes

scored mango halves

raspberries, bananas, figs

red Bartlett pears and figs

Chunky Honey Applesauce (page 34)

Cider-Baked Apples (page 34)

Stewed Prunes

Who would have thought! One of those menu items that always gets a reaction, these prunes are so popular they are featured daily on the breakfast menu.

2 pounds pitted prunes

2 cups orange juice

1 cup tawny port

10 to 12 cinnamon sticks

2 oranges, washed, rind left on, sliced in half circles
    and seeded

Place all ingredients in a heavy stainless pot. Cover and bring to a boil. Stir gently! Simmer uncovered over low heat for 1 to 2 minutes.

Remove from heat and set aside to plump the prunes. Stir gently every 10 minutes or so until cool. The juices will thicken as they cool and form a nice glaze. Serve warm. Each serving should have 2 half slices of orange and a cinnamon stick for interest. Garnish with fresh mint for additional color.

Extra stewed prunes will keep for weeks in the refrigerator. Cool completely before refrigerating and reheat before serving as they are most flavorful when warm.

{ We've changed a lot of minds about prunes! }

Damson Plum Jam

This is our all-time favorite. Damson plums are small purple plums that grow wild in Oak Creek Canyon. They usually ripen in mid to late September. While not really good for eating off the tree, they make the most wonderful jam. It is a gorgeous deep purple color, and despite the sugar used, the jam is tart and fruity.

3 pounds plums, rinsed

1 cup water

Put plums in a heavy stockpot, adding enough water to keep the fruit from scorching. Bring to a boil over high heat, then immediately lower heat to simmer until the plums split and the fruit is tender, approximately 15 to 20 minutes. When cool, put the mixture through a food mill, which separates the fruit from the pits and skins. (We do this in huge batches, then refrigerate or freeze the puree until we have time to make the jam.)

From this point, follow standard jam recipes:

Either the traditional method:

4 cups purée

4 cups sugar

Cook, stirring constantly, until thickened.

Pour into sterilized jars.

Or:

4 + 1/2 cups purée

7 + 1/2 cups sugar

1/2 teaspoon butter to reduce foaming (optional)

1 pouch liquid Certo pectin

Follow the directions in the pectin package. Boil for one minute and pour into warm sterilized jars. Makes about 8 cups of jam. This method is quicker and very reliable.

THE CHOCOLATE ECLAIR GOT THE BEAR

The past seven years of drought have brought hungry black bears down from the mountains in search of food. Various peaceful strategies were tried, such as piling less than perfect fruit in the far reaches of the property for the taking. But one year a particularly aggressive bear insisted on more than his share, ripping branches off the peach trees and wreaking an intolerable level of havoc. Nora, the resident Akita, was on alert, insistently barking to warn the bear to stay off. Finally, our friend from the Game and Fish Department hauled a huge cylindrical trap up to the upper orchard, confessing that no one had ever caught a bear in this ungainly thing.

But in good faith the trap was set with trout innards and bacon grease. The first night passed, and then the second. This discerning bear would have nothing of it, continuing to feast on our precious peaches.

Finally we decided to up the ante, making a Hansel and Gretel-like trail of pancakes drizzled with maple syrup, then strategically placing a sample of the previous night's dessert right where a bear swipe might trip the trap door. And sure enough, the following morning we'd caught our prey! The chocolate eclair got the bear!

Cider-Baked Apples

You know it's fall when warm baked apples are on the breakfast menu. These are a great thing to prep the day before when you are having a group.

6 apples, preferably Romes, which have the perfect texture for baking
1/2 cup brown sugar
1 teaspoon cinnamon
1/2 teaspoon lemon rind
1/4 cup raisins (optional)
1/4 cup chopped walnuts (optional)
3 tablespoons butter
1 cup apple cider
1/2 cup water

Wash the apples and remove the core to within a half-inch of the bottom of each apple.

Mix the sugar, cinnamon, lemon rind, raisins, walnuts, and pack the mixture into the cavities in the apples. Dot the filled cores with butter. Put the apples in a baking dish.

Preheat the oven to 350°. Combine water and cider in a pan and bring to a boil. Pour into the baking dish. Cover the dish tightly with foil. Carefully place in the oven and bake 30 to 40 minutes, until just tender. Serve in individual bowls, spooning the pan juices over the apples.

Chunky Honey Applesauce

This is a favorite on crisp fall mornings. We like chunky applesauce served warm.

5 pounds apples (preferably a tart variety or mix of varieties—Jonathans, Granny Smiths, Pippins, or Winesaps), peeled and sliced
1 + 1/2 cup water or cider
3/4 cup sugar or honey
dash of lemon juice (optional)
dash of cinnamon to taste
dash of vanilla to taste

Combine apples, water and sugar in a heavy saucepan. Cover and bring to a boil. Reduce the heat and simmer until just tender. Mash a bit with a potato masher for a chunky texture. Add lemon, cinnamon, and vanilla, as desired.

Smoothies

Fruit smoothies are a good way to use leftover fruit. We stash unused fruit in gallon-size ziplock bags and freeze for later use. Thaw the fruit halfway; combine in the blender with a banana, apple cider, or other juices, and throw in a bit of yogurt for a creamier texture. Delish! Some of our favorites are strawberry and banana, and the tropical smoothie which combines mangoes, bananas, pinapple juice and unsweetened coconut milk. Avoid blending stringy fruit like pineapple, "skin-y" fruits like grapes, or too much melon. Bananas add a nice smooth texture. Experiment! You can't go wrong!

Garland's Granola

This recipe came to us from Stabo, our invaluable veteran assistant cook, who worked at Macy's Coffeehouse in Flagstaff. We substituted almond butter for their mixture of peanut butter and tahini, finding that too many people were allergic to peanuts and most tahini was too dominant in taste. We go through a lot of this granola, and consequently make it in huge batches. The recipe is easily reduced if you prefer, or make the whole batch and freeze for later use. Consider it for the Birkenstock types on your holiday list. Give it in a pretty quart jar with a big bow—and include the recipe, because this stuff is addicting!

14 cups Old-fashioned Quaker Oats
   (*not* quick cooking oats)

3 cups chopped mixed nuts (walnuts and
   slivered almonds, pecans optional)

1 cup sesame seeds

1 + 1/2 cups almond butter, or almond
   and peanut butter, mixed

2/3 cup honey

1 cup maple syrup

2/3 cup canola or vegetable oil

2 tablespoons vanilla

2 scant teaspoons cinnamon

1/2 teaspoon nutmeg

Preheat the oven to 300°.

Toast the oats in two 2- to 3-inch-deep baking pans for 30 minutes. Add the nuts and toast 30 minutes more. Stir occasionally and rotate the pans in the oven as the top pan will brown more quickly. The idea is to toast it all lightly and bring out the nutty flavors before adding the wet ingredients.

Whisk the nut butter, honey, syrup and oil together in a large saucepan. Heat until very hot and smooth, then add the vanilla, cinnamon, and nutmeg. Toss with the oat mixture. Toast at 300° for another half hour, turning the mixture every 10 to 15 minutes and rotating the pans as needed. The goal is to cook it slowly until it all is a deep golden brown. Cool. Break up any large chunks before sealing tight in plastic containers or glass jars.

GRANOLA PARFAIT: Layer Granola in a parfait glass with berries and yogurt. Very pretty. (Although many of our guests have granola or the parfait as an appetizer before their main course, Garland's Granola can be a perfectly hearty breakfast on its own, with the addition of milk or yogurt and fresh berries.)

GRANOLA WITH DRIED FRUIT: Add 3 to 4 cups raisins, dried cherries, cranberries, or other dried fruit to the toasted and cooled granola for a nice addition of texture and color.

{ Give it in a pretty quart jar with a big bow—
and include the recipe, because this stuff is addictive! }

French Toast with Garden Honey Rhubarb Sauce

FOR FOUR TO SIX

A Saturday morning favorite is French toast, using up some of our yummy breads. We soak thick slices for half an hour or so, which makes them "custardy" and delicious. Take care to cook slowly so the toasts cook all the way through.

8 eggs

1/2 teaspoon salt

2 cups buttermilk

1 tablespoon sugar

1/2 teaspoon vanilla

1/2 teaspoon cinnamon

12 thick slices of bread (3/4 to 1 inch), crusts left on,
    preferably homemade with a fine texture

Beat the eggs. Add the salt, buttermilk, vanilla, and cinnnamin. Soak the bread slices 5 minutes on each side. On a preheated griddle, brown the toasts on each side. Sprinkle with powdered sugar and serve immediately with Garden Honey Rhubarb Sauce or warm maple syrup.

Chunky Honey Applesauce (page 34) and a smattering of fresh berries are nice on the side.

Garden Honey Rhubarb Sauce

1 + 1/2 pounds fresh or frozen rhubarb,
    cut in 1/4-inch pieces

3/4 ounce fresh ginger root, peeled and grated,
    a knob about the size of your thumb

1/2 cup honey

3 tablespoons sugar

2 cinnamon sticks, broken in halves

1 cup Garland's apple cider

1/2 cup fresh orange juice

2 pints fresh strawberries, cut in half, then sliced

1 teaspoon vanilla extract

1/2 teaspoon kosher salt

In a medium saucepan, bring rhubarb, ginger, honey, cinnamon sticks, and juices to a boil. Reduce the heat and simmer uncovered, stirring occasionally until tender, approximately 10 to 15 minutes. Add the strawberries and simmer one minute, then add the vanilla extract.

This sauce can be prepared up to three days in advance and kept refrigerated. When warming, stir constantly. Freeze any extra for later use. It is delicious as a sauce for ice cream or with shortcake.

Georgie's Buttermilk Waffles

FOR FOUR TO SIX (MAKES SEVEN TO EIGHT SIX-INCH WAFFLES)

Stephen Benedict, a.k.a. "Benny," one of our breakfast cooks with a noteworthy appetite, invented one variation of Buttermilk Waffles, called the "Train Wreck Waffle," as a creative way to use up leftovers from breakfast. The essential ingredient was the waffle, of course, then just about anything and everything else that appealed—a pile of fruit, some bacon bits, yogurt or whipped cream. If you try it, let your imagination and not your conscience be your guide.

2 cups all purpose flour

1 tablespoon baking powder

1/2 teaspoon soda

1/4 teaspoon salt

3 tablespoon sugar

2 eggs separated, yolks and whites beaten separately

1/4 cup oil or melted butter

2 cups buttermilk, at room temperature

Combine flour, baking powder, soda, salt, and sugar, and set aside. In a separate bowl, whisk egg yolks until pale yellow. Add melted butter and buttermilk to yolks. In a third bowl, beat egg whites until they form soft peaks.

Add egg mixture to flour mixture, folding just to blend. Add beaten egg whites, folding gently by hand until just blended. Do not overmix.

Spray waffle iron with cooking spray. Ladle batter onto hot waffle irons. Remove from the iron when nicely browned. Trim edges. Garnish with berries (optional) and serve with warm maple syrup.

FRESH PUMPKIN AND CINNAMON WAFFLES WITH CHUNKY HONEY APPLESAUCE: Make the basic recipe, adding 3/4 cup canned or fresh pumpkin purée, 1 teaspoon cinnamon, 1 teaspoon ground dried ginger, and 1 teaspoon nutmeg to the batter. Serve with Chunky Honey Applesauce (page 34).

BANANA NUT WAFFLES: To the basic recipe add 2 bananas, cut into half-inch dice, plus 1/2 to 3/4 cup chopped pecans.

Georgie's Buttermilk Pancakes

FOR FOUR TO SIX

This recipe, along with those for waffles, pie crusts, and so many other great basics, came from Georgiana Garland's early days in Flagstaff.

2 cups all purpose flour

1 tablespoon baking powder

1/2 teaspoon soda

1/4 teaspoon salt

3 tablespoon sugar

2 eggs, lightly beaten

1/4 cup oil or melted butter

2 cups buttermilk, at room temperature

In a medium bowl, sift together flour, baking powder, soda, salt, and sugar. Set aside. In another medium bowl, blend the eggs, oil or butter, and buttermilk. Make a well in the dry ingredients (the flour mixture) and add the egg mixture, stirring gently until just blended. The batter should have a medium thick consistency to make nice lofty cakes.

Preheat the griddle over medium heat. Spray lightly with vegetable oil. Spoon batter in approximately 4- to 5-inch circles. When bubbles on the surface pop, turn the cakes. Adjust heat if too pale or too dark. When the bottoms are nicely browned, serve immediately.

BANANA-NUT PANCAKES: Add 1 diced banana and 1/2 cup chopped nuts (macadamias are festive) to the batter.

OATMEAL BUTTERMILK PANCAKES: Increase the buttermilk to 2 + 1/2 cups. Soak 1 cup Old Fashioned Quaker Oats in the buttermilk for 30 to 60 minutes before combining with the other wet ingredients. You may need a dash or two of extra buttermilk to get the right consistency.

PANCAKES WITH FRUIT: Fold into the basic batter 1 cup chopped apples, peaches, or blackberries plus 1 teaspoon lemon zest or a dash of vanilla extract. (Use individually frozen berries to keep their juice from bleeding into the batter.)

Oak Creek Trout with Corn Fritters

FOR SIX

Unusual to some, fresh trout for breakfast became a delicious custom at the Garlands' Pine Flats summer cabin when proud young fishermen and women brought home their early-morning catch. These have been such a hit at the Lodge that we offer them every other day as one of the entrees, always smiling pleasantly when the guests ask, "Did you catch these for us this morning?"

The recipe for these corn cakes came from Anne Howe Garland, Bill's mother. Alternately called "fritters" or "oysters," they were an easy and inexpensive staple during the Depression, and the grandkids loved them, no matter what they were called.

Food and Wine magazine sent a crew out in 1980 to do an article on the Lodge. The chef loved the "corn oysters" that accompanied the trout and asked for the recipe. Gary obliged. The chef replied, "Your forgot something. When do you add the oysters?"

1/4 cup canola oil

6 fresh trout, 8 to 10 ounces each, rinsed

2 cups yellow cornmeal

6 tablespoons butter, cut into pieces

pinch kosher salt

pinch black pepper, freshly ground

Preheat oven to 250°. In a large frying pan or griddle, bring 1/4 cup oil to temperature over medium heat. Roll the trout in cornmeal to cover the outside, then put one tablespoon of butter, plus a pinch of salt and pepper in the center of each trout. When the oil is hot, place trout in the pan. Cook covered, 8 to 10 minutes on each side, until the flesh is opaque.

Hold in warm oven until the fritters are done. Serve with Corn Fritters, lemon wedges, and maple syrup.

Corn Fritters, a.k.a. Corn "Oysters"

2 eggs

1 + 1/2 cups (1 can) creamed corn

1/2 cup buttermilk

2 + 1/2 cups saltine crackers crushed to a coarse meal

pinch black pepper

1/3 cup canola oil for frying

Combine all the ingredients except the oil in a medium bowl and stir until well mixed. The batter should be thick enough to hold its shape. If too thin, add a bit of flour.

In a 10-inch frying pan, heat oil over medium heat. Check the temperature—the batter should crackle when it touches the pan. Using a large tablespoon, drop dollops of batter onto the pan and let cook 5 minutes or so on each side, until dark golden brown and cooked through. Flip them often to make sure that they don't burn.

You can make the batter for these up to 4 hours in advance. Refrigerate it until you're ready to make fritters.

Canyon Scramble

FOR FOUR TO SIX

8 slices bacon, cooked well, drained,

    cut into half-inch pieces

1/2 cup chopped green onions

2 tablespoons butter

8 eggs, beaten

salt and pepper

2 to 3 tablespoons chopped parsley

4 ounces cream cheese, cut into quarter-inch squares

    (dip your knife in hot water between each cut

    to eliminate sticking)

Place bacon, green onions, and butter in a large nonstick pan over medium heat. Stir with a wooden spatula until the butter is bubbly (but not brown) and the onions and bacon are heated through. Add the eggs, salt, pepper, parsley, and cream cheese.

Push the mixture to the center as it cooks, letting the uncooked eggs flow to the outside of the pan. Cook to taste very slowly (slow cooking creates large soft curds of scrambled egg). Transfer to a warm plate and serve immediately.

On cooking bacon for a group: Lay good quality bacon slices on a parchment-lined baking sheet. Preheat the oven to 350°. Bake for 30 to 40 minutes, or until evenly browned and crisp. Remove and drain on paper towels. Keep warm until ready to serve.

OAK CREEK SCRAMBLE: Instead of the bacon, add 1 cup smoked trout, carefully deboned, or 1 cup smoked salmon.

SOUTHWEST SCRAMBLE: Add 1/2 cup diced green chiles (such as Anaheims), 1/3 cup Cotija cheese, 1/3 cup chopped green onions, and 2 to 3 tablespoons of cilantro in place of the parsley.

THE BREAKFAST PANTRY

Tomatillo Sauce

Like Roasted Red Chile Sauce, this is a great sauce to have on hand. Make a big batch and freeze for later use. Wonderful as the base for chilaquiles, great on breakfast enchiladas as well. This recipe came from Sylvia and Yesi, two lovely Hispanic women who take care of our cabins.

2 pounds tomatillos, husked and stemmed,
    washed and cut in half

4 cloves garlic, peeled and chopped

2 jalapeños, stemmed and seeded

1 medium onion, chopped

2 small poblanos, seeded

1 teaspoon salt, or to taste

1/2 cup lightly packed chopped fresh cilantro

olive oil

Preheat the oven to 400°. Spread the tomatillo halves, garlic, jalapeños, poblanos, and onion on an oiled pan. Brush the veggies with olive oil and sprinkle with salt.

Roast in the oven 15 to 20 minutes until the edges are browned. Purée with the cilantro in a food processor or blender. Adjust salt to taste.

Roasted Red Chile Sauce

Roasting the vegetables concentrates moisture in the tomatoes, brings out the natural sugars of all the veggies, and deepens flavors. It also facilitates removal of tough chile skins, which can be bitter.

10 to 12 Roma tomatoes, cut in half
    (about 2 + 1/2 pounds)

6 cloves garlic, peeled and roughly chopped

1 medium yellow onion, peeled and quartered

1 red bell pepper, quartered, stemmed and seeded

1 to 2 jalapeños, stemmed and seeded

1 teaspoon kosher salt, or to taste

1 canned chipotle chile with a tablespoon of the adobo
    sauce (canned chiles in adobo are available in the
    Hispanic section of many groceries)

1/2 cup chopped fresh cilantro

Preheat the oven to 400°. Spread the tomato halves, garlic, onion, pepper, and jalapeños on an oiled sheet pan. Sprinkle with salt. Roast in the oven until the veggies begin to blacken on the edges, about 20 to 25 minutes. Turn as needed. Purée in the blender with the chipotle and cilantro until smooth.

This sauce can be prepared up to 3 days in advance, puréeing all ingredients except cilantro. Purée with cilantro just before using.

Guacamole

FOR FOUR TO SIX (TWO CUPS)

3 large ripe avocados

2 to 3 tablespoons chopped fresh cilantro leaves

1/2 cup diced red onion

2 jalapeños, stemmed, seeded and minced

2 tablespoons freshly squeezed lime juice, to taste

1 teaspoon salt, to taste

> Cut the avocados in quarters; remove the pits and skins. Mash with a fork or potato masher to a chunky texture. Add the other ingredients. Adjust the seasonings.

Salsa Fresca

FOR FOUR TO SIX (FOUR CUPS)

We make this good basic salsa in large quantity. It holds well and is a nice complement to Southwesten egg dishes.

2 tablespoons finely diced white onion

2 tablespoons finely diced red onion

8 Roma tomatoes, chopped evenly into half-inch dice

3 jalapeños, stemmed and seeded, finely diced

(about 1/4 cup)

2 to 3 tablespoons fresh cilantro leaves

1 teaspoon salt, to taste

1 to 2 tablespoons fresh lime juice, to taste

pinch of sugar (optional)

> Combine all the ingredients in a medium bowl. Add sugar if needed to balance the acidity.

> The salsa keeps 3 days in the refrigerator in a non-reactive container.

Hash Browns

We serve hash-browned potatoes with most of our egg dishes. They are crisp, lightly seasoned, and irresistible. The potatoes are boiled until they are not quite cooked through. A fork should penetrate the potato without any crunchy feel. They should be allowed to cool completely (best if refrigerated overnight), then peeled, grated, and tossed with salt and pepper and chopped green onions.

A thoroughly heated grill or skillet is critical. Heat canola oil until hot but not smoking. Drop handfuls of the potato mixture into the skillet and cook just enough to create a nice brown crust. Flip when medium brown and finish the other side. Serve immediately.

4 large baking potatoes, cooked until slightly
   underdone, thoroughly cooled, then grated

1 teaspoon kosher salt

1 + 1/2 teaspoons freshly cracked black pepper

1/4 chopped green onions

1/4 cup canola oil

Black Beans

These beans are integral to Huevos Rancheros and are a great side dish for any Southwestern breakfast.

8 cups water

2 cups dried black beans, rinsed well

1 large yellow onion, diced

3 garlic cloves, minced

1 tablespoon chile powder

1 tablespoon whole cumin seeds

1 tablespoon kosher salt

In a large saucepan, combine all ingredients except salt.

Over high heat, bring to a boil, then reduce to low, cover and let simmer for two and a half to three hours, stirring regularly and checking the water level. Add half the salt just as beans are beginning to soften. Cook until tender. Pour off excess water if needed. Taste and add more salt as needed.

Eggs Florentine

A delicious dish and relatively simple once all the components are prepared: poached eggs served on spinach, ham, and English muffins, with Mornay Sauce. For a veggie option, add some sautéed mushrooms to the spinach and skip the ham.

1/4 cup chopped onion

2 cloves garlic (optional)

1/4 cup olive oil

2 pounds baby spinach, well washed and dried
    (a salad spinner works well for drying)

kosher salt

pepper to taste

FOR THE MORNAY SAUCE

4 tablespoons butter

3 to 4 tablespoons flour

1/4 cup chopped onion

2 cups milk

1/4 cup Parmesan cheese, grated

1/4 cup Gruyère cheese, grated

salt

white pepper

nutmeg (optional)

1/4 cup chopped chives

TO FINISH THE DISH

12 eggs

12 slices ham

6 English muffins, split

4 tablespoons butter

In a heavy skillet, sauté onion and garlic in olive oil just to soften. Add the spinach and cook until barely wilted and still bright green. If you have to hold the spinach for a while, blanch first, rinse in cold water, and drain (in order to hold the color) before adding to the sautéed veggies. Add salt and pepper to taste. Set aside.

Make the sauce. In a heavy saucepan (or, preferably, a double boiler), melt the butter over low heat. Sauté the chopped onion until softened. Whisk in the flour and cook for 3 to 4 minutes, stirring constantly. Slowly whisk in the milk. Stir until thickened, then strain the sauce. You can continue with the sauce or set it aside at this point. When you are ready to use the sauce, reheat it. When it is hot, whisk in the cheese, salt, white pepper, and nutmeg to taste. Thin with a bit more milk if needed.

Poach the eggs. Fill a deep sauté pan with water, add the tablespoonful of vinegar, and bring to a simmer. Crack the eggs into the water. Hesitating for just a moment as you release the cracked egg into the water will help the egg white coagulate and the egg retain its form. Simmer 4 to 5 minutes until the white is firm and the yolk is still soft. Remove eggs with a slotted spoon and place on a warm plate for a moment or two until ready to assemble the dish. Practice! This is a skill worth learning.

Grill the ham.

Assemble on warm plates: toasted muffins with a dab of butter, grilled ham, sautéed spinach, then the eggs, and the whole thing topped with a spoonful of sauce. Garnish with chopped chives.

Eggs Blackstone

FOR SIX

We first ran across this variation of Eggs Benedict—kind of a breakfast BLT—at Perry's on Union Street in San Francisco. We thought it was named for some illustrious local character and that we were being sneaky stealing the recipe, only to come home and find it in *The Joy of Cooking!* Still no idea who eggs Blackstone and Benedict are named for. In the meantime, ignorance is bliss.

10 slices bacon, cut into half-inch pieces,
   sautéed and drained

12 large rounds of beefsteak tomato,
   sliced half-inch thick

12 eggs

3 tablespoons butter

salt and pepper

2 tablespoons finely chopped fresh chives

Blender Hollandaise

Cook the bacon, drain, and set aside. Toast the English muffins. Top with dabs of butter. Grill the tomato slices, sprinkle with salt and pepper, set aside. Poach the eggs. Fill a deep sauté pan with water, add the tablespoonful of vinegar, and bring to a simmer. Crack the eggs into the water. Hesitating for just a moment as you release the cracked egg into the water will help the egg white coagulate and the egg retain its form. Simmer 4 to 5 minutes until the white is firm and the yolk is still soft. Remove eggs with a slotted spoon. Quickly assemble the components on warm plates: muffin, bacon, tomato slice, poached egg, Hollandaise, pinch of chives.

Blender Hollandaise

We make Blender Hollandaise that waits patiently till you are ready for it, is easily thinned, and coats the eggs nicely.

3 egg yolks

1 tablespoon freshly squeezed lemon juice

1/4 pound butter, melted, bubbly hot, but not browned

very small amount of hot sauce (if you like a little
   spice in your life)

Whip the egg yolk and lemon juice in a blender for a few seconds. Remove the blender jar from its base and place it, still filled with the mixture, in a pan of very hot water for 10 to 15 minutes.

Return the blender jar to its base and add the hot melted butter. Whirl until the Hollandaise begins to thicken. Return the blender jar to the hot water bath to keep it warm until you are ready to serve. Thin the sauce with a bit of very warm water if it gets too thick.

Eggs Benedict with Blender Hollandaise

This dish is a bit old hat but remains a favorite on Sunday mornings. Prep is critical here; have all your ingredients at hand when you begin.

1 tablespoon white vinegar

12 eggs

12 thin slices ham or Canadian bacon

6 English muffins, split and toasted

3 tablespoons butter

Blender Hollandaise (page 49)

2 tablespoons finely chopped fresh chives

Fill a deep sauté pan with water, add the tablespoonful of vinegar, and bring to a simmer. Crack the eggs into the water. Hesitating for just a moment as you release the cracked egg into the water will help the egg white coagulate and the egg retain its form. Simmer 4 to 5 minutes until the white is firm and the yolk is still soft. Remove eggs with a slotted spoon and place on a warm plate for a moment or two until ready to assemble the dish.

Grill ham until heated through.

Place two toasted muffins halves on each warm plate, with a dab of butter on each. Lay a hot grilled slice of ham on top, then gently transfer the drained eggs on top. Spoon a big tablespoon of Hollandaise Sauce on top of each egg. Sprinkle with chives and serve immediately.

Swiss Baked Eggs

FOR SIX

3 cups grated Swiss or Gruyère Cheese

3/4 cup heavy cream

12 eggs

2 tablespoons chopped chives

1 teaspoon salt

1 teaspoon white pepper

1/2 teaspoon nutmeg (optional)

12 English muffin halves, toasted

12 slices ham or Canadian bacon

Spray 6 individual baking dishes or ramekins with cooking spray. Line each dish with 1/4 cup of the grated cheese. Make circular wells in the cheese. Carefully crack and place one egg in each well. Place a tablespoon of cream over each yolk. Sprinkle one teaspoon chives over each dish, along with a pinch of salt, white pepper, and nutmeg. Finish with a sprinkle of the remaining cheese. Place a small dab of butter on top of each yolk. Bake at 350° until just set, approximately 10 minutes. Meanwhile toast the English muffins. Lightly fry the ham or Canadian bacon.

Place 2 English muffins halves on each warm plate, with warm ham on top. When the cheese is just melted and the eggs begin to set, remove from the oven. Loosen the the sides of the mixture from the ramekins. Slide the eggs onto the muffins and ham. Serve immediately.

CHEDDAR BAKED EGGS: Substitute 1 + 1/2 cups sharp Cheddar and 1 + 1/2 cups mild Cheddar for the Swiss cheese. Whisk 2 tablespoons Dijon mustard into the heavy cream before spooning over the yolks. Delete the nutmeg.

Huevos Rancheros

1/4 cup olive oil

1 +1/2 cups sliced yellow onion

1 teaspoon chile powder

1 +1/2 cups sliced yellow bell pepper

1 +1/2 cups sliced red bell pepper

1 +1/2 cups poblano or Anaheim chiles,
    seeded and cut in strips

12 yellow corn tortillas, sautéed in a bit of canola oil,
    covered and kept warm

butter for cooking eggs

8 to12 eggs, cooked sunny side up or scrambled

1 + 1/2 cups Roasted Red Chile Sauce (page 44)

1 cup grated mild white Cheddar or Cotija

Black Beans (page 46)

In a large sauté pan, heat the olive oil until smoking and add onions and chili powder, stirring constantly until wilted. Add peppers and salt with heat still on high, stirring constantly until they start to soften, approximately 8 to 10 minutes. Set aside to keep warm. Put warmed tortillas in the center of the plate and place two sunny side up or scrambled eggs on top.

Surround the eggs alternately with pepper mixture and black beans. Spoon a bit of sauce over the eggs and pepper mixture, then sprinkle with cheese and put in oven or under the broiler until melted. Serve immediately. Hot plates!

Great served with additional warm tortillas, fresh salsa and/or guacamole.

Breakfast Chilaquiles

Chilaquiles made with shredded poached chicken are a classic supper dish. For this breakfast version, we omitted the chicken. We like to serve tasty chilaquiles (chee-lah-kee-lays) with Southwest Scramble (page 43) and Black Beans (page 46).

8 to 10 corn tortillas (day old are best),
    cut or torn into strips

1/4 cup canola oil

2 cups Tomatillo Sauce (page 44)

2 tablespoons crema or sour cream

2 tablespoons butter

1/2 cup diced roasted green chiles

1/3 cup chopped green onions

8 eggs, beaten

1/3 cup Cotija cheese

2 to 3 tablespoons chopped fresh cilantro

Sauté the tortillas until crisp. Set aside to drain.

Add the Tomatillo Sauce to the skillet, then the crema or sour cream. Return the tortillas to the sauce, cooking until softened.

Heat the butter. Sauté green chiles and green onions. Add the eggs. Cook until tender and fluffy (cook eggs slowly for large soft curds).

Divide the tortillas and sauce among warm plates, the top with the eggs. Garnish with Cotija and fresh cilantro.

Breakfast Enchiladas

We use Roasted Red Chile Sauce for this dish too. It is very versatile. The mellower Tomatillo Sauce is delicious as well. Better yet, both!

8 to 12 corn tortillas

1 cup canola oil

2 tablespoons butter

1/2 cup diced roasted green chiles

1/3 cup chopped green onions

2 to 3 tablespoons chopped fresh cilantro

8 to 12 eggs

1/3 cup Cotija cheese

salt and pepper to taste

Tomatillo Sauce or Roasted Red Chile Sauce (page 44)

    or both

sour cream, chopped green onions

    and cilantro for garnish

Heat the oil in a small sauté pan. When the oil is hot, dip the tortillas one at a time to soften. Drain on paper towels and keep warm.

Melt the butter in a large non-stick pan over medium heat. Add the chiles and onions and sauté until heated through.

Add the eggs, salt, pepper, cilantro and Cotija. Push the mixture to the center as it cooks, letting the uncooked eggs flow to the outside of the pan. Cook to desired doneness very slowly (slow cooking creates large soft curds of scrambled egg).

Fill each tortilla with a portion of the cooked eggs and roll to close. Ladle Roasted Red Chile Sauce or Tomatillo Sauce (or both) over the enchiladas. Garnish with a dollop of sour cream, chopped green onions, and a bit of cilantro.

Guacamole and Salsa Fresca (page 45) are nice accompaniments for the Breakfast Enchiladas.

Huevos Borrachos

The name of this dish means "Drunken Eggs." The basis for this recipe is the Roasted Red Chile Sauce, which is blended to a fine purée, then thinned to make the poaching liquid for the eggs. It is yummy.

8 eggs

2 to 3 tablespoons olive oil

3 cups Roasted Red Chile Sauce (page 44), puréed

3 cups chicken broth

12 corn tortillas, sautéed in a bit of canola oil,

    covered and kept warm

1 cup yellow Cheddar or Cotija cheese

1/2 sour cream, for garnish

chopped green onions for garnish

In a deep large frying pan, heat the oil. Add the puréed Roasted Red Chile Sauce and the chicken broth, mix well, and bring to a simmer. Crack the eggs into the simmering liquid and cook 4 to 5 minutes, basting the eggs occasionally with the hot broth. Remove the eggs and set aside for a moment.

Place 2 tortillas in each ramekin or soup bowl. Put one or two eggs on top. Spoon some sauce over. Sprinkle with cheese and finish under the broiler. Garnish with a dollop of sour cream and chopped green onions.

Garland's Garden Frittata

FOR FOUR

At the Lodge, we make individual frittatas to order, using two or three eggs and an 8-inch non-stick pan. To serve four to six, use a 10-inch pan. A frittata and a fresh green salad can be perfect for a simple dinner as well.

2 tablespoons olive oil

1/3 cup chopped red onion

2 cloves garlic, minced

1/3 cup sweet red peppers, thinly sliced

1/3 cup sweet yellow peppers, thinly sliced

1/3 cup tomatoes, peeled, seeded, and chopped

salt and pepper to taste

1 tablespoon finely chopped fresh basil

1 tablespoon finely chopped fresh parsley

2 tablespoons olive oil

8 eggs, beaten together lightly

1/2 cup feta or goat cheese, crumbled

1/4 cup Parmesan cheese, grated

Preheat the oven to 350°.

Heat olive oil in a 10-inch non-stick pan. Sauté veggies until slightly softened (about one minute). Season with salt and pepper and add basil and half the parsley. Drain the vegetables and add to the beaten eggs. Wipe out the pan, add olive oil. Heat over a hot flame. When the oil is very hot, add your egg and veggie mixture.

Sprinkle the cheese over the surface. Move the egg mixture to the middle with a spatula, allowing the uncooked egg to move to the outside of the pan.

When the frittata is starting to firm up, and the bottom is light brown, flip the frittata, and either finish in a moderate oven (350°) for 3 to 4 minutes, or turn the heat *very* low, and cook until the bottom is also light brown (3 to 4 minutes). Transfer to a warm plate and garnish with the remaining chopped parsley.

Frittata combinations are endless. Some of our favorites include Mushroom, Gruyère, and Sweet Onion; Tomato, Basil and Red Onion; Fresh Garlic-Sautéed Spinach and Feta Cheese; Yukon Gold Potato, Onion, and Cheddar; Broccoli, Bacon and Cheddar; and Asparagus Tips, Goat Cheese, and Dill.

Blue Corn Piñon Cakes

1 + 1/2 cups all purpose flour

1/2 cup blue cornmeal

1 tablespoon baking powder

1/2 teaspoon soda

1/4 teaspoon salt

3 tablespoons sugar

2 cups buttermilk

1/4 cup canola oil or melted butter

2 eggs, separated, yolks and whites beaten separately

2/3 cup pine nuts (piñon nuts), toasted at 325° for 8 minutes (careful not to burn)

Place flour, cornmeal, baking powder, soda, salt, and sugar in a large bowl and whisk to blend. In a separate bowl combine oil or butter, buttermilk, and beaten egg yolks. Stir into the flour mixture just to mix. In a third bowl, beat egg whites until stiff, then fold into the batter gently but thoroughly. Add nuts.

Heat the griddle thoroughly. Ladle batter onto the griddle for each cake. Cook until small steam holes begin to appear in the surface of the cakes, then flip to cook the other side. Serve immediately, with warm maple syrup.

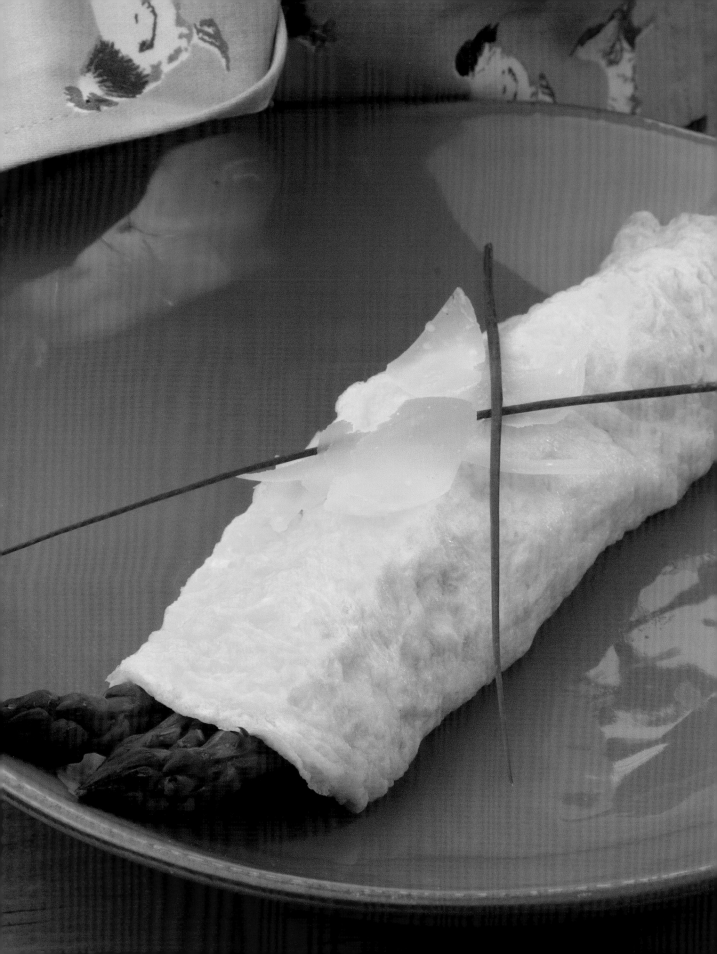

Omelettes

Gary's favorite was a roasted green chile and sour cream omelette, so it showed up on the menu a lot, and thus became "a Garland classic." We roast our chiles in advance, usually red and green Anaheims, sometimes mixing in some poblanos, which are a bit hotter. Roast close to the flame until the skins are evenly blackend. Set aside to cool before removing skin, ribs, and seeds, then slice lenghwise into strips. If fresh chiles are not available, canned whole chiles can be similarly roasted to bring out their flavor. Since they are already skinned, take care not to blacken them.

We like our omelettes fluffy and just cooked through, no brown edges or crusts. Technique is the critical element. Beat the eggs lightly, pour over two tablespoons of hot, but not browned, melted butter in a non-stick pan. Move the cooked egg at the edges to the center of the pan, working counterclockwise. When most of the egg is congealed and almost cooked, flip the omelette to finish the raw side, top with filling, and roll onto a warm plate.

A heavy non-stick pan is critical, and the proportion of eggs to the size of the pan will definitely effect the outcome—usually two or three eggs to an eight-inch pan is about right.

1 to 2 tablespoons butter, melted

3 eggs, beaten lightly

2 roasted chiles, skin, ribs and seeds removed

2 tablespoons sour cream, preferably room temperature

1 teaspoon chopped chives, for garnish

Serve with hash browns or black beans and salsa fresca.

VARIATIONS Omelettes are a cook's playground. Let inspiration guide. Some of our favorites:

~ Spinach, Bacon, and Gruyère

~ Asparagus and Shaved Parmesan

~ Mushroom, Ham, and Swiss

~ Avocado, Bacon, and Cheddar

Adventures in Animal Husbandry

{ No need to bring pets, we've got 'em }

Susan Garland was laid up after foot surgery in the summer of 1971, and whiled away her time reading *Mother Earth News* and *Organic Gardening* magazines.   It turned out to be time well spent when the following summer the Garland family purchased Todd's Lodge. Susan cared for, even to the extent of naming, each of the original batch of chickens. A trip to the county fair that fall brought home Izzy the goat. Mary loaded her into the Jeep Wagoneer to be bred at the Goat Lady's in Cornville. Mary, an ingenue in agrarian ways, was mystified as to how anyone could tell when the girl goat was "ready" for breeding and so relied on the Goat Lady's assurance that the deal was secure.

The ride home proved disastrous for the out-going mail, which was devoured by the goat while Mary dashed in for groceries at the Grasshopper Shopper. But Geoffrey was born five months later, testimony to the Goat Lady's expertise. Geoffrey proved to be as obstinate as his mother has been docile and sweet, climbing in and defoliating the apple trees—the end of the goat phase.

Later experiments included a rabbit in a moveable bottomless cage whose task was to nibble the weeds as his cage was moved down the garden rows. But Mr. Rabbit somehow escaped, leading an undoubtedly short but independent and happy life.

The "moveable feast" concept was tried again with sheep, corralled in a light-weight pen which could be moved periodically between apple trees, saving us the trouble of mowing. Alas, Mario's little lambs were mightier than the stick fence, and the havoc they wrought quickly put an end to that "labor saving" trial.

Lodge staffers Mari Pattison and Rainy Lautze thought raising pigs would be just the ticket for wet garbage reduction and a little cash for the long winter vacation. Affectionate and creative names were assigned to our snouted friends—Ham, Bacon, and Sausage, Ted and Willie, Mary and Gary (a bit of passive aggression?). Rainy and Mari humanely released the pigs for regular romps around the orchard, whistling to round them up. Every now and then they'd roam a bit farther afield and trot up to the front lawn. One day we got a call from the Department of Public Safety saying two large pigs had been sighted on Highway 89A right outside our entrance. Panic ensued. I cluelessly headed out in Gary's and my Volkswagon bus only to realize that a posse of pig wranglers would be required to herd them back into their pens.

Disposing of the porcines ourselves was out of the question, so the annual slaughter was jobbed out every fall. Even listening to them squeal as they were carted away in the butcher's truck was excruciating, further entrenching the resolve of the vegetarians on premise. Eau de pig became significant in the lower orchard, though any respectable pig farmer will tell you that pigs are brighter than dogs and really will keep a clean pen, if given the chance. We must not have provided the right setting, as the rank odors soon ruined the ambiance of the snazzy new clay tennis court. The bloom was off the proverbial rose, and the pig era went the way of that of the goats and the sheep.

Clucking chickens and crowing roosters in the old rock coop are and have always been a fixture at the Lodge, delighting suburban children and grownups alike. In Todd's Lodge times, they produced eggs, and ultimately ended up plucked and succulently fried in cast iron skillets, served with mounds of mashed potatoes and gravy, at communal tables for the "Who's Who of Flagstaff." Desserts made with home-grown fruit were served with cream from the family cows. These simple meals evoked reverie, even poetry, from loyal guests returning season after season.

There is one four-legged creature whose tenure at the Lodge has been completely successful yet who does not lay eggs or give milk. That would be any one of the succession of lucky canines who have lived here. Just think of it . . . endless green grass, fawning guests, doting children. Guests, forbidden to bring their animals, adopt ours, and sometimes invite them in, even stooping so low as to bribe them with treats. Most returning guests politely ask about the Garland family and staff when they arrive. Returning children, not bound by such formalities, get right to the point: Where and how are the dogs? Especially Rosie, a 14-year resident Keeshond and friend to many of our guests. Rosie loved to eat and would often convince guests that she hadn't been fed for days. As a result, we had to fit her with a little sign saying "Please do not feed me"!

Felines were also a fixture at the Lodge before the arrival of our Akita, Nora, the cat terrorist. Kitty Pudy and Geoffrey had some lovely years here, cultivating the guests like nobody's business. Whenever they wanted some attention, they would paw (bang) the screen doors of the cabins, until some soft-hearted soul invited them in for a visit.

When Nora came and put an end to Cat Nirvana, they simply migrated up the canyon to the neighboring resort, Junipine. Patient office staff there would call to report their guests' complaints about pesky critters banging their screen doors. So up we would drive to retrieve our pets, with cookies or muffins to make amends.

Even spring floods did not deter them. We would bring them "home" over the raging creek, only to find that they had swum upstream yet again to escape canine harassment and cultivate the neighboring clientele. Garland's guests who missed them would go up to the Junipine office and "borrow them" for the week-end. After Sunday morning breakfast, the cats checked out along with the guests, and headed back up the canyon to their new home. I am not really sure when it happened. There was no formal transfer of ownership, but somehow those wily cats wheedled their way into our neighbors' hearts. Soon they were living in the lap of luxury in the Junipine office, served canned tuna in pretty bowls, far far away from Nora and all the other Lodge dogs.
— MG

Orchards in the Red Rocks

{ Some of our trees are eighty years old. }

Oak Creek has been an apple growing area since the early homestead days. Jess, Dan, and Albert Purtymun built the irrigation ditch that still runs through the Junipine and Garland orchards during the era when apples were hauled by wagon to Flagstaff and Jerome.

Luckily for us, Walter Jordan was shutting down his operation on Jordan Road just as we were starting up. When Dan and Gary Garland purchased a diesel storage tank from Walter, they were treated to a seminar in the use of orchard contraptions such as the funny-looking heaters that were everywhere. In beat-up overalls, Walter peered over his Coke-bottle–thick specs as he patiently explained the home-devised alarm that woke him up when temperatures dipped. Diesel prices were low enough then to warrant firing up all those heaters to protect tender fruit from frost. That first year we lucked out and had a bumper crop. Forty pound-bushels of apples brought only $8 in those days, marketed out of the back of our brand new Ford pickup.

Some of our oldest trees are eighty years old. Heirloom varieties ripen at different times and so extend the harvest time. Each variety is extolled for its various virtues. Gravensteins and Jonareds are early and crisp; Grimes Golden were Papa Isham's favorite for pie; Romes made the best baked apples, and Arkansas Blacks, late and self-waxing, kept well in root cellars over the winter.

Rob Lautze and Mario Valeruz transitioned the orchard to organic methods starting in the 1990s. Out went the Alar and chemical fertilizers. Instead they amended the soil with compost and nurtured the trees with various organic nutrient sprays. When the trees were doused with fish emulsion and seaweed, you could close your eyes and swear you were at the beach!

The most dreaded pest in the orchard is the coddling moth, whose eggs become worms in apples. Sheaths of cardboard are wrapped around the trees in winter to host the larvae of the moth, then are removed and burned. Triangular orange moth traps hang in the trees, indicating when the hatch is on. The most asked question at the Lodge is "What are those little red curlycues hanging on those wires strung from tree to tree?" The little gizmos are pheromone emitters, which disrupt the mating cycle of the moths. Additionally, trees are sprayed with a biological insecticide to deter the moth worms from boring into the cores of the apples. Instead of using chemical thinners, the trees are hand thinned. Each cluster of baby apples is examined, and damaged fruit is discarded. Pride and conviction keep these organic farmers going. It is truly a wonder organic fruit does not cost much more! —MG

TEATIME

Afternoon tea became a mainstay after Gary Garland came home from a fishing trip on the Spey River in northern Scotland. At Tulchan Lodge Gary not only acquired a taste for single malts, but also got hooked on the civilized tradition of offering tea and snacks every afternoon. Amanda and staff graciously obliged Gary's request to begin a new tradition, and our guests were delighted.

After breakfast, satiated Lodgers swear they'll never eat again. . . a lot of that swearing goes on around here after meals. But after a brisk hike up one of the local trails and a couple of hours reading on the porch, miraculous amnesia occurs, and stomachs begin to rumble.

So guests file in at four in the afternoon for a hot or iced tea, curious to see what sweet and savory nibbles might tide them over till dinner. A casual affair, it is another opportunity to mingle a bit with fellow guests. Then there is just enough time for a little nap or a massage, a quick shower, and a bit of primping before cocktails.

Mr. and Mrs. Frank E. Snider,   Flagstaff
Genevien M. Owens Hollywood Calif—
Mr & Mrs. Hubert Richardson Cameron
Eleanor & Tommy Knoles. Flagstaff

Pauline Robertson _____ Winslow, Ariz.
Laura Harris Winslow, Arizona 5/19/40.
Helen Mooney - Winslow, Ariz.
Mary Breckenridge - Winslow, Arizona
Nell Doggett - Winslow, Arizona

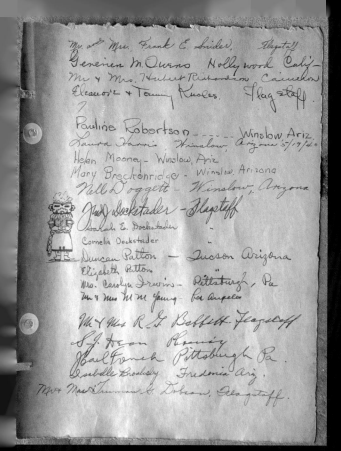

Jno Dockstader - Flagstaff
Sarah E. Dockstader   "
Cornelia Dockstader   "
Duncan Patton — Tucson Arizona
Elizabeth Patton
Mrs. Carolyn Irwin - Pittsburgh, Pa
Mr & Mrs W. M. Young - Los Angeles

Mr & Mrs R. G. Babbitt Flagstaff
S. J. Dean Phoenix
Earl French Pittsburgh Pa.
Isabelle Brodsby Fredonia Ariz.
Mr & Mrs Truman G. Dobson, Flagstaff.

Laura M. Albers Cincinnati, Ohio July 24
Florence C. Albers   "   "

Paul Coze - Phoenix - Arizona
Paris - France

Marjorie Scheumann
Mr. and Mrs. Bob Luenske

Dr. and Mrs. Altemeister 7/4 to 7/16—1941 Louis

O. D. Miller?
Mrs. O.D. Miller 142 S. Windsor Dr Phoenix
Mrs Laura Richard - 325 So Wilmer, Los Angeles, Calif

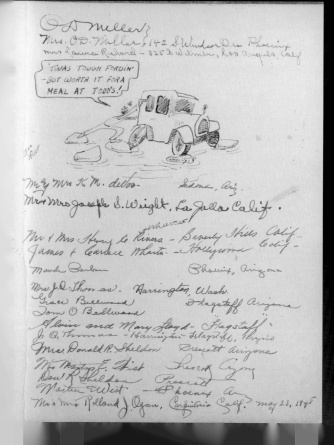

"TWAS TOUGH FORDIN'
- BUT WORTH IT FOR A
MEAL AT TODD'S!

Mr & Mrs K. M. Dellos —   Sedona, Ariz.
Mr & Mrs Joseph S. Wright, La Jolla Calif.

Mr. & Mrs Henry L. Rivers - Beverly Hills Calif—
James & Carrie Whorts. - Hollywood   Calif—
Maude Barlow   Phoenix, Arizona
Mrs J. D. Thomas - Harrington, Wash.
Grace Bellward   Flagstaff Arizona
Tom O Bellward
Alvin and Mary Floyd - Flagstaff.
J. Q. Thomas - Harrington Flagstaff. Arizona
Mrs. Donald R. Sheldon Prescott Arizona
Mrs Marion E. Hist Prescott Ariz
Don R Sheldon Prescott
Marten West - Phoenix Ariz
Mr & Mrs Rolland J. Ogan, Carpinteria Calif. may 23, 1945

Frank A Nelson Cleveland Ohio
& wife
Dick Hull   do
Alice Bowler - Kelley Bar Harbor Maine
Meyer Tighe   14460 Chatsworth St. San Francisco
Gordon Bolisko   Hampstead, Essex England   California
Mrs Ora Frankenberg   Jumpa Aug 5/18
Mrs Chris Stude
Harry & Mabel Moore   Flagstaff

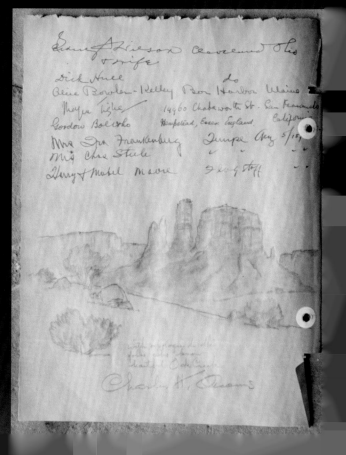

Charley H. Owens

{ *All* our guests are famous to us! }

We are often asked if we have had any "famous guests." Just the other day a fifty-something-year-old, returning with his family after thirty years, asked if his memory was right. In 1975, the year he passed the bar exam, he remembered being seated at dinner with Joan Fontaine. Indeed that lovely lady *was* here with a gentleman escort, booked in a duplex with adjoining rooms, giving us much to speculate about. Prior to their arrival we hooted with laughter when they inquired about "boating guides" on Oak Creek. They must have been sorely disappointed when they forded our little stream in their touring car.

Kingdom of the Spiders, a B movie starring William Shatner, known to most as Captain Kirk in *Star Trek,* was filmed here prior to our official season in March of 1977. The screenplay was written Alan Caillou, a talented and imaginative local author. The gist of the plot involves a mutation in the genetic code of the local tarantulas, making them carnivorous, ultimately decimating all animal and human life forms in the Verde Valley. Shatner is the trouble shooting sheriff, Tiffany Bolling his romantic interest. In the final scene,

the camera pans up and away, showing the Lodge and its environs shrouded in cobwebs. We all had loads of fun watching the movie being made. The spider wrangler stayed in cabin #8, with stacks of specimens ready for action. It was a little creepy going in to make those beds! We were most amused when all the *Kingdom's* stars chose to stay in town rather than in our rustic cabins. The King's Ransom had been home to Elvis, Henry Fonda, and other famous actors in the early Westerns filmed in Sedona. But as soon as they got wind of the fabulous dinners the crew were enjoying at the Lodge, we were begged to accommodate them all, which of course we did.

Beautiful Lynda Carter, alias Wonder Woman, and a Phoenix native, came to stay at the Lodge in the early 1980s. Her fame was lost on us Canyon hicks who had no TV reception. When introduced to the star, Gary Garland embarrassed himself by asking if she was connected with the Flagstaff temp agency by the same name!

Richard Chamberlain, a.k.a. "Dr. Kildare," was observed jogging into the Lodge to book a dinner reservation. Nosy and more worldly guests roused from

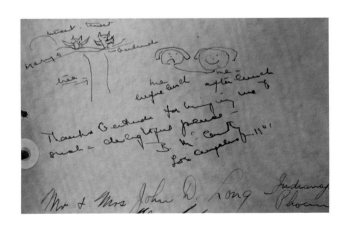

their chaise lounges and rushed into the office to ask Rainy, the receptionist, "Was that *the* Richard Chamberlain?" She blankly checked the name and offered, "Well, yes! I guess it could be! The reservation *is* in the name of "Chamberlain." Later that evening he returned for dinner, charmed all the guests, happily autographing their menus, their napkins, and anything else they could think of.

Michael Richards from the *Seinfeld* show had a brief, nervous night here. He was so fearful people might notice him that you couldn't help but! Katherine Ross, from *The Graduate,* and Sam Elliot stayed a couple of times and were delightful, "regular" folks.

And then there was Martha Stewart. . . In May of 1998, we were contacted by a location scout to see if Martha and Co. could use our creek crossing for a KMart ad for her linens, in a rustic version of the work of installation artist Christo. As we were closed that Monday morning until check-in time, we said Yes, provided we, our employees, and any deliveries had

right of way through her entourage of camera crews, makeup artists, production assistants, and their commissary trailer. And a production it was! A few days prior, the scout inquired if we would like to provide breakfast for Martha. We asked all of the employees about working to accommodate this famous lady, but the response was politely negative. After all, it was their morning off.

Martha was scheduled to be coifed in one of our quaint little log cabins. I had the good fortune to meet her while she was having her hair poufed. She was pleasant, charming, and appreciative of the Lodge, contrasting it with places she had been that advertised authenticity and had prices to match, but whose fireplaces were fake stone and whose linens had a lower thread count than her KMart line. We laughed as I described our own experiences with haughty waiters and their unnecessary pretensions in such places. I guess it was a form of shop talk. Again she chuckled, and I thought her a fine woman.

{ A defining and accidental attribute of the Lodge is its size. }

Early guest registers were fashioned of wood and leather with copper embossing. At right, Joan Sheff, avid fisherwoman and loyal lodger.

When Judy Walker, the *Arizona Republic* travel writer, called that afternoon to find out what was new at the various lodges in Oak Creek, I reminded her that nothing much ever changed here. Our guests are so proprietous about "their cabins" that they squawk whenever we change much of anything. Then it dawned on me. . . Martha Stewart had been here! Now that was news! Judy responded, "Oh my God! You have got to talk to my friend!" Moments later I got a call asking what was Martha like, how did she look, and so on. When I answered that she was charming, pretty, and funny, the woman quizzed me further. "What did she say that was funny?" At that moment I realized that this "friend" was also a columnist at the *Arizona Republic* who covered celebrity sightings in the state. I stammered, not wanting to report a conversation about the foibles of the hospitality business. Fortunately the columnist was adept and made a witty little story out of my babble.

The magazine called back the following year to ask if we would be interested in doing a feature story for *Martha Stewart Living*. Never one to look a gift horse in the mouth, I assured them that of course we were interested. Scheduling the entire Garland family for a midsummer shoot with such short notice was a little dicey, and there were mixed reactions to the proposal, not unlike the reaction of our staff. But finally all agreed and so ensued our fifteen seconds of fame. Needless ot say, we got a lot of mileage out of "The Martha Experience."

All our guests are famous to us! So many return each season, we have gotten to know them and count them as friends. Each annual visit is an opportunity to review the year's events, both happy and sad. We have watched children progress from cradle through college. Some now return with their own young families.

One of the truly magical elements of the Lodge is the interaction between the guests. Many a friendship has begun at a table shared by strangers in our dining room. Initial hesitation dissipates with the passing of warm bread and a review of the dinner to come. Invariably travel tales and other culinary adventures are swapped. We are frequently asked how we "match" people so well. Our office staff is astute, and the Lodge just seems to be a place where people can relax and be themselves. A defining and accidental attribute of the Lodge is its size. Somehow the scale of this place encourages intimacy. There is time and space for solitude and reflection, but also plenty of opportunities for conversation and camaraderie. Free of the usual daily distractions, long-married couples hold hands while strolling the grounds. It is a joy to behold and to be a part of.

Chocolate Zucchini Bread

TWO LOAVES

Chocolate Zucchini Bread came to us through Mike the Knife (also known as Michael Brosnahan) from his lovely wife-to-be Mary Lou Parker. It's a great snack or tea bread, and almost sweet enough to have for dessert, perhaps with some mascarpone and orange zest. It's a good keeper.

4 ounces unsweetened chocolate

1 + 1/2 cups canola oil

4 eggs

2 + 1/2 cups sugar

3 cups grated zucchini

3 cups all purpose flour

1 teaspoon baking soda

1 teaspoon salt

1 cup ground pecans or almonds

Preheat the oven to 350°. Melt the chocolate and oil together, either in a glass measuring cup in the microwave, or in a small double boiler on the stove. Set aside. In a medium mixing bowl, whisk the eggs and sugar together very well, until lightened and pale. Stir in the melted chocolate. Stir in the grated zucchini, mixing well.

Whisk the flour, soda, and salt together in a separate small bowl, then stir into the chocolate mixture. Fold in the nuts.

Divide the batter between two greased and floured 9- by 5-inch loaf pans and bake for 45 to 55 minutes, until the top of the loaf springs back when pressed gently. Cool on a rack in the pans for 10 minutes, then remove from the pans and cool 30 minutes more, at least, before slicing.

Zucchini Spice Bread

ONE LOAF

A very easy and delicious bread, a relic from the early 70s in Jackson, Wyoming. A good use of that summer bounty!

2 cups whole wheat flour

1 tablespoon cinnamon

1 teaspoon salt

1 teaspoon soda

1 teaspoon baking powder

3 eggs

1/2 cup oil

1/2 cup sugar (or 3/4 cup honey)

2 teaspoon vanilla

2 cups grated zucchini

Preheat the oven to 350°. Coat two 9- by 5-inch loaf pans with cooking spray and dust with flour.

Whisk the flour, cinnamon, salt, soda, and baking powder together in a small bowl and set aside.

Beat the eggs, oil, sugar, and vanilla together with a whisk in a medium bowl. Add the dry ingredients and the zucchini.

Scrape the batter into the loaf pan and bake for 55 to 65 minutes, until the the top of the loaf springs back when pressed gently. Cool on a rack for 5 minutes in the pan, then unmold and cool for 30 minutes more before slicing.

Molasses Gingerbread

FOR EIGHT TO TWELVE

This is certainly one of our mainstay teatime sweets, very good any time of the year, but especially in fall. The batter comes together so quickly and with a minimum of fuss and dishes, and the result is so good. Sometimes I bake this in a cake round and serve it warm with caramelized apples and ice cream—hard to beat!

1 cup butter, melted

1/2 cup warm water

1/2 cup orange juice (or coffee)

1 cup brown sugar

1/2 cup maple syrup

1/2 cup molasses

3 eggs

2 +1/2 cups flour

1 teaspoon salt

1 teaspoon soda

1 teaspoon ginger

1 teaspoon cinnamon

1 teaspoon nutmeg

1/4 teaspoon allspice

Preheat oven to 325°. Combine the butter, water, juice, sugar, syrup, and molasses in a medium bowl and whisk together well. Add the eggs and whisk in very well.

Combine the flour, soda, salt, and all spices together in another bowl and whisk to mix completely.

Whisk the dry ingredients into the wet ingredients, mixing very well. Coat a 9-inch square pan or round cake pan with cooking spray and dust lightly with flour. Scrape batter into the pan and bake for 35 to 40 minutes, or until top springs back lightly when pressed with your finger.

Cool on a rack for 10 minutes. Unmold and serve in squares or wedges with whipped cream or lemon sauce or softened sweet butter (another favorite!)

This is not a great keeper, in my opinion—maybe a day or two, but that's it. Only make half a recipe if you don't think it will all be eaten in a day.

Banana Nut Bread

TWO LOAVES

A very good recipe for banana bread, moist and rich with great banana flavor. We always have overdone bananas on hand and the ones that don't go into the freezer for smoothies go into this bread for our teatime. At home I like it for breakfast, lightly toasted (butter is optional!) When completely cooled and double wrapped, it freezes very well.

6 ripe bananas, cut into one-inch slices

2 + 1/2 cups sugar

4 eggs

1 tablespoon vanilla

1 cup canola oil

3 cups all purpose flour

1 teaspoon salt

1 teaspoon baking soda

1 cup finely chopped nuts, toasted

Preheat oven to 350°. Combine the bananas and sugar in the bowl of a stand mixer fitted with a paddle. Beat on medium speed very well, for about 2 minutes. Add the eggs and vanilla and mix well. Add the oil.

Whisk together the flour, salt, and baking soda, taking care to mix the soda in completely. Stir into the banana mixture, mixing well. Fold in the chopped nuts.

Coat two 9- by 5-inch loaf pans with cooking spray and dust lightly with flour. Divide the batter between the pans and bake in 350 oven 50 to 60 minutes. Cool 30 minutes before slicing.

Lindsey's Pumpkin Bread

TWO LOAVES

This simple and totally delicious sweet bread came to us from Lindsey Riibe, one of our amazing assistant cooks.

2 cups fresh or canned pumpkin purée

4 eggs

3 cups sugar

1 cup canola oil

2/3 cup water

3 + 1/2 cups all-purpose flour

2 teaspoons baking soda

1 teaspoon salt

1 teaspoon ground cinnamon

1 teaspoon nutmeg

1/2 teaspoon allspice

1/2 teaspoon ground ginger

1/8 teaspoon ground cloves

Preheat oven to 350°. Combine the pumpkin, eggs, sugar, and oil in a large bowl. Whisk together very well, then mix in the water.

In a separate small bowl, whisk together the flour, soda, salt, and all the spices. Whisk into the wet mixture, mixing well. Coat two 9- by 5-inch loaf pans with cooking spray and dust lightly with flour. Pour the batter into the pans and bake for 45 to 50 minutes, until top springs back when pressed gently with a finger.

Cool on a rack 10 minutes, then unmold the breads. Cool 20 minutes more before slicing, if you can handle the wait.

This bread is a great keeper. It also multiplies easily and freezes very well. Makes an excellent little holiday gift.

Lemon Almond Crescents

TWO DOZEN

The perfect, elegant little cookie for any occasion, or no occasion at all! Very delicate, so handle gently.

2/3 cup blanched, slivered almonds

1/3 cup sugar

1 cup butter, in cubes

1/2 teaspoon vanilla

1 tablespoon lemon zest

1 + 2/3 cups flour

1/4 teaspoon salt

1 cup sugar

Preheat oven to 325°. Line a baking sheet with parchment. Grind the almonds and the sugar in a food processor until very fine but not pasty. Add the butter cubes, vanilla, and zest and pulse until combined. Add the flour and salt and mix until just combined. Transfer the dough to a small bowl and chill for one hour, until firm. Shape small balls into crescents on the parchment. Bake 10 to 12 minutes until barely colored. Cool 2 minutes, then roll gently in the sugar.

VARIATION Add half a teaspoon of freshly grated nutmeg or cinnamong to the sugar used for dusting the warm cookies.

Ginger Scones

SIXTEEN SCONES

Lovely little biscuits, wonderful for breakfast, tea, or anytime! They are great on their own but you could serve them with a little lightly sweetened whipped cream cheese if you like.

3 + 3/8 cups flour

1/2 cup sugar

1 + 1/2 teaspoon baking powder

2 teaspoons finely grated lemon zest

8 ounces very cold butter cubes (2 sticks)

2/3 cup finely chopped crystalized ginger

1 + 1/8 cup heavy cream

Preheat oven to 350°. In the bowl of a stand mixer fitted with a paddle, combine the flour, sugar, and baking powder. Stir to mix. Add the lemon zest and butter cubes, and mix on low speed until mealy.

Transfer to a medium bowl, mix in the ginger and the heavy cream. Mix only until the dough barely comes together. Turn out onto a lightly floured work surface and knead very gently 8 to 10 times.

Divide dough in two portions and gently roll out in half-inch thick rounds. Cut each round into 8 wedges and place one inch apart on a parchment-lined sheet pan. Brush tops with a touch of cream and sprinkle with a pinch of white or raw sugar.

Bake 13 to 15 minutes, till golden brown and beautiful. Serve warm.

Oat Chocolate Chip Cookies

This is our standard cookie dough. It never fails and lasts two weeks in the fridge. We nearly always add some kind of nut, but they're optional, as are the cherries, cranberries or raisins.

1 cup butter

1 cup brown sugar

1 cup sugar

2 eggs

2 tablespoons milk

2 teaspoons vanilla

2 + 1/2 cups flour

1 teaspoon baking powder

1 teaspoon baking soda

1 teaspoon salt

2 cups rolled oats

12 ounces chocolate chips

1 cup chopped pecans, walnuts or almonds or 1/2 cup nuts and 1/2 cup dried tart cherries, cranberries or raisins (optional)

Preheat oven to 350°. In the bowl of a stand mixer fitted with a paddle, cream the butter and both sugars together until light and fluffy, 2 to 3 minutes. Stop the machine and scrape down the sides of the bowl once during mixing. Beat in the eggs one by one, then mix in the vanilla and milk.

Whisk the flour, baking powder, soda, and salt together, then add to the butter mixture, blending well. Mix in the oats, then the chips, nuts, and optional dried fruit. Drop by tablespoons full on a parchment lined sheet pan. Bake for 8 to 10 minutes, till light brown and still a little gooey. Cool on a rack.

Christie's White Chocolate Chip Cookies

Christie Helm came to us the season after Mike the Knife left, a beautiful young woman who was due to be married that summer. We lost her after the wedding, but she keeps in touch from her home in Dallas, where she's busy raising three kids. In her short time here, she left us with several great recipes.

1 cup butter

3/4 cup sugar

3/4 cup brown sugar

2 eggs

1 teaspoon vanilla

3 cups flour

1 teaspoon baking soda

1/4 teaspoon baking powder

1 teaspoon salt

12 ounces white chocolate chopped in small chunks

Preheat the oven to 350°. Cream the butter and both sugars till fluffy, then add the eggs and vanilla. In a separate bowl whisk the flour, soda, baking powder, and salt together, then add to the butter and eggs until well blended, and finally fold in the white chocolate bits.

Scoop mounds of cookie dough onto a greased cookie sheet or a sheet pan lined with parchment. Bake 12 minutes.

Peanut or Almond Butter Cookies

An excellent cookie and a good keeper. A glass of cold milk is the perfect thing with these!

2 + 1/2 cups flour

1/2 teaspoon baking powder

1/2 teaspoon baking soda

1/2 teaspoon salt

1/2 cup butter

1 cup brown sugar

1 cup sugar

1 cup peanut or almond butter

2 eggs

2 teaspoons vanilla

Preheat oven to 350°. Whisk the flour, baking powder, soda, and salt together in a small bowl. In a stand mixer fitted with a paddle, cream the butter and both sugars together until very smooth and light. Add the nut butter and cream until very light. Add the eggs, one by one, mixing well after each. Add the vanilla. With the machine on low, add the dry ingredients slowly, until well blended and smooth.

Using a small scoop or two spoons, form one-inch balls and place on a parchment-lined sheet pan. Flatten the cookies with a floured fork or the bottom of a flat glass. Bake for 8 to 10 minutes, until just set. Cool on a rack.

VARIATION Add 1 cup chocolate chips, or finely chopped toasted peanuts or almonds, or raisins.

Kendra's Gingersnaps

Our daughter Kendra came home after culinary school to do her externship at Sedona's Enchantment Resort. Along with the pleasure of having her with us again for a bit, she brought us some pretty good recipes.

1 cup butter

1 + 1/2 cups brown sugar

2 eggs

1/3 cup molasses

1 + 1/2 teaspoon baking soda

3/4 teaspoon salt

1 tablespoon ground cinnamon

2 teaspoons ground ginger

1/2 teaspoon nutmeg

1/8 teaspoon ground black pepper

4 cups flour

1/2 cup chopped crystallized ginger

2 teaspoons orange zest

Preheat the oven to 350°. In the bowl of a stand mixer fitted with a paddle, cream the butter and brown sugar together until very light and fluffy. Add the 2 eggs, one by one, mixing well after each. Add the molasses. Whisk the soda, salt, cinnamon, ginger, nutmeg, and pepper with the flour until well blended. Add to the butter mixture with the machine running on the lowest speed, mixing in completely. Mix in the chopped ginger and orange zest. Chill the dough for one hour. Form cookies into one-inch balls, roll in sugar, place 2 inches apart on a parchment lined sheet pan, and bake for 10 to 12 minutes. Cool on a rack.

The cookies keep for a week, well wrapped and in a cool spot. The dough keeps two weeks, at least, in a cold fridge.

Aunt Dodo's Apple Cookies

This is an old family recipe, named for Gary's aunt, Dorothy Pickrell, and makes a couple dozen light and cakey cookies. The kind your aunt might have kept in a tin with waxed paper between the layers.

2 cups sifted flour

1 teaspoon baking soda

1/2 teaspoon salt

2 teaspoons cinnamon

1 teaspoon cloves

1/2 teaspoon nutmeg

1 + 1/3 cup brown sugar

1/2 cup soft shortening or butter

1 egg

1/4 cup milk or apple juice

1 cup walnuts, coarsely chopped

1 cup raisins

1 cup chopped apple, skin on is fine

Preheat the oven to 350°. Combine the flour, soda, salt, cinnamon, cloves, and nutmeg in a small bowl. Cream the brown sugar and shortening together in another bowl till light. Add the egg, then the milk or juice. Stir in the dry ingredients, then fold in the nuts, raisins, and apples.

Drop by tablespoons full on a parchment lined sheet pan and bake for 10 to 12 minutes. Cool on a rack. Spread with Vanilla Glaze (recipe at right) while still warm.

Sour Milk Chocolate Cookies

Another delicious recipe from the same aunt, also cakey and glazed.

1 cup shortening or butter

1 + 1/2 cup sugar

2 eggs

1 teaspoon vanilla

1/2 cup cocoa

3 cups flour

2 teaspoons baking powder

1 teaspoon baking soda

pinch salt

1 cup sour milk

2 cups pecans or walnuts, chopped

FOR THE VANILLA GLAZE

1 + 1/2 cup powdered sugar

1 tablespoon soft butter

1/4 teaspoon vanilla

pinch of salt

1 tablespoon milk or more, to make the right consistency

Cream the shortening and sugar together. Add the eggs and vanilla. In a separate bowl, sift the cocoa, flour, baking powder, and salt together. Add the flour mixture to the creamed shortening-sugar mixture alternately with the sour milk till all the ingredients are incorporated, then add the nuts. Bake at 350° for 10 to 12 minutes, removing the cookies from the oven while they are still a bit soft. Transfer to a rack and spread with Vanilla Glaze or ganache while still warm.

Stabo's Chocolate Orange Bars

TWENTY-FOUR BARS

Stabo, a.k.a. Steve Hosmer, my incomparable assistant for 18 years (!) loves chocolate and orange together. This is one of his many fine offerings.

2 cups flour

1/2 cup powdered sugar

1/4 teaspoon salt

1 + 1/2 stick cold butter, cubed

zest of 2 oranges

1 + 1/3 cup sugar

1/2 cup orange juice

6 eggs

1/3 cup flour

1/2 teaspoon baking powder

1 teaspoon orange extract

1 teaspoon vanilla

1 + 1/4 cups Ganache, slightly warm,

pourable (page 244)

Preheat the oven to 325°. Combine the flour, sugar, and salt in a food processor and pulse to blend. Add the cold butter and pulse several times more until mealy. Spread evenly in a 9- by 13-inch baking pan and press lightly. Bake for 20 minutes, till golden brown. Meanwhile, combine the zest and sugar in the food processor and pulse to blend. Add the remaining ingredients except the ganache and pulse. Pour over the warm cookie crust and bake for 15 to 20 minutes, until just set. Cool on a rack.

Pour the Ganache over the cooled orange bars, tilting the pan to spread the chocolate evenly. Chill until just set, about 30 minutes. Cut into rectangles.

Grodzinsky's Apple Cake

We met Jack Grodzinsky in 1976, when his wife forced him to take a much needed sabbatical from his stressful job running several Miracle Mile Delicatessens in Phoenix. A friendly but fidgety fellow, Jack did not relish the peace and quiet of his solitary stay at Garland's Lodge. With no television, but even worse, no telephones, he thought he might go crazy. So he hung out in the kitchen, where he fell in love with Susan Garland while teaching her to braise a brisket and sharing old family recipes, like this apple cake. After a week with Susan, he called his son, Alan, in Berkeley, California, to tell him that he had found The Girl For Him. Even though Alan lived in another state and was in a relationship with another girl, Jack was right. Susan and Alan were married in November, 1980.

4 cups finely chopped peeled apples

1 + 1/2 cups sugar

2 cups flour

2 teaspoons cinnamon

2 teaspoons baking powder

1/2 teaspoon salt

2 eggs , beaten

3/4 cup oil

2 teaspoon vanilla

1 cup chopped walnuts

1/2 cup raisins

Vanilla Sauce

Preheat the oven to 350. Butter and flour a 9-by 11-inch pan. Chop the apples; combine with the sugar and set aside.

In a separate bowl, sift the dry ingredients. Add the beaten eggs, the oil and vanilla, the apples, walnuts, and raisins. Pour the batter into the baking pan and bake for 45 to 50 minutes until a knife or toothpick is clean at the center. Cool and divide into squares. Serve with vanilla sauce and whipped cream or vanilla ice cream.

Vanilla Sauce

1/2 cup butter

1 + 1/2 cups cream

1/2 cup sugar

1 + 1/2 teaspoons vanilla

Combine ingredients in a heavy saucepan and bring to a boil. Cook until thickened. Serve warm.

Snickerdoodles

Snickerdoodles are very old-fashioned, but still good after all of these years. Sometimes we add half a cup of currants to this dough, and I think it's a great variation.

2 + 1/2 cups all purpose flour

2 teaspoons cream of tartar

1 teaspoon soda

1/4 teaspoon salt

1 cup butter

1 + 1/2 cups sugar

2 eggs

1/2 cup sugar for glazing

1 teaspoon each cinnamon, nutmeg

Preheat the oven to 350°. Sift the flour, cream of tartar, soda, and salt together. In the bowl of a stand mixer fitted with a paddle, cream the butter and sugar together until very light and fluffy. Add the eggs, one by one. Add the flour mixture in four additions, with the machine running on low speed. Chill the dough for one hour.

Mix the sugar and cinnamon/nutmeg together in a small bowl. Form the dough into one-inch balls, roll in the sugar mix, place two inches apart on a parchment lined sheet pan and bake for 8 to 9 minutes. Cool on a rack.

These cookies keep for three to four days. The dough keeps two weeks under refrigeration.

Almond Streusel Coffeecake

FOR THE STREUSEL

1/2 cup brown sugar

2 tablespoons flour

2 tablespoons butter

1/4 cup unsweetened coconut

1/4 cup sliced almonds

2 tablespoons ground almonds

FOR THE COFFEECAKE BATTER

2 cups all purpose flour

1 teaspoon baking powder

1 teaspoon baking soda

1/4 teaspoon salt

1/4 pound butter

1 cup sugar

2 eggs

1 teaspoon vanilla extract

1 teaspoon almond extract

1 + 1/2 cup sour cream

Preheat the oven to 350°. Coat an 8- by 8-inch baking pan wtih cooking spray and dust with flour.

Prepare the streusel topping first. Mix the brown sugar and flour together. Cut in the butter, then stir in the coconut and almonds. Stir the dry ingredients together for the coffeecake batter; set aside. Cream the butter and sugar together. Add the eggs, and then the extracts.

Alternately beat in the flour mixture and the sour cream in three additions, beginning and ending with the flour mix. Spread half of the batter in the baking dish, then streusel in the middle, more batter and and then more streusel on top. Bake at 350° for 30 to 40 minutes or until a toothpick comes out clean.

Brie and Pear Quesadillas

FOR EIGHT TO TEN

This is a Lodge original and a favorite I make often for weddings. It is simple and delicious, combining sweet, crisp pear, luscious Brie, and spicy chiles.

6 ten-inch flour tortillas

3 large firm-ripe Anjou or Bartlett pears
   (cored but no need to peel)

1/4 wheel semi-firm Brie cheese, with rind

4 to 5 medium jalapeños, seeded and minced

Lay out tortillas on the work surface (as many at a time as your space will allow). Slice 4 eighth-inch wedges of Brie for each tortilla and lay across one half of tortilla. Press four to five thin slices of pear into the Brie. Sprinkle about one hefty tablespoon minced jalapeños over the pears and fold the tortilla in half, pressing the halves together firmly. The filled quesadillas can be stacked, slightly overlapping, wrapped well, and refrigerated for 24 hours before proceeding.

Heat a griddle or skillet over medium high heat. Spray lightly with cooking oil. Lay quesadillas in the skillet, without crowding (quesadillas should not touch), and cook until crisp and lightly browned, flipping once, about three minutes per side. Repeat for remainder of quesadillas, placing them on warm sheet pans in a single layer as they are finished. Alternatively, the quesadillas can be sprayed directly with the cooking oil, laid on sheet pans in a single layer, then baked in a preheated oven at 350° until crisp. Cut each quesadilla into five wedges and serve warm.

Quesadillas can be browned and crisped, then held for up to an hour, uncut. Reheat quickly in a hot oven, cut into wedges and serve.

Oak Creek Trout Pâté

ABOUT TWO CUPS

A great use for our leftover breakfast trout. We collect these in our freezer and try to do a big smoking every few months, along with any extra salmon filets we may have.

8 ounces cream cheese, softened

1 tablespoon capers

1 tablespoon ketchup or chili sauce

1 tablespoon chopped Italian parsley

1 to 2 tablespoons fresh lemon juice, to taste

1/2 teaspoon hot pepper sauce, to taste

1/2 cup smoked trout, flaked

1/2 teaspoon dill weed

3 green onions, chopped

Combine the cream cheese, capers, ketchup, parsley, juice, and pepper sauce in a food processor and pulse to mix until very smooth. Add the trout, dill and green onions and pulse to mix in well. Correct seasoning for salt, lemon juice, and pepper sauce. Pack into a small crock or souffle dish and allow to chill for one hour. Serve with slices of baguette or pumpernickel. Finely diced red onion and additional capers may also be served with this and are delicious.

Smoked salmon can be substituted for the trout. Use wood-smoked salmon rather than lox.
This keeps for four to five days in the fridge, well wrapped in the freezer for a month. Thaw in the fridge five to six hours or overnight.

Cheddar Biscuits

ABOUT 20 TINY BISCUITS

A simple biscuit recipe with lots of flavor and a very forgiving texture. These could be cut larger to serve with supper. They also could be split, and filled with ham or smoked turkey, and a little habanero jam. I love them best like this, tiny and fresh from the oven.

3 cups unbleached all purpose flour

1 + 1/2 tablespoons baking powder

1 tablespoon sugar

2 + 1/4 teaspoons salt

1 cup (packed) grated sharp Cheddar cheese

2 + 1/2 cups heavy cream

2 to 3 tablespoons melted butter

Preheat oven to 350°. Combine the flour, baking powder, sugar, and salt in a large bowl. Add the cheese and toss lightly to combine. Pour the cream around the edges of the bowl and mix everything together with your hands thoroughly but gently.

Turn out onto a lightly floured board and knead very gently, two to three strokes only. Pat or roll out to a 3/4-inch thickness. Cut into 1 + 1/2-inch rounds or squares, using a small biscuit cutter or a very sharp knife. Place on a sheet pan lined with parchment paper. Set aside for 10 minutes. Brush with melted butter. Bake 15 to 20 minutes, until puffed and golden brown.

VARIATIONS Add 1 tablespoon chopped chives, fresh dill, chopped jalapeños or finely chopped crisp bacon along with the cheese and mix in well. Proceed as above. Each a little different, all delicious.

Parmesan Scones

Another delicious little biscuit. These are good by themselves as just a bite, or cut larger as an accompaniment to soups and stews.

2 + 3/4 cups flour

4 teaspoons baking powder

2 teaspoons salt

3/4 cup grated Parmesan cheese,
    plus a little more for topping

1 stick cold butter, cut in 8 pieces

1/4 cup minced green onions or chives

1/2 cup sour cream

1/2 cup heavy cream, plus more for topping

Preheat oven to 350°. In the bowl of a stand mixer fitted with a paddle, combine the flour, baking powder, salt, and Parmesan. Mix at low speed to combine well. Add the cold butter and mix at low speed until the dough looks sort of mealy. Transfer the mixture to a medium bowl and stir in the chives or green onions. Mix the sour and heavy creams together until smooth and loose and pour over and around the flour mixture, tossing and mixing gently with your hands until just combined.

Turn out onto a lightly floured work surface, knead gently 3 or 4 times and pat out into a rectangle, approximately half-inch thick, 12 inches long and 4 inches wide. Cut the rectangle in half lengthwise, then cut each half again lengthwise, to make 4 strips. Cut each strip with right and left angle cuts to make triangles or just cut into one-inch squares. Place one inch apart on a parchment lined sheet pan, brush with a touch of heavy cream, sprinkle with more Parmesan and bake for 15 minutes.

The scones should be golden brown, firm yet tender. Serve warm.

This dough can be mixed in a food processor if you prefer. The same method and sequence applies, using the pulse button to mix the flour and cut in the very cold butter. Just be sure not to over-process the butter! The biscuits can be frozen unbaked; allow to thaw completely and bake when needed. The baked biscuits can be frozen and thawed and reheated reasonably well, although lacking that fresh tender flakiness.

Cheddar Crisps

A Lodge favorite, one- or two-bite flavor punches that are good any time of the year, but seem best to me for cooler weather. We like to serve them slightly warm, in a basket lined with a colorful napkin. They're wonderful served with apples, grapes and other fall fruits, and of course, a good bottle of wine.

3/4 cup butter, softened (1 + 1/2 sticks)

4 + 1/2 cups grated sharp Cheddar, preferably yellow

3 egg yolks

1 teaspoon salt

1 + 1/8 cups flour

1 + 1/2 teaspoons freshly cracked black pepper

Preheat oven to 350°. In the bowl of a standing mixer fitted with a paddle, combine the butter and grated Cheddar cheese. Cream together on medium speed until fluffy. Add the egg yolks and mix until smooth and creamy. Whisk the flour, salt and pepper together in a small bowl, then add it to the mixing bowl with the machine running on the slowest speed. Mix just until the dough comes together in a ball. Remove the bowl from the mixer, scraping all the dough from the paddle, and chill the dough, covered, for 1 hour or until firm. Preheat oven to 350°.

Form one-inch balls with a small cookie scoop and place on a parchment lined sheet pan. Flatten with a fork that has been dipped in flour, making a crisscross pattern.

Bake for 15 minutes at 350°, until well browned and a little crispy at the edges. Cool on a rack 10 minutes. They can be re-heated once.

Pimiento Cheese

ABOUT THREE AND A HALF CUPS

This is a memory from my Texas years, and I don't mean that negatively at all! This is, of course, great as a sandwich spread, but it's also really good with all sorts of crackers. This will keep for four or five days in the fridge, but does not freeze well.

4 ounces cream cheese, softened

1/3 cup mayonnaise

1/2 pound grated sharp Cheddar, about 2 + 1/2 cups

4 ounces canned roasted red bell peppers,

    drained, diced

1 teaspoon salt, to taste

1/8 teaspoon cayenne pepper, to taste

1/4 teaspoon thyme

1/4 teaspoon sage

1/4 cup chopped green onions, black olives,

    or green chiles (optional)

Combine cream cheese and mayonnaise in the bowl of a mixer fitted with a paddle attachment. Mix on low speed until well blended, 1 to 2 minutes. Add the Cheddar and mix until just combined, then stir in the red peppers, herbs and seasonings. Stir in any of the optional ingredients at this point. Place in the fridge for 30 minutes to an hour to allow the flavors to blend a bit.

Serve with crusty bread slices or good crackers.

Pimiento Cheese can be mixed in the food processor, but it tends to purée the whole thing, and that's not the texture you want. It would be better to mix it up in a bowl with a wooden spoon or spatula if a stand mixer is not available; that's certainly how they do it in Texas.

Gougere—the Classic

This is a classic French appetizer, a great accompaniment to wine, of course, but good with soups and stews as well. This dough is simply a savory version of pâté a choux, which is used to make cream puff and éclair shells. It's really one of those magical combinations of flour, butter, eggs and heat that transforms into this wonderful and delicious little puff. They are also easy to make but do follow the directions on this one!

2 cups water

1 cup butter

2 teaspoons salt

2 cups flour

7 eggs

3 cups grated Gruyère or sharp Cheddar or pepperjack/
   Cheddar mix

1/2 teaspoon cayenne pepper

1 teaspoon dry basil, dill or caraway seed (optional)

Preheat oven to 400°. Bring water, butter, and salt to a boil in a heavy bottomed 4-quart saucepan. Remove from the heat, and stir in the flour all at once. Turn the heat back to medium and stir the mixture with a wooden spoon until very smooth and shiny (3 minutes). Transfer to the bowl of a stand mixer fitted with a paddle. Mix on low speed about one minute, then raise to medium speed; add the eggs one at a time, mixing each one in before adding the next. Reduce back to low speed and add in all the cheese and cayenne; mix in well. Add in any herbs you wish or one of the other optional ingredients.

Using two spoons, form small, 1- to 1 + 1/2-inch mounds on a parchment lined sheet pan. Bake for 15 minutes, till puffed. Reduce oven to 350 and bake 15 minutes more until golden and firm, but not hard. Serve warm or at room temperature.

V A R I A T I O N S Add to the gougere dough 1/4 cup finely chopped sun-dried tomatoes or 1/4 cup chopped jalapeños and 1/2 teaspoon cumin or 1/2 cup finely diced ham (excellent!).

Scalloped Poppyseed Shortbread

TWO DOZEN

Lovely little tea bites, not too sweet or rich. Substituting a tablespoon of lavender buds for the poppy seeds is a great variation, do try it!

1/2 pound butter, room temperature

3/4 cup powdered sugar

1 teaspoon vanilla extract

2 cups flour

12 teaspoon salt

1 tablespoon poppyseeds

Preheat oven to 325°.

Combine all in a food processor, or an electric mixer with the paddle, until the dough just comes together. Pat and roll out gently about a quarter-inch thick on a lightly floured surface. Cut into pretty two-inch rounds and bake on a baking sheet lined with parchment for 20 minutes or until the edges are just beginning to brown.

Garlicky Artichoke Spread

ABOUT THREE CUPS

Probably our fail-safe teatime snack, the one thing we always have tucked away to pull out in a hurry. So, accordingly, make a double batch, pack into four-inch soufflé dishes and bake them all. When cool, wrap the extras well with plastic film and freeze. In spite of the mayonnaise, they keep very well in the freezer. Thaw overnight in the fridge if possible, or in the microwave in a pinch!

4 cloves garllc, peeled and minced

1 cup mayonnaise

3/4 cup grated Parmesan

1 tablespoon freshly squeezed lemon juice

1/4 cup chopped Italian parsley

1/2 teaspoon freshly ground pepper

1 17-ounce can artichoke hearts, drained

　　(not the marinated variety)

Preheat the oven to 350°. Combine the garlic, mayo, Parmesan, juice, parsley, and pepper in a food processor. Pulse to blend, 4 to 5 times. Add the choke hearts and pulse to blend, leaving it a little chunky. Transfer to an oven proof souffle dish. Bake 10 to 15 minutes until browned and bubbling.

Serve with baguette slices, lightly brushed with olive oil and toasted.

V A R I A T I O N S Add about a fourth cup chopped sundried tomatoes or chopped ripe black olives along with the artichoke hearts. Pulse to blend.

Garland's Tapenade

TWO AND HALF CUPS

Our version of the traditional olive spread of the south of France. Sometimes we make it with more green olives than black, and a few roasted peppers for a different look and flavor. The addition of a little fresh basil or oregano is also good.

2 cups chopped mixed pitted olives (Kalamatas, green
　　Greek, pimiento-stuffed, ripe)

2 cloves garlic, peeled and pressed

1 tablespoon capers

1 anchovy, chopped

1 tablespoon minced chives

1 tablespoon chopped Italian parsley

1 to 2 tablespoons freshly squeezed lemon juice,
　　to taste

1 tablespoon cognac or brandy, to taste

1/4 to 1/3 cup extra virgin olive oil, to make spreadable

freshly ground pepper

Combine olives, garlic, capers, anchovy, chives, and parsley in a food processor. Pulse only enough to blend! Turn out into a bowl. Then add lemon, brandy and oil to make a nice, slightly loose spread.

Correct for salt and pepper. Allow to sit one hour to meld the flavors.

Serve at room temperature with baguette slices.

Brandied Wild Mushroom Pâté

TWO CUPS

I first made this in the early 70s when I worked in Jackson Hole at the Steak Pub. At that time we used basic white mushrooms. I recalled it after my first wild mushroom foray into the San Francisco Peaks with Bogomir Pfeifer, the owner of Slide Rock Lodge, and an old forager from way back in Slovenia. He very generously took me to many great spots to find *Boletus Edulis*, or King Boletus. Also known as porcini (in Italy) or cepes (in France). If you ever have the opportunity to go with someone who knows the mushrooms, please take it; it's a gift and a great experience.

1/2 ounce dried shitake or porcini mushrooms

    or a blend

1 cup hot water

1/4 pound butter

2 cloves garlic, minced

1/2 medium yellow onion,

    finely chopped

6 ounces fresh crimini (Italian

    brown) mushrooms, sliced

1 tablespoon chopped

    Italian parsley

1 teaspoon thyme

1/2 teaspoon sage

salt, pepper to taste

1/2 cup dry white wine

1/8 cup sherry or brandy

Soak the dried mushrooms in a cup of hot water for 10 minutes, until very tender. When draining, pluck mushrooms gently from the top of the container to avoid unsettling the grit that may have drifted to the bottom. Drain well.

Melt the butter in a heavy skillet. Sauté the onions and garlic until beginning to color. Add mushrooms, parsley, herbs, salt and pepper. Sauté over medium heat until very juicy. Reduce until some of the liquid evaporates; add wine and brandy, reducing until it thickens and most of the liquid is gone. Cool. Taste, then puree very smooth. Correct salt and pepper again. Pour into a small crock or soufflé dish and chill until set. Serve with lightly toasted French bread slices or a good rye bread.

Remember to slightly over-season this before chilling; chilling mutes flavors.

BANJO BILL & LODGE LIBATIONS

Bill Garland, our business manager and director of marketing at the start of Garland's Lodge, insisted we had to have a signature house drink. To name it, we "embroidered" a bit on the story of a local character, Banjo Bill Dwyer, who lived here in 1885 and was known both for his musical abilities and his homemade whiskey. As Bill Garland told it, neighbors and travelers alike looked forward to refreshment from the still—and thus the concoction was named "Banjo Bill's Anticipation."

Forest Hunter, a.k.a. Captain Vacation, invented the rum mixture that is the spicy soul of a Banjo Bill. Forest showed up on a motorcycle with a kerchief covering his balding pate. . . a free spirit with roots in Chicago, stints behind him in Key West, New York and Tucson. He lit here and served as dining room manager, enlivening our lives for ten or so years.

Guests would ask the "secret" to the Banjo Bill, to which we replied, "Captain Vacation's Rum, of course." Many a perplexed guest would return the following season to ask again, after scouring the liquor store, whether we had meant "Captain Morgan" rum, not realizing that ours was a home brew. We still brew the rum mixture for our Banjo Bills, steeping gallons of light Bacardi rum with lemon peel, cloves, and cinnamon sticks for several weeks, until it is "done," then decanting it for later

use. A hefty shot of spiced rum mixed with our own apple cider (hot in the winter, cold in the summer) is a perfect cocktail. Forest is also responsible for the Vortex, named for Sedona's famous energy centers.

It has worked well here for the majordomo to pick his successor. Forest was succeeded by John MacArthur. Their mutual friend Donald Zealand was next in line. Donald had come here for years as a guest, crossing over to staff side in 1996. Appropriately, his main hobby is dining, traveling and dining, and reading about dining. A huge fan of M. F. K. Fisher, the celebrated food writer, he has compiled an exhaustive bibliography of her work. A self-made sophisticate from Minnesota, he is Amanda's biggest champion, support, and hiking buddy.

Donald puts together an interesting wine list every season, and is responsible for selecting the recommended wine to match each evening's meal. He also came up with another popular house drink, The Cosmic Cosmo. A returning guest recently complained, "Donald, I followed your recipe exactly when I got home, but my martini just doesn't taste the same as yours." To which Donald replied, "Perhaps that's because you're not drinking it on the lawn at Garland's."

For those who care to try to replicate their Garland's experience, we offer these recipes.

Banjo Bill's Anticipation

1 + 1/4 ounce spiced rum

6 ounces Garland's apple cider

In the early spring and fall, we serve this hot, in a mug with a cinnamon stick. During warm weather we pour it over ice and garnish with a lime or sprig of mint.

The Vortex

1 ounce of apple cider

5 to 6 ounces dry sparkling wine

squeeze of lime

Serve in a champagne flute.

Cosmic Cosmo

1 + 1/2 ounce Grey Goose vodka

1/2 ounce cranberry juice

1/2 ounce Cointreau

Chill a martini glass. Put the drink ingredients in a shaker over ice, shake, then strain into the chilled glass. Garnish with a lemon twist.

Dark and Stormy Night

This delicious and very popular coffee concoction was created by Lynn Mikula, a seven-year veteran of our dining room, and Stabo's partner in life.

3/4 ounce Frangelico

3/4 ounce Chambourd

5 to 6 ounces hot coffee in a Garland's mug

whipped cream to finish

Peach Daquiris

This quintessential summer drink is offered only during peach season, usually the end of July when we pick the Early White Giants, through late August when the Elbertas ripen. Because we never make just one of these, we prepare a large batch of peach purée each day in anticipation of the evening cocktail hour.

FOR THE PURÉE

8 large peaches, about 8 cups

1 + 1/3 cups sugar

1 cup limeade

(made with frozen limeade concentrate)

Wash the peaches well, removing as much of the fuzz as possible. Cut the peaches, leaving skins on (for color), and blend into a purée.

For each daquiri, blend:

6 ounces ice

1 + 1/2 ounces light rum

1/3 cup peach purée

1 + 1/2 ounces limeade

BREAD, SOUP & SALAD

We begin the dining experience with warm, truly fresh-from-the-oven bread, made with exceptional ingredients and served with wonderful sweet butter; it's absolutely the best. With the current carb phobia many of us have strayed away from bread. Really *good* bread, though—now that's a different thing altogether, and something we celebrate and enjoy in moderation as part of a good meal.

Our menus are planned with flavors that work together, and, with that in mind, the baker plans the bread to accompany the soup. It's such an integral part of the meal here that we are offering a small collection of our breads for you to try.

We realize, of course, that everyone is very busy, but all of these breads are easy and fast to proof. If you do try a recipe or two, please mix the dough with a mixer and your hands and not one one those bread machines—you really need to feel and shape these loaves to get the very best from your dough, and, therefore, the whole experience.

Soups and salads at Garland's are a showcase for the constantly changing bounty of goodness that Mario delivers throughout spring, summer and fall from our organic gardens and orchards along the creek. We hope you will enjoy making them from your own local gardens and farmers' markets.

Every good chef needs willing assistants and Stabo has certainly filled the bill. We have been blessed to have Steve Hosmer, a.k.a. "Stabo" with us for 18 years.

An Air Force kid raised mostly in Montana, Stabo said "no way" when his parents moved to Kansas. After a brief stint in college, he and a friend hit the road. "Brazil or Bust" was their ambitious plan, but a misadventure in California thwarted their plan. While on the loose, they spent a night in a roadside patch of iceplant outside of Cardiff-by-the-Sea. An Aikido sensei took them under his wing, seeing the potential in the young men. Stabo's delightfully calm temperament was strengthened by years of martial arts practice.

A book by Paolo Soleri entitled *City in the Image of Man* so impressed Stabo that he made a pilgrimage to Arcosanti, the site of Soleri's visionary city-to-be in the high desert of Northern Arizona. He participated in the commune's agricultural programs and learned to bake wonderful bread under the tutelage of the master baker Charlie McClein. One of the "industries" in the experimental city was the production of Soleri bells, heavy hand-cast wind chimes. Somewhere along the line his pals dubbed him "Stabo," and it stuck. A rift occurred at the foundry one year between the "Heads" (the businessmen) and the "Hearts" (the hippies, who wanted more of a say in how things were done), causing a diaspora of talent.

Early seeds sown in fertile soil, the friendships and experiences at Arcosanti, led Stabo to Jerome, then to Flagstaff, where he gardened at the Flagstaff Arboretum and cooked at various restaurants and bakeries. While picking apples at our neighboring orchard, Stabo was drafted to wash dishes at Garland's, and he quickly graduated to cooking. His attention to detail made him an astute apprentice and a willing and precise teacher. He makes sure to pass on all the little tips and tidbits that make each step of creating a dish successful.

Multi-talented, Stabo was also a beekeeper before coming here. He came to the rescue one day when a swarm of bees showed up in our upper orchard. In proper garb, wielding a smoker, he calmly collected the bees and moved them into a hive, where they produced honey for the kitchen for years. Stabo has been an invaluable asset to Amanda and to the Lodge. He is a sweet soul.

at Garland's Lodge   95

In the early years, a Flagstaff dairy made biweekly deliveries to the Lodge. Each delivery included a five gallon jug of sweet cream. Every afternoon we whisked a batch of butter in our Hobart bowl. If the cook was distracted, a deluge of buttermilk would slosh out of the bowl when the butter solidified. The occasional mess was worth the payoff of soft sweet butter, which we mounded into ramekins for the dinner tables. About the same time, loaves of perfectly browned bread emerged from the oven and were lined up on racks to cool. All that bread and divine butter were a terrible temptation to everyone in the kitchen. It was all over as soon as the first sample slice was cut. Invariably each passerby cut another and slathered it with butter. Before you knew it the loaf was gone! Even svelte young Tricia Garland succumbed, putting on a good ten pounds in her first weeks here as a new bride.

People who like to cook usually like to eat, and nibbling was a problem for some of the early cooks. Kitchen conversations weighed the merits of various diets and the health benefits of fasting as toasty warm herb croutons mysteriously disappeared and the edges of the brownie pan were "tidied up." Susan Garland and her assistants Jenny Devaney and Joanne Mullen solved the problem by wearing piggy-cheeked half masks to block the hand-to-mouth reflex.

Focaccia

Focaccia is the easiest bread ever to mix and bake up, and the fastest. It's similar to pizza dough, but much more flavorful. I definitely encourage the addition of fresh herbs or 2 teaspoons of coarse black pepper. The salt is important here.

2 cups warm water

1 tablespoon yeast

3/8 cup olive oil

6 + 1/2 cups flour

1 rounded tablespoon kosher salt

extra olive oil for pans

Preheat the oven to 375°.

Whisk the yeast into the warm water in a standing mixer bowl, fitted with a dough hook, and allow to proof. Add the olive oil and then 5 or so cups of the flour, and the salt. Add the herbs, or pepper or onions if you like. Mix well, then gradually add more flour to make a soft pizza-like dough. Transfer to a well-oiled medium large bowl, cover with plastic wrap and set aside in a warm spot to rise for 40 minutes, till doubled.

Drizzle a heavy sheet pan with olive oil. Work the dough out evenly over the pan surface. Drizzle more extra virgin olive oil and sprinkle with more kosher salt over the top of the dough. Set aside in a warm spot to rise until light and puffy. Bake for 40 to 45 minutes until browned. Cool on a rack before slicing.

V A R I A T I O N S Add a tablespoon of chopped herbs or coarse ground pepper, or 1/3 cup of dried onions.

Red Chile Bread

TWO LOAVES

Brick-red and packed with tons of flavor. This would make an incredible grilled cheese sandwich.

1 tablespoon yeast

3/4 cup warm water

1/4 cup butter, melted

2 teaspoons chipotle powder

1/3 cup honey

3/4 cup canned tomatoes puréed with their juice

1 cup buttermilk

1 tablespoon salt

5 to 6 cups bread flour

1 cup grated sharp Cheddar cheese

Sprinkle the yeast over the warm water in a small bowl and stir. Set aside to proof (the mixture should become frothy).

In a separate bowl melt the butter, then add the chipotle powder, honey, and tomato purée. (Note: Choose good quality canned tomatoes that do not contain additional sugar or other seasonings.)

Pour the buttermilk into a stand mixer bowl fitted with a hook, then add the warmed butter mixture. Add the yeast-water mixture and the salt. With the mixer on low, add 2 cups bread flour, then the grated cheese. Mix well, then add 2 more cups of flour and mix until the dough begins to come together.

Add additional flour bit by bit, with the machine running on low until the dough comes together in a smooth mass and cleans the edge of the bowl (you may not need the full 6 cups).

Turn the dough out into a lightly oiled medium-large bowl and cover well with plastic wrap. Set aside in a warm spot in your kitchen.

Allow to rise for 2 hours or until doubled. Save the plastic wrap for later.

Punch down the dough with your fist and fold the dough over on itself. Turn the dough out onto a clean work surface. (We really like a wood surface for this.) Very lightly sprinkle a little flour over and around the dough and knead the dough just enough to work out any excess air. Divide the dough into 2 equal portions and mound them into smooth balls with both hands. Set aside on your work surface, covered with plastic wrap, for 10 minutes.

Preheat the oven to 350°.

Form the loaves by patting the dough out into 2 rough rectangles, pressing out as much air as you can. Fold the dough over on itself, rolling towards you, sealing with your thumbs as you go. Put the loaves seam side down in two lightly oiled 9- by 5-inch bread pans. Place the pans in a warm spot, covered with plastic wrap, and let rise for 40 minutes to one hour, or until well risen above the top edges of the pans and puffy to the touch.

Make three diagonal cuts across the top of each loaf to let the steam escape. Place them in the middle of the oven. Bake 40 to 50 minutes, or until deep golden brown. When fully baked, the loaves will sound hollow if you tap them on the bottom. Cool completely on a rack.

Oat Sunflower Bread

TWO LOAVES

A beautiful, slightly sweet loaf, great for sandwiches and toast.

3/4 cup rolled oats (old-fashioned, not quick)

1 + 1/4 cups very hot water, not boiling

1/4 cup warm water

1 tablespoon yeast

1/2 cup honey

1/4 cup olive oil

1 tablespoon salt

2 cups whole wheat flour

3 cups bread flour

1/2 cup toasted sunflower seeds

additional flour for kneading the dough

In the bowl of a stand mixer fitted with a dough hook, mix the oats and hot water together just until moistened. Let sit and cool and soften the oats for 5 to 8 minutes. Meanwhile, whisk the yeast into the 1/4 cup of warm water and allow to proof while the oats are cooling. Add the honey, oil, and salt to the oats and mix on low speed for a minute. Add the yeast mixture and mix a bit. Add the wheat flour and 2 + 1/2 cups of the bread flour and mix on low speed until the dough begins to come together. Add additional flour bit by bit with the machine running on low until the dough comes together in a smooth mass and cleans the edge of the bowl. Add the sunflower seeds and mix gently to incorporate them into the dough.

Turn the dough out into a lightly oiled medium large bowl and cover well with plastic wrap. Set aside in a warm spot in your kitchen. Allow to proof for 2 hours or until doubled and very light. Save the plastic wrap for later.

Punch the dough down with your fist and fold the dough over on itself. Turn the dough out onto a clean work surface. Very lightly sprinkle a little flour over and around the dough and knead the dough just enough to work out the excess air. Divide the dough into 2 equal portions (relatively) and mound them into smooth balls with both hands. Set aside on your work surface and cover them with the wrap for 10 minutes.

Preheat the oven to 350°.

Form the loaves by patting the dough out into a rough rectangle, pressing out as much air as you can. Fold the dough over on itself, rolling towards you, and sealing with your thumbs as you go. Place the loaves seam side down in two lightly oiled 9- by 5-inch bread pans. Place the pans together in a warm spot, cover with the plastic wrap and let rise for 40 minutes to one hour, or until well risen above the pans and very light when you touch the surface. Make three diagonal cuts across the top of each loaf to let the steam escape and place in the middle of the oven. Bake 40 to 50 minutes, or until deep golden brown and the loaf sounds sort of hollow when tapped on the bottom. Cool completely on a rack.

V A R I A T I O N Try exchanging the sunflower seeds for toasted sesame seed. It makes for a delicious and very different flavor.

Blue Thunder Bread

TWO LOAVES

Blue Thunder Bread is the brainchild of Stabo and Mike the Knife, the incomparable baker and the taste wizard playing together in the kitchen.

1/2 cup warm water

1 tablespoon yeast

1/4 cup honey

1/4 cup vegetable oil

1 tablespoon cumin

1/4 teaspoon red pepper flakes

1 tablespoon salt

1 + 1/2 cups very warm water

1 + 1/2 cups blue cornmeal

1 + 1/2 cups whole wheat flour

1/4 cup diced hot green chiles

    (frozen Baca's or Bueno are best)

4 cups bread flour

3/4 cup pine nuts, toasted

Whisk the yeast into the 1/2 cup water and set aside to dissolve. In the bowl of a stand mixer fitted with a dough hook, combine the honey, oil, cumin, pepper flakes, salt, and the 1 + 1/2 cups very warm water. Add the blue cornmeal and mix to blend and cool a bit. Add the yeast and the wheat flour and mix one minute. Add the green chiles and 3 cups of the bread flour.

Mix on low speed until the dough begins to come together. Add more flour slowly, bit by bit, until the dough forms a smooth mass and cleans the side of the bowl. Add the pine nuts slowly, working them into the dough.

Turn the dough out into a lightly oiled medium large bowl, cover well with plastic wrap and set aside in a warm spot. Let rise about 2 hours, or until doubled and very light.

Remove the wrap and save it for later. Punch the dough down and turn it out onto a clean work surface. Knead it 3 or 4 times. Divide into 2 equal portions, set aside on the work board and cover with the wrap for 10 minutes.

Preheat the oven to 350°.

Form the loaves by firmly pressing the dough into 2 rough rectangles, each about 8 by 10 inches. Roll the dough down tightly towards you, from the top, pressing at the edge of the roll with your thumbs to seal.

Place the loaves, seam side down, in 2 lightly oiled 9- by 5-inch bread pans. Set the pans together in a warm spot, cover with the wrap and let rise for 40 minutes to one hour, or until above the edge of the pans and very light.

Make 3 diagonal cuts across the tops and place in the middle of the oven. Bake 40 to 50 minutes, or until very deep golden and hollow when tapped on the bottom.

{ There's no reason ever to have a bad loaf of bread! }

Nutty Bread

TWO LOAVES

An old Lodge recipe, rich with nuts and vanilla, absolutely delicious. This is not like the usual breads that we eat now or that bakeries even make these days, so do try this one. It's worth the splurge.

1 tablespoon yeast

1 tablespoon brown sugar

1/2 cup warm water

1/3 cup butter

3/4 cup brown sugar

3 eggs

1 cup warm milk

1 tablespoon salt

2 teaspoons vanilla extract

1 teaspoon almond extract

1 + 1/2 cups whole wheat flour

4 to 5 cups bread flour

1 cup ground mixed nuts, a mix of pecans, walnuts,

    hazelnuts and almonds

egg wash: 1 egg whisked with 1/2 teaspoon water

Whisk the yeast and one tablespoon brown sugar into the warm water and set aside to dissolve.

In the bowl of a stand mixer with a paddle, cream the butter and brown sugar till light. Add the eggs one by one, beating after each. Add the yeast mixture, then the warm milk, the salt and extracts.

Change from the paddle to a dough hook. Add the wheat flour and 4 cups of bread flour, mixing on low speed until dough begins to come together. Add the ground nuts and mix a minute more. Add more flour bit by bit, on low speed, until dough forms a smooth mass that cleans the side of the bowl. Turn out into a lightly oiled large bowl, cover well with plastic wrap and set aside in a warm spot. Let rise for 2 hours or until doubled and very light.

Remove the wrap and save it for later. Turn the dough out onto a clean work surface and punch down with your fist. Sprinkle a little flour around the dough if too sticky and knead briefly, 3 or 4 times. Divide the dough into two portions, set aside on the work surface and cover with the wrap for 10 minutes.

Preheat the oven to 350°.

Form the loaves by pressing each ball out into a rough rectangle, about 8 by 10 inches. Roll the dough down tightly from the top, rolling towards you, pressing at the edges with your thumbs to seal. Place the loaves, seam side down, in two lightly oiled 9- by 5-inch bread pans.

Set the pans together in a warm spot, cover with the wrap and let rise for 40 minutes to one hour, or until well risen over the top of the pans.

Brush the tops with egg wash, make 3 diagonal cuts across each, and place the loaves in the middle of the oven. Bake 45 to 55 minutes, or until deep golden brown, and hollow when tapped on the bottoms. Cool completely on a rack.

Rosemary Raisin Bread

TWO LOAVES

Fragrant and flavorful, wonderful with soups—and, of course, toasted and buttered.

1 tablespoon yeast

1/2 cup warmish water

1 cup warm milk

1/4 cup sugar

1 tablespoon salt

1 tablespoon chopped fresh rosemary leaves

3 eggs, beaten

1/4 cup olive oil

2 cups whole wheat flour

4 cups bread flour

1 cup raisins, soaked in 2 cups warm water 5 minutes, drained very well

Whisk the yeast into the 1/2 cup water to dissolve.

In the bowl of a stand mixer fitted with a dough hook, combine the warm milk, sugar, salt and rosemary. Add the beaten eggs and mix on low speed for one minute. Mix in the olive oil, then add the yeast. Add the wheat flour and 3 cups of the bread flour. Mix on low speed until the dough begins to come together. Add more flour a little at a time, on low speed, till dough forms a smooth mass and cleans the sides of the bowl. Add the well-drained raisins slowly, sprinkling them over the dough with the machine still on low. Remove the dough from the mixer into a lightly oiled large bowl, cover well with plastic wrap and set in a warm spot. Let rise for 2 hours, or until doubled and very light.

Remove the wrap and save it for later. Turn the dough out onto a clean work surface and lightly sprinkle flour over and around the dough. Knead the dough briefly, working some of the flour in to make it very smooth and elastic. Divide into 2 equal portions, set aside on the work surface and cover with the wrap for 10 minutes.

Preheat the oven to 350°. Form the loaves by firmly pressing each dough ball out into a rough rectangle, about 8 by 10 inches. Roll the dough down tightly from the top, towards you, pressing at the edge with your thumbs to seal. Place the loaves, seam side down, in two lightly oiled 9- by 5-inch bread pans. Place the pans together in a warm spot, cover with the wrap and let rise for 40 minutes to one hour, or until well risen above the pans. Make 3 diagonal cuts across the tops and place in the middle of the oven. Bake 40 to 50 minutes, or until very well browned and hollow when tapped on the bottom. Cool completely on a rack.

Orange Cinnamon Swirl Bread (Ian's Brown Sugar Bread)

TWO LOAVES

This delicious breakfast bread was the favorite of my son Ian and all the other kids who grew up here at the Lodge. Wonderful for toasting and fabulous for French toast. Easy to make.

1/2 cup warm water

1 tablespoon yeast

1 cup very warm water

1/2 cup sugar

1/4 cup butter, softened (1/2 stick)

1 tablespoon salt

zest of I medium orange

1/2 cup orange juice

1 egg, beaten

1 cup whole wheat flour

4 to 5 cups bread flour

FOR THE FILLING

About 3 tablespoons softened butter

2/3 cup brown sugar mixed with 2 teaspoons cinnamon, 1/2 teaspoon nutmeg and 1/4 teaspoon salt

egg wash: 1 egg whisked with 1/2 teaspoon water

Whisk the yeast into the 1/2 cup water and dissolve.

In the bowl of a stand mixer fitted with a dough hook, combine the hot water, sugar, butter, salt, zest and juice. Mix on low speed one minute until the butter is melted. Add the yeast mixture. Add the beaten egg and one cup wheat flour. Mix on low one minute. Add 4 cups of bread flour and mix on low speed until dough begins to come together. Add more flour bit by bit, on low speed, till dough forms a smooth mass and cleans the sides of the bowl. Turn out into a very lightly oiled large bowl and cover well with plastic wrap. Set aside in a warm spot to rise, 2 hours or until doubled and very light.

Remove the wrap and save it for later. Punch the dough down with your fist and fold the dough over on itself. Turn the dough out on a clean work surface and knead the dough briefly, three or four times. Divide the dough in 2 portions, set aside and cover with the wrap for 10 minutes.

Preheat the oven to 350°.

Form the loaves by firmly pressing the dough out into a rough 8- by 12-inch rectangle. Spread one half of the butter over the top two-thirds of the rectangle. Sprinkle half the brown sugar mixture over the butter. Roll the rectangle down tightly from the top, sealing the seam well at the bottom.

Place the loaves, seam sides down, in 2 lightly oiled 9- by 5-inch bread pans. Press down on the tops of the loaves with the flat of your hand. Place the pans together in a warm spot, cover with the wrap and let rise for 40 minutes to one hour, or until well risen above the pans and very light when you touch the surface.

Brush the top of the loaves with some egg wash, make 3 diagonal cuts across each and place in the middle of the oven. Bake 45 to 55 minutes, or until deep golden brown and hollow when tapped on the bottoms. Cool completely on a rack.

Day-old Orange Cinnamon Swirl Bread makes great French toast (page 36). Soak briefly on both sides in a well-whisked batter made with buttermilk, eggs and a pinch of salt, and fry in butter till crispy on both sides.

THE JOY OF SOUP

It was so perfect to arrive here and find that I would be able to make a different soup *every* day, and the bread to go with it! Although I had made some of both at other restaurants where I'd worked, they weren't nearly so varied, nor such an integral part of the meal. The truth is that I love soup and practically live on it at times. It' s also really fun to make and easy, and the big payoff is you nearly always have leftovers! Mary is the queen of leftovers, transforming a little soup and dressing from the Lodge into very delicious and healthy meals for her family with simple additions of rice, tofu, maybe some pasta, more veggies, and beans. Our staff also makes most of their meals of soup, salad, bread and, of course, dessert. Not necessarily in that order, either!

A few notes on soups and the recipes that follow: First, a good rich stock has long been considered the basis for a successful soup. Having said that, as you go through these recipes you will notice that many of our soups are based on only water. The basic reason for this is our desire to accommodate vegetarians. We actually don't get that many strict vegetarians here at the Lodge, and many of them (including Gary Garland) don't react to a small amount of good stock in their soup. But rather than querying each diner or making a second soup we just started making a lot more of them without chicken stock!

The way we do this is with lots of aromatics, such as onions, garlic, celery and carrots, pure olive oil, good quality dried herbs, and a slow sweat to develop all the flavors. I believe this method of slowly cooking the veggies and herbs allows them to break down more completely before adding the liquid. The use of dried herbs in soups is preferable for their more concentrated flavor, and of course, convenience and availability. Fresh herbs are best chopped and added during the last 10 to 15 minutes of cooking, for the best flavor and color.

The other all-important ingredients are a good quality salt and freshly cracked pepper. We salt judiciously at every stage of cooking for full integration of flavors.

Good, rich chicken stock is still an essential ingredient to have on hand (or in your freezer) and really is best for some of the soups in this book. In the recipes where I believe stock is required I have listed it first, and often with some portion of

water. I think it's okay to have a good quality canned broth in your cupboard, because the reality is that it's just hard to do all the things we'd like to do in a day. Swanson's consistently wins the taste tests nationwide, and it has now come out with low-sodium, no-MSG, and organic versions; ask your grocer to stock them. In my experience, the organic brands from natural food stores have been pretty bad, so don't waste your money.

Chicken Stock

A good basic stock to have on hand for sauces and to enrich soups. This can be reduced to make a sort of "chicken demiglace" or very rich base that keeps very well in the freezer.

1 chicken, organic or at least naturally raised,
    4 to 5 pounds, cut up

1 cup coarsely chopped celery

2 cups coarsely chopped carrots

2 cups coarsely chopped onions, with some of the skins

6 stems and leaves of Italian parsley

2 teaspoons black peppercorns

1 + 1/2 gallons cold water, divided

Rinse the chicken pieces in cold water. In a 10-quart stockpot, combine the chicken, vegetables, parsley, and peppercorns. Add one gallon of water, bring to a slow boil, skimming the foam that forms on the surface. Adjust heat to keep at a steady simmer and cook until volume is reduced by about one half. Add the remaining water and 1 tablespoon of salt. Continue cooking until reduced again by one third. Strain the stock, cool in a water/ice bath, then refrigerate overnight. Skim the fat layer off the top, strain again through a double layer of cheesecloth into a clean pot. Divide into smaller containers for storage. Keeps in the refrigerator three to four days, in the

freezer two months. Makes about three quarts.

To make a chicken glacé: Reduce de-fatted and strained stock down to one quart. Cool, refrigerate, then divide into one-cup containers and freeze. This can be used as a base, with additional water and/or stock and wine to make sauces.

Ancho Purée

This recipe makes about two to three cups of fabulous ancho purée that you can use in soups, stews, and sauces. It freezes really well. Of course, you can always use ground ancho chile powder, often found in the Hispanic spices section of the grocery store, generally near the produce. It's also a very great product, just not as complex in flavor.

1 teaspoon each cumin seed, oregano, sage,
    kosher salt

10 ancho chiles, stemmed and rinsed

1/2 medium onion, chopped

4 garlic cloves

Toast the spices, salt, and garlic together in a heavy skillet over medium heat for five minutes or until they become slightly fragrant. Add the onion and chiles and sauté the whole thing together for 5 minutes or more, again until toasty fragrant. Transfer the mixture to a saucepan and add water to cover. Cook over medium high heat, partially covered, 15 to 20 minutes. Cool a bit. Transfer to a blender and process until very smooth.

Pour the purée through a strainer, whisking the mixture to force every bit of the puree to come through and leaving the bits of skin and seeds behind.

Coconut Seafood Chowder

FOR EIGHT TO TEN

Coconut Seafod Chowder is a year-round favorite, rich in flavors and textures, yet surprisingly light to eat. It has a vaguely Asian taste but goes with many different entrées, except, perhaps, really Mexican or Southwestern dishes.

2 tablespoons olive oil

1 + 1/2 cups celery, sliced 1/4 inch

1 + 1/2 cups leeks, sliced 1/4 inch

1 + 1/2 cups carrots, sliced 1/4 inch

1 tablespoon ginger, minced

1 tablespoon garlic, minced

1 teaspoon each thyme, marjoram, kosher salt

1/4 teaspoon red pepper flakes

1/2 cup blanched slivered almonds, toasted and ground in a processor

1/2 cup unsweetened coconut, toasted and ground in a processor (toast and grind the nuts and coconut together to a rough meal)

1 cup canned tomatoes, chopped in medium pieces

2 cups clam juice

3 cups water

1 cup unsweetened coconut milk

2 tablespoons lemon and/or lime juice

2 tablespoons cilantro, chopped

Drops of hot pepper sauce, 2 to 3 to taste

1 full cup crabmeat, picked over for shell

In a 4- to 6-quart stockpot, warm the oil over medium heat. Add the celery, leeks, carrots, ginger, garlic, herbs, salt, and pepper flakes. Cover and sweat for five to 10 minutes until a bit juicy.

Add the ground nuts and coconut, chopped tomatoes, clam juice, and water, cover, and bring to a very gentle boil. Reduce the heat some and cook until the veggies are tender.

Remove from heat. Add the coconut milk, lemon and lime juice, and cilantro. Add the crabmeat, mix well. Add salt if needed and the pepper sauce to taste. Serve immediately garnished with sliced scallions or chives.

VARIATIONS

~ Add 1 + 1/2 cups chopped raw small shrimp.

~ Or add 1 + 1/2 cup corn kernels along with the chopped tomatoes. Substitute chicken stock or water for the clam juice.

Black-Eyed Pea Soup with Kale

FOR EIGHT TO TEN

One of many nods to my mother's Southern roots, Black-Eyed Pea Soup with Kale is especially satisfying in fall and winter, but we serve it all year, simply adding more veggies in the summer.

2 tablespoons olive oil

2 to 3 stalks celery, about 1 + 1/2 cups chopped

2 medium carrots, peeled and sliced, 1 + 1/2 cups

1 medium leek, white and tender green parts only,
    sliced

1/2 medium each red and yellow bell pepper, diced,
    about 1 to 1 + 1/2 cups

2 teaspoons minced garlic

1 teaspoon kosher salt, more later

1 teaspoon each thyme, oregano, marjoram

1/2 teaspoon each sage, dill weed, dill seed, cumin

1/8 teaspoon (scant) cayenne pepper

1 + 1/4 cups dried black-eyed peas

9 cups water or half stock/water

2 cups packed kale, Swiss chard or
    other greens as you wish

about 1 teaspoon liquid pepper sauce,
    such as Crystal or Tabasco

about 2 teaspoons apple cider vinegar, to taste

1 to 2 tablespoons chopped Italian parsley

In a 4- to 6-quart stockpot, warm the olive oil over medium heat. Add the celery, carrots, leeks, peppers, garlic and one teaspoon salt, mix well, cover and sweat for a few minutes. Add the herbs and spices, cover and sweat again for a few minutes more. Stir in the black-eyes and add the water, mix well. Cover, bring up just to the boil, reduce the heat to a brisk simmer and cook for 20 minutes or so.

When black-eyes just begin to soften add another teaspoon of salt. Cook slowly another 20 minutes or until everything is nice and tender. Stir in the greens, and depending on the type of greens, cook another five to ten minutes. Add the pepper sauce and vinegar to taste, and a touch more salt if needed. Stir in the fresh parsley just before serving.

The soup could take longer to cook depending on the age of the peas. If you happen to have fresh black-eyes, use 2 cups of them and add half the water to the veggies to cook for 15 minutes before adding the peas and remaining water. Fresh or dried, they eventually will break down like other legumes, so mind the cooking times so the peas retain their shape. Wonderful with chunks of ham, smoked turkey, spicy sausage, or bacon.

My favorite hot pepper sauce is Crystal brand, from Louisiana. It's not always easy to find so if you see it at the grocery be sure and pick some up. Tabasco is also good. There are tons of hot sauces out there, but in this case you need a vinegar-based hot pepper sauce.

Asparagus-Pea Soup with Lemon Chive Cream

FOR EIGHT TO TEN

Fresh asparagus soup of one style or another turns up on literally every opening weekend menu at Garland's. Actually, I think it's so essential to spring that I often will have it in a salad or pasta the next evening—and, very possibly it will turn up in an omelette at breakfast! When it's in season, we cook with it a lot, and then it's over until the following spring.

1 tablespoon butter

1 tablespoon olive oil

2 small yellow onions, chopped, about 1 + 1/2 cups

2 stalks celery, sliced, about 1 cup

2 medium cloves garlic, minced

3 tablespoons Basmati rice

1 teaspoon each thyme, marjoram, kosher salt

1/8 teaspoon white pepper

6 cups stock/water mix (3 cups of each)

2 cups chopped asparagus

3/4 cup small green peas (frozen is fine,
    we use the "petite" peas)

about 1/3 cup half and half

kosher salt and white pepper

Lemon Chive Cream

In a 4- to 6-quart stockpot, heat the butter and olive oil over medium heat. Add the onions, celery and garlic, stir well, cover and sweat for a few minutes. Add the herbs, salt and pepper, rice, and 6 cups stock/water mixture. Cover and cook over medium heat to a brisk simmer for about 20 minutes, or until the veggies and rice are tender. Add the asparagus and peas and cook uncovered for about 5 to 8 minutes until the asparagus is tender but still bright green. Remove from the heat and let cool for 10 minutes. Add one cup cold water and purée in a blender in batches. It needs to be very smooth.

Return to a clean stockpot and add about 1/3 cup half and half. Add salt if needed and a pinch of white pepper. Serve in warm shallow bowls, garnished with a small scoop of Lemon Chive Cream and serve immediately.

Lemon Chive Cream

1/3 cup heavy whipping cream

pinch of kosher salt or to taste

1 teaspoon lemon juice

2 rounded teaspoons chopped chives
    (or mint, dill or basil)

Whip the cream and salt together in a mixing bowl until the mixture has very soft peaks. Add the juice and whip again until cream is firm. Fold in the chives with a spatula, mixing completely. Chill until serving time. Use a very small cookie scoop or 2 teaspoons to form small mounds to float on the surface of the soup. It will begin melting right away, so float these just before serving!

Sweating those veggies. . . A classic first step in soup making and other cooking combines veggies, usually celery, carrot, and onion and/or leeks (also called a mirepoix) with a little salt and oil in a saucepan. The pan is covered with a heavy lid so the veggies "sweat" out their moisture and become juicy and yummy. This begins the marriage of flavors and creates a medium for adding dried herbs and other ingredients.

Fresh Carrot Soup
with Mint Cream

FOR EIGHT TO TEN

This soup is a light but very stimulating beginning to a big-flavor meal. The soup itself is very simple and is completed, I think, by the garnish. It's excellent cold as well.

1 tablespoon each butter and olive oil

2 cups chopped yellow onion

5 cups sliced, peeled carrots

1 teaspoon each thyme and marjoram

1 teaspoon curry powder

1 + 1/2 teaspoons kosher salt

1 tablespoon honey

2 tablespoons Basmati rice

7 cups chicken stock/water (4 cups/3 cups)

1/4 cup orange juice

2 tablespoons lemon juice, or to taste

1/2 cup half and half

kosher salt and white pepper

Mint Cream

In a 4- to 6-quart stockpot, warm the butter and olive oil over medium heat. Add the onions and carrots, stir well, cover, and sweat five minutes. Add the herbs, curry powder, salt, honey, and stock/water mixture, cover and cook at a brisk simmer for 15 minutes. Add the rice, cover and cook 15 minutes more.

Remove from heat and cool 10 minutes. Purée in a blender in batches to a very smooth texture. Transfer to a clean stockpot, and add a little water if the purée is too thick. Add the orange juice and one tablespoon of lemon juice, mix well, and add the half and half. Add a touch more salt if needed and a pinch of white pepper, taste, and add more lemon juice at this point if it needs a bit of acidity.

Serve in warm shallow bowls with a small scoop of Mint Cream added just before serving.

Mint Cream

1/3 cup heavy whipping cream

pinch kosher salt

1 generous teaspoon chopped mint

Whip the cream and salt together in a mixing bowl until cream has firm peaks. Fold in the mint with a spatula, mixing completely. Chill until serving time.

Red Lentil Chowder

FOR EIGHT TO TEN

A lovely soup, warm with Indian spices, great to precede a lighter dinner entrée, or perfect as a meal with some whole grain sourdough and a salad.

2 tablespoons olive oil

2 to 3 stalks celery, sliced , about 1 + 1/2 cups

2 medium carrots, peeled and sliced, 1 + 1/2 cups

1 medium yellow onion, diced, 1 + 1/2 cups

1 tablespoon minced garlic

1 teaspoon minced gingerroot

1 teaspoon kosher salt, more later to taste

1 teaspoon each leaf thyme and marjoram

1 teaspoon cinnamon

2 teaspoons ground coriander

1 + 1/2 teaspoons ground cumin

1/4 teaspoon cayenne

1 cup canned pear tomatoes, chopped

1 + 1/2 cups red lentils, well washed in cold water

8 cups water or half stock/half water

1 + 1/2 cups yellow summer squash,
        cut in 1/4-inch dice

2 to 3 tablespoons chopped cilantro

2 tablespoons lemon juice or to taste

In a 4- to 6-quart stockpot warm the olive oil over medium heat. Add the celery, carrots, onions, garlic, ginger, and salt, stir well, cover and sweat for 5 minutes. Add the herbs and spices and chopped tomatoes, cover, and sweat again for a minute or two.

Add the red lentils and water, stir well, and cover. Bring to a gentle boil, reduce heat to a simmer and cook another 15 minutes. Add squash and cook another 15 to 20 minutes or until the lentils have broken down and the veggies are tender. Stir in the cilantro, add a bit of salt and pepper if needed, and add lemon juice just to brighten.

You may wish to thin this soup with a bit of water.

Six Onion Soup

FOR EIGHT TO TEN

Loaded with immunity-building alliums, based with rich chicken broth and finished with a good slug of brandy, it's like a cold remedy in a bowl..

2 tablespoons olive oil

2 medium yellow onions, quartered, then sliced 1/8 inch thick

1 medium red onion quartered, sliced 1/8 inch thick

1 large leek, cleaned, split and sliced 1/8 inch thick

2 small white onions quartered, sliced 1/8 inch thick

1 tablespoon minced garlic

1 teaspoon each kosher salt, thyme, sage and marjoram

1/2 teaspoon each dry mustard and dill seed

1/4 teaspoon fresh pepper

7 cups chicken stock (or beef stock)

1 cup dry red wine (Merlot or Pinot Noir)

1 piece Parmesan rind, about 2 inches square

1/4 cup brandy

shredded Parmesan and green onions

or chives for garnish

In a 4- to 6-quart stockpot, warm the olive oil over medium high heat. Add the veggies and garlic, cover, and sweat for 5 minutes until beginning to get juicy. Add the salt, herbs, and spices, cover, and cook over medium low heat for 25 to 35 minutes. Take care to adjust heat and stir occasionally to prevent sticking.

When all the onions are nice and golden, add the stock, wine, and rind, cover, and cook 20 minutes more. Add the brandy; add kosher salt and fresh pepper to taste (which it will need). Simmer 10 minutes.

Serve in warm bowls garnished with shredded Parm and green onions or chives.

Really good rich beef stock is, of course, wonderful here but we generally don't use it in soups at the Lodge because of the dietary restrictions some guests have. This soup is great with croutons also, the cubes rather than the traditional rounds.

A product that we sometimes use at the Lodge in lieu of beef stock is called Bragg's Aminos, found at any good health food store. It has a flavor somewhere between soy sauce and beef stock, though not as strong or salty as either one; it's a good item to have on hand.

Garland's Garden Minestrone

This vegetable soup/stew is simply based upon the seasons and the cupboard. We do a summer version well laden with tomatoes, peppers, and basil and a fall version with pumpkin, sweet potatoes, and cabbage. Or whatever. And they're all delicious.

2 tablespoons olive oil

1 + 1/2 cups celery, sliced into 1/4-inch half-moons

1 + 1/2 cups leeks, sliced into 1/4-inch rounds

1 + 1/2 cups carrots, sliced into 1/4-inch rounds

1 cup canned tomatoes, chopped

1 tablespoon each kosher salt, thyme,
   marjoram, basil

1/4 teaspoon red pepper flakes

6 cups water, to start

1 piece Parmesan rind, about 2 inches square
   (optional but great if available)

1 + 1/2 cups cooked white beans

1 cup asparagus pieces, 1/2 to 3/4 inch lengths

3/4 cup baby green beans, cut into 3/4 inch lengths

3/4 cup fennel bulb, cut into 1/2-inch dice

3/4 cup spring peas (frozen is fine)

2 cups baby spinach leaves, chopped lightly

kosher salt and fresh pepper

fresh Italian parsley, about 2 tablespoons chopped

freshly hand-grated Parmesan cheesse for garnish

In a 4- to 6-quart stockpot, warm the oil over medium heat. Add the celery, leeks, and carrots, cover, and sweat 5 minutes. Add the tomatoes, salt, herbs, pepper flakes, and water to cover well. Add the Parmesan rind if you have it. Cover and bring to a gentle boil, then reduce heat and simmer for 15 minutes. Add the white beans and cook 10 minutes more. Add the asparagus, beans, fennel, peas and spinach. Cook uncovered until the veggies are tender, 10 to 15 minutes.

Stir in the fresh parsley; add salt and fresh pepper to taste. Remove the Parmesan rind. Serve in warm bowls, garnished with long shreds of Parmesan.

When and how to salt? All stories have a beginning, a middle, and an end, and the same is true for salt in a dish. It's important to salt at each major stage of the preparation of any savory dish. If you salt only to taste at the end of cooking, the salt flavor cannot penetrate the dish. It just "lays on top" of the dish's flavor and often tastes too salty. Types of salt make a difference, too. We use kosher salt, primarily, for its nice clean taste, and we like to keep a stash of special salts such as fleur de sel, the "flower of the salt." Check out the markets these days for a variety of salt choices.

Good canned white beans are a great staple to have in the pantry. Try to buy one of the organic brands, many of which are available at the local supermarket. Of course, if you're making fresh beans for this soup, please make more to have on hand for other great uses, like salads, or hummus, or chili.

About the Parmesan rind—this is the greatest stuff for flavoring a soup or beans or even rice. It's the perfect thing to use in lieu of meat stock in dishes where you want that full flavor. Just cut off the rind (the printed edge) of the cheese and store in a ziplock bag in the freezer. Cut or break off a piece and add it to your next minestrone. Just remember to fish it out before serving! It will melt some but not really break down completely.

Roasted Red Pepper-Tomato Soup with Cheese Croutons

FOR EIGHT TO TEN

This soup is like summer in a cup. Vitamin and mineral packed, very low fat but tasting very rich, it's a perfect beginning to a summer meal. It's also great for lunch with a grilled cheese sandwich— and it's excellent cold. Any number of other garnishes would work.

About 1/4 cup olive oil

3 medium tomatoes (or 4 plum tomatoes) halved

3 medium red bell peppers, halved and seeded

1 + 1/2 cups coarsely chopped yellow onion

1 small yellow squash, halved lengthwise

1 cup sliced celery

1 cup sliced carrots

1 teaspoon kosher salt

1 teaspoon each basil, thyme, oregano

1/4 teaspoon crushed red pepper flakes

1/2 teaspoon ground cumin

8 cups water

1/4 to 1/3 cup half and half

1 to 2 tablespoons lemon juice, to taste

Preheat oven to 400°. Spread the tomatoes, peppers, onion, and yellow squash on an oiled sheet pan. They can be slightly overlapping. Brush the veggies with some of the olive oil, sprinkle with a good pinch of salt and a bit of coarse pepper. Roast 15 to 20 minutes or until browning well at the edges.

Meanwhile, heat the remaining oil in a 4- to 6-quart stockpot, add the celery, carrots, salt, herbs and spices, cover and sweat for 15 minutes over low heat.

When the roasted veggies are cool enough to handle, cut or tear into medium chunks and add to the stockpot. Add seven cups of the water, cover and cook at a brisk simmer until very tender, about 25 to 30 minutes more.

Set aside off the heat for 10 minutes to cool, then add one cup of cold water. Purée in batches to a very smooth consistency.

Transfer to a clean stockpot. Add the half and half and a bit more salt if needed. Add a touch of lemon, and a little water if too thick. Serve with Cheese Croutons or Basil Cream (page 118).

{ This soup is like summer in a cup. }

Cheese Croutons

3 cups bread cubes preferably cut from sourdough

  or other rustic bread

2 tablespoons extra virgin olive oil

2 tablespoons butter

1 clove garlic, pressed

1/8 teaspoon kosher salt

small pinch cayenne pepper

1/4 cup finely grated Parmesan, or 1/3 cup finely

  grated sharp white Cheddar

Preheat oven to 325°. Spread the bread cubes on a heavy sheet pan and toast in the oven for 10 minutes or so, until beginning to dry but still slightly moist. While the bread is toasting, heat the oil, butter, garlic, salt and cayenne together until very warm. Pull the sheet pan from the oven, drizzle the warm oil/butter mixture over the croutons and mix with a heatproof spoon to blend. Return to oven for another 10 minutes or until crisp but tender; do not over bake! They will continue to dry and crisp as they cool. Remove from oven and transfer into a 2-quart bowl. Sprinkle the cheese over the croutons while stirring to blend. Spread the croutons on another sheet pan to fully cool.

Garden Squash Dill Chowder

FOR EIGHT TO TEN

A chance to use up some of that zucchini! Remember to cook without a lid after adding the squash. This helps preserve their pretty color as long as possible (veggies cooked in a covered pan for a prolonged period lose their bright color). Lemon juice, lime juice, and other acids can have the same graying effect, so add these at the end of cooking.

2 tablespoons olive oil

1 + 1/2 cups celery, sliced 1/4 inch thick

1 + 1/2 cups leeks, sliced 1/4 inch thick

3/4 cup carrots, sliced 1/4 inch thick

3/4 cup red bell pepper cut in 1/2-inch dice

1 teaspoon kosher salt

1 teaspoon thyme

1/2 teaspoon each sage, marjoram, dill weed, basil

1/4 teaspoon dill seed

1/4 teaspoon red pepper flakes

1 + 1/2 cups red or yellow potatoes,

  diced into 1/2-inch cubes

7 cups chicken stock and/or water mixed

2 cups green and/or yellow squash,

  diced in 1/2-inch cubes

3/4 cup heavy cream

kosher salt, hot pepper sauce to taste

lemon juice to taste

chives or green onions, fresh dill for garnish

In a 4- to 6-quart stockpot, warm the oil over medium heat. Add the celery, leeks, carrots, peppers, salt, herbs, and spices, mix well, cover and sweat for 10 minutes until juicy.

Stir in the potatoes and stock/water mix, cover and bring to a gentle boil. Reduce heat to a simmer and cook until veggies are tender, about 15 minutes more. Stir in the squash cubes and cook uncovered until squash is just tender.

Add heavy cream, mix well and add salt and pepper sauce to taste. Add a touch of lemon juice, maybe a few teaspoons, just to brighten up the flavors. Serve in warm bowls, garnished with fresh chopped dill, if available, and chopped chives or scallions.

Roasted Eggplant-Tomato Soup with Basil-Lemon Cream

FOR EIGHT TO TEN

The original springboard for this soup came from *The Greens Cookbook* by Deborah Madison, a truly phenomenal book that was really an inspiration for me. This soup and many of the vegetable purées that we do at the Lodge might as well be called Roasted Some-kind-of-Vegetable Soup, because that's how they can be in the middle of August when we have tons of eggplant and tomatoes and squash and peppers. We like to serve this with a very garlicky saffron aioli sometimes, but I think it's best with Basil-Lemon Cream.

1 medium eggplant, unpeeled, sliced 1/2 inch thick

1 medium yellow onion, sliced

1 small yellow bell pepper, halved, seeded

1 small red bell pepper, halved, seeded

2 medium or 3 small tomatoes, halved

2 tablespoons olive oil

1 cup carrots, peeled and sliced

1 cup celery, sliced

2 large cloves garlic, minced

1 teaspoon kosher salt

1 teaspoon each thyme, marjoram, ground coriander

2 teaspoons basil

1/4 teaspoon crushed hot red chile flakes

8 cups water

lemon juice, about 1/4 cup

Basil-Lemon Cream

Preheat oven to 400°. Spread eggplant, onion, peppers, and tomatoes out on an oiled sheet pan. Brush with a little olive oil and sprinkle with some salt. Roast veggies for 15 to 20 minutes, or until browning and softening on the edges and tops. Meanwhile, heat two tablespoons oil in a 4- to 6-quart stockpot, add the carrots, celery, garlic, salt, herbs, and spices, cover and sweat on medium low heat for 15 minutes. When the veggies are roasted, set aside for a few minutes until cool enough to handle. Cut into large chunks and add to the stockpot. Add the water, cover and bring up to a brisk simmer. Cook until all the veggies are very soft, about 30 minutes. Cool for 10 minutes, then purée in batches to a very smooth consistency. Thin with a little water if too thick, add lemon juice to taste and salt if needed.

Drizzle with Basil-Lemon Cream on each serving.

Basil-Lemon Cream

1/2 cup sour cream, regular or low fat

3 to 4 leaves of fresh basil, torn

1/2 teaspoon fresh lemon juice, to taste

pinch of kosher salt, to taste

1 to 2 teaspoons water, to blend

Combine all together in a mini food processor or a glass measuring cup.

Process to blend to a very smooth, pale green sauce. If using a measuring cup, you will need a hand-held immersion blender, or stick blender. A very nifty tool, and inexpensive, too. I think everybody should have one.

Sopa de Posole

This is our very untraditional version of a favorite Mexican stew that is both called posole and is made with posole! It's very sturdy and filling in spite of being entirely vegetable, so I like to serve it before a lighter entrée such as halibut or bass. Cook the posole first, then start your soup!

2 tablespoons olive oil

1 + 1/2 cup sliced celery

1 + 1/2 cup sliced leeks

1 medium white onion, diced

1 cup sliced carrots, 1/4 inch rounds

2 tablespoons chopped hot green chiles

1/2 cup diced canned plum tomatoes

1 teaspoon each kosher salt, thyme, sage, oregano, ground red chile

2 teaspoons ground cumin

1 + 1/2 cups cooked posole (see instructions for cooking posole at right)

2 cups posole cooking water

5 cups water

1/2 cup orange juice

2 to 3 tablespoons fresh lime juice

1/4 cup cilantro

1 + 1/2 cups very thinly sliced green cabbage

1/2 cup sliced green onions

In a 6-quart stockpot, heat the olive oil over medium heat. Add the celery, leeks, onions, and carrots, cover and sweat until juicy, about 5 minutes. Add the chiles, tomatoes, salt, herbs and spices; cover and cook gently a few minutes more. Add the posole, the posole cooking water, and 5 cups water or stock. Bring just to a boil, reduce heat, and simmer 30 to 40 minutes, until very tender. Add the orange juice, lime juice to taste, and a touch of salt if needed. Stir in the cilantro.

Mix the cabbage and green onions together gently. Mound a small bundle on top of each serving. Thinly sliced radishes and finely diced jalapeños are another traditional and delicious garnish, adding even more flavor and texture. Serve immediately.

Posole

1 package frozen nixtamal (posole)

1 tablespoon ground red chile

2 teaspoons oregano

1 tablespoon kosher salt

Cover the posole with 4 inches of water; add the other ingredients. Simmer until very tender, generally 1 to 1+ 1/2 hours, but sometimes taking two to three hours, depending on the brand of posole. Add additional water as needed to keep it covered.

A note on posole: Posole or *nixtamal* or hominy is a special lime-treated corn which is a cornerstone of Hispanic cooking. It is the same corn that's used to make masa, the basis for tortillas and tamales. It's especially rich in calcium. It comes fresh or frozen, uncooked, and often labeled *nixtamal*. This is a great product. It also comes dried and I've had less success with that. It's also available cooked and canned. If at all possible, cook up your own batch to get the very best flavor and texture, plus the fabulous cooking stock. You can cook the whole package and freeze what you don't use in this soup for another meal next month!

Albondigas de Pollo in Spicy Tomato Broth

Albondigas, or Mexican meatballs, are a Lodge staff favorite, probably because they can be a meal in themselves, with salad and dessert. Bathed in a fragrant Mexican vegetable broth, they are a substantial first course, so best to pair them with a lighter entrée. Of course, the dish can be great on its own for your next meal, too!

1 pound ground chicken or turkey

3 cloves garlic, pressed

2 teaspoons kosher salt

1 teaspoon fresh pepper

1/2 cup chopped green onions

2 tablespoons chopped cilantro

1 tablespoon chopped jalapenos

3/4 cup cracker meal (saltines, about 1/3 sleeve)

3 eggs, lightly beaten

Spicy Tomato Broth

First, crush the saltines in a food processor. Measure out three-fourths cup; save any remainder to use on another occasion for a quick breading. Combine the chicken, garlic, salt, and pepper, green onions, cilantro, and chiles in the processor. Pulse 3 to 4 times just to blend. Add meal; pulse to blend. Add the eggs; pulse again until smooth. Scrape mixture out into a small bowl; cover and chill while poaching water comes to a boil.

Bring 4 quarts water to a boil. Reduce heat slightly, then, using a small ice cream scoop, form balls of the chicken mixture and release at the surface of the simmering water.

Cook gently in batches of 10 or so until firm (about five minutes). Transfer the cooked meatballs to a clean bowl with a slotted spoon. Cover with a clean towel and keep warm until all the mixture is used.

Spicy Tomato Broth

1 cup sliced celery

1 + 1/2 cups sliced carrots

1 1/2 cups diced yellow onion

1 teaspoon kosher salt

1 teaspoon each thyme, sage, oregano

2 teaspoons ground cumin

2 teaspoons ground red chile

1 + 1/2 cups chopped canned tomatoes

7 cups water

1 to 2 tablespoons lime juice (to taste)

kosher salt to taste

In a 4- to 6-quart soup pot, heat the oil over medium heat. Combine celery, carrots, and onions, cover and sweat until juicy, about 5 minutes. Add salt, herbs and spices, cover and cook a few minutes more. Add tomatoes, water and/or stock; cover and simmer till veggies are tender and flavorful. Add lime juice to taste, and a bit of salt if needed.

Place warm albondigas in each soup bowl, 2 to 3 per bowl, then ladle broth over, making sure meatballs are covered by the hot broth. This method assures a neater serve-up than than trying to fish each meatball out of the soup pot. If this is not a concern for you, just add the meatballs to the soup and serve, garnished with sliced green onions.

Tomatillo Bisque with Tortilla Crisps and Lime Crema

FOR EIGHT TO TEN

Tomatillo Bisque is great with tomatillos from your local supermarket, but really wonderful with truly ripe, slightly yellow ones from the local farmer's market. The Hispanic markets are a good source as well. It's a light but stimulating beginning to a spicy and substantial meal. It's very good cold too.

3 stalks celery, sliced 1/4 inch

1 medium yellow onion, chopped

2 small carrots, peeled, chopped

1 pound tomatillos, soaked in warm water, skin

   removed, cut in quarters

2 cloves garlic

2 tablespoons diced hot green chilies (we use a frozen

   product that's excellent, Baca's or Bueno brands)

1 teaspoon each thyme, sage, oregano

1 teaspoon ground cumin

1 + 1/4 teaspoons kosher salt

7 cups chicken stock/water, approximately

1 small zucchini cut in quarters,

   center white core removed (we want

   the outside 1/3 of the squash)

1/2 of a small bunch of cilantro,

   well washed, chopped, about 1/3 cup

3/4 cup orange juice

lime juice to taste, approximately 2 tablespoons

Tortilla Crisps

Lime Crema

In a 4 or 5-quart stockpot, warm 2 tablespoons olive oil over medium heat. Add the celery, onions, carrots and tomatillos. Cover and sweat the vegetables 5 minutes, until they become a bit juicy. Add the garlic, chiles, herbs, cumin, and salt. Cover and sweat again while you're prepping the squash. Set squash and cilantro aside in a bowl. Add water/stock to cover well, 6 cups at this point. Cover, simmer until very tender, about 20 minutes. Uncover, add the squash and cilantro, cook uncovered at a bare simmer another 5 minutes to soften the squash. Off the heat, add the remaining cup of water, cool 10 minutes, and then purée in batches to a very smooth texture. Transfer to a clean heavy saucepan. Add orange juice, correct for salt; add lime juice bit by bit just to brighten the flavors. If too thick for your liking, thin with a little more water.

Tortilla Crisps

6 yellow corn tortillas

vegetable oil for frying

kosher salt

Stack tortillas, cut in half to make two half circles. Cut each stack into quarter-inch strips. Fry the strips in batches in one inch of hot oil. Scoop the crisps out onto a sheet pan lined with layered paper towels, and sprinkle them lightly with salt.

Lime Crema

1/3 cup sour cream, regular preferably, but low fat is

   okay (forget the nonfat!)

1 teaspoon lime juice, or to taste

pinch of salt

Whisk together until smooth. Serve bowls of soup with a small pile of crisps on top, drizzle with the crema and sprinkle with a few sliced green onions.

Lentil and Sweet Potato Soup with Chopped Greens

FOR EIGHT TO TEN

A fall and winter soup, a meal in itself. Quite often we will use pumpkin or another autumn squash in this, which lightens it up a bit. Either way, with the lentils and all the veggies and greens it's a nutritional powerhouse.

2 to 3 stalks celery, sliced, about 1 + 1/2 cups

2 medium carrots, peeled and sliced

1 medium yellow onion, diced, about 1 + 1/2 cups

2 teaspoons minced garlic

1 teaspoon kosher salt

1 teaspoon each thyme, marjoram, sage,
    ground coriander

1/2 teaspoon fennel seed or caraway seed

1/4 teaspoon crushed red pepper flakes

1 + 1/2 cup brown lentils, rinsed and drained

8 cups water or stock/water

1 cup chopped, canned pear tomatoes

1 + 1/2 cups sweet potato, cut into 1/2-inch dice

2 cups packed chopped spinach leaves

1 to 2 teaspoons hot pepper sauce

green onions, sliced, for garnish

In a 4- or 6-quart stockpot, warm the olive oil over medium heat, add the celery, carrots, onions, garlic, and salt, stir well, cover and sweat for five minutes. Add the herbs, spices, lentils, and stock/water. Cover and bring to a brisk simmer. Adjust heat to keep at a medium simmer for about 15 minutes.

Add the tomatoes and sweet potatoes, cover and cook at a slow simmer for 20 minutes or until all the veggies are very tender and the lentils are beginning to break down. Stir in the spinach, cook uncovered 5 minutes, add salt and hot pepper sauce to taste. Garnish with sliced green onions to serve.

This soup would also be great with small bits of smoked ham, crispy bacon, or turkey sausage.

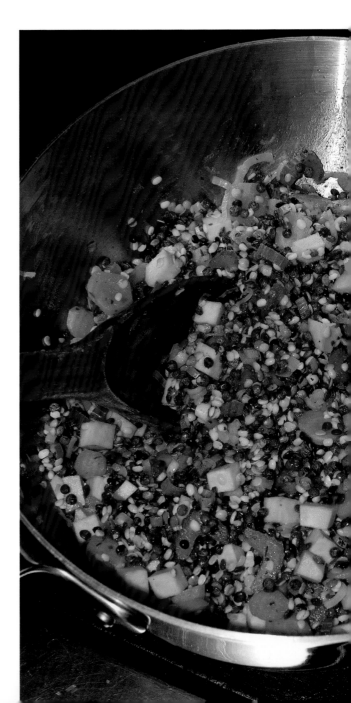

Butternut Squash–Apple Soup with Toasted Pecan or Nutmeg Cream Garnish

This is the essential autumn soup. We have several variations of this soup, with flavor ranges from Southeast Asia to Mexico to Morocco. This slightly Southern version is one of my favorites. Works great with pears instead of apples too.

1 tablespoon each butter and olive oil

3 to 4 cups butternut squash, peeled, seeded,
    cut in 1-inch chunks

1 cup chopped celery (about 2 stalks)

2 cups chopped yellow onion

1 cup peeled and chopped carrots

1 + 1/2 cups tart apple, peeled and cut into 1/2-inch
    dice (Macintosh, Jonathans, Romes)

1 teaspoon each thyme and marjoram

1/2 teaspoon each ground cumin and cinnamon

1/8 teaspoon cayenne

1 teaspoon kosher salt

7 cups stock / water

1 cup apple cider

1/4 cup heavy cream

salt and white pepper

Toasted Pecan Garnish

Nutmeg Cream

In a 4- to 6-quart stockpot heat the oil and butter over medium heat. Add the squash, celery, onions, carrots, and apple, mix well, cover and sweat 5 minutes. Add the herbs, spices, and one teaspoon salt. Cover and sweat again for 5 minutes more. Add the stock and water, bring to a gentle boil, reduce heat slightly and cook for about 30 minutes. Remove from heat and cool for 10 minutes. Add the apple cider. Purée in batches until very smooth and transfer to a clean heavy-bottomed pan. Add the heavy cream. If the soup is too thick, thin with a little water. Add salt and white pepper to taste.

Toasted Pecan Garnish

1/2 cup chopped pecans

about 1 teaspoon olive oil,
    enough to just coat the pecans

pinch salt

pinch sugar

tiny pinch cayenne

Toss all ingredients together, spread in a pie tin and bake for five minutes at 350°, or until fragrant. This can also be done in a small heavy skillet on the stove, but mind the temperature and make sure to toss the nuts to avoid burning. Toasting nuts is a very good time to use a kitchen timer!

Nutmeg Cream

1/3 cup heavy cream

good pinch kosher salt, to taste

pinch nutmeg

Whip cream to soft peaks, add salt and nutmeg, whip to stiff peaks. Chill until serving time.

At dinner, serve soup in warm shallow bowls, top with a small scoop of cream and serve immediately.

MTK's Tortilla Soup with Tortilla Crisps

MTK is the acronym for Mike the Knife, the nickname given to Michael Brosnahan, a great guy who we were fortunate enough to have with us in the kitchen for four years. Mike was a tremendous support, inspiration, and teacher for me, and although he no longer cooks professionally, I still consider him to be one of the most instinctive and innovative cooks I know. We also miss his on-the-floor sense of humor, always a good addition in a sometimes chaotic kitchen.

2 tablespoons olive oil

1 + 1/2 cups sliced celery

1 + 1/2 cups sliced carrots

1 + 1/2 cups sliced leeks

1 teaspoon kosher salt

1 teaspoon sage

1 teaspoon thyme

1 teaspoon oregano

2 teaspoons ground cumin

1 tablespoon Ancho Puree (page 107) or 2 teaspoons ancho powder

1/3 teaspoon cinnamon

1 + 1/2 cups canned tomatoes, chopped

7 cups water

1 cup diced zucchini

1 + 1/4 cups diced sweet potato

2 tablespoons diced hot green chiles (jalapeños or frozen green chiles)

1/2 cup orange juice

1 to 2 tablespoons lime juice

1/3 cup chopped cilantro

1 to 1 + 1/2 cups grated sharp white Cheddar or Cotija

4 green onions, sliced for garnish

Tortilla Crisps

In a 4- to 6-quart stockpot, warm the olive oil over medium heat. Add the celery, leeks and carrots, cover and sweat 5 minutes. Stir in the salt, herbs, spices, purée and tomatoes, cover and cook 5 minutes more. Add the water, cover and bring to a very gentle boil, reduce heat a bit and cook 20 minutes.

Add the zucchini, sweet potato, and green chiles and cook 15 minutes more or until the potato is tender.

Add the orange and lime juices and cilantro, taste and add salt if needed. Serve in warmed bowls, adding a small bundle of chips to each serving and sprinkling with cheese and finally green onions. Delicious!

Tortilla Crisps

6 yellow corn tortillas

vegetable oil for frying

kosher salt

Stack tortillas, cut in half to make two half circles. Cut each stack into quarter-inch strips. Fry the strips in batches in one inch of hot oil. Scoop the crisps out onto a sheet pan lined with layered paper towels and sprinkle lightly with salt.

Corn and White Cheddar Chowder

FOR EIGHT TO TEN

A great summer soup, of course, when corn is happening, but actually just as great all year with a good quality frozen brand. This version has Southwest flavors but we often do a version with dill and sage, and sometimes caraway, leaving out the cumin, chiles, and cilantro. Instead of lime juice I use hot pepper sauce, for the little acid kick. They're both delicious anytime.

2 tablespoons olive oil

1 + 1/2 cups sliced celery

1 cup sliced carrots, thin rounds

1 + 1/2 cups sliced leeks, thin rounds

1 cup diced yellow and red bell peppers (or all red)

2 + 1/2 cups corn kernels (about 4 to 5 ears, or frozen)

1 cup chopped canned plum tomatoes, drained

1 teaspoon each kosher salt, sage, thyme, oregano

2 teaspoons ground cumin

2 tablespoons hot green chiles

7 cups water and/or chicken stock

1 + 1/2 cups diced yukon gold or red potatoes

   (I like to leave the skins on)

1 tablespoon lime juice

1/4 cup chopped cilantro

1 cup heavy cream

1 + 1/2 cups grated white sharp Cheddar, for garnish

1/2 cup sliced green onion, for garnish

In a 4- to 6-quart stockpot, heat the olive oil over medium heat. Add the celery, carrots, leeks, peppers, and corn, cover and sweat 5 minutes, until very juicy. Add the tomatoes, salt, herbs, spices, and chiles. Cover and cook a few minutes more. Add water; bring to a gentle boil, then reduce heat and simmer 20 minutes. Add the potatoes; cook 15 to 20 minutes more till very tender. Add the lime, and maybe a touch of salt, then stir in the cilantro and heavy cream. Serve in warm bowls, sprinkled with white cheddar, then green onions.

KNOT PAINTING

By 1985 four new cabins had been built in the upper orchard and the dining room was getting a bit cramped. We knew we needed to expand, but were afraid of ruining the integrity of the old structure. After a heavy snow in early November, an old English walnut keeled over and damaged the front entrance. Now we had to do something! New young architects at the Design Group in town were consulted and helped us figure out a way to expand and improve this venerable old building. Deep sills and American Craftsmen details created a beautiful new facade. In the process we found a 1943 buffalo nickel in the foundation, a clue to the date of the last dining room addition. Tim O'Malley, a Lodge guest affiliated with O'Malley Lumber in Phoenix, replicated the historic paned and transom windows. The scored concrete floors were painstakingly matched, as was the dark stain on hand-hewn walls.

At some point Gary realized that the knots in the addition had not taken the stain and were glaringly light, while those in the old part had aged to a rich dark brown. Knot painting ensued, and along with it, lots of punchy banter. What to do? What knot to do? Are you painting or knot painting? Maybe it was the fumes, but it made us laugh and we got it done and the end result was perfect.

Mushroom Chowder with Sherry and Salted Whipped Cream

FOR EIGHT TO TEN

This soup has a rather autumnal feel about it, with the woodsy mushrooms and wild rice and the sherry; somehow sherry and port just have a kind of cold-weather, comforting effect about them, so I tend to use them only in the fall and winter, sometimes very early spring. This soup can be lighter and just as delicious without the wild rice. The heavy cream garnish, however, is the key.

2 tablespoons butter

2 tablespoons olive oil

1 + 1/2 cups leeks, sliced 1/4 inch thick

1 + 1/2 cups diced yellow onion

1 cup carrots, sliced 1/4 inch thick

3 cups crimini mushrooms, sliced 1/4 inch thick

1/2 cup dried porcini or shitake
   or forest blend mushrooms

1 cup very hot water

1 teaspoon kosher salt

1 teaspoon thyme

1 teaspoon marjoram

1/4 teaspoon freshly ground black pepper

6 cups stock/water mix

3/4 cup cooked wild rice

1/2 cup sherry

kosher salt and black pepper

1/4 cup finely chopped chives

Salted Whipped Cream

Soak the dried mushrooms in the hot water while beginning to prepare the soup. In a 4- to 6-quart stockpot, warm the butter and oil over medium heat. Add the leeks, onions and carrots, cover and sweat for 5 minutes. Add the sliced crimini mushrooms, salt, herbs and pepper, cover and sweat again until the mushrooms soften and become juicy.

Drain and save the liquid from the dried mushrooms. Add this liquid and the stock mix to the veggies, mixing well. Cover and bring to a brisk simmer while trimming and slicing the drained mushrooms. Add these to the soup and cook gently for 20 minutes.

Add the wild rice, the sherry and two cups of water and cook 10 minutes more. Remove from the heat. Add a pinch of kosher salt and a few good grinds of black pepper. Serve in warm bowls, adding a small scoop of Salted Whipped Cream on top and chopped chives. Serve immediately.

Dried mushrooms of several varieties are increasingly available in the produce section of the supermarket. For this soup, dried mushrooms are preferable to fresh for the intensity of flavor they impart.

Salted Whipped Cream

1/3 to 1/2 cup heavy whipping cream

pinch kosher salt

Whip the cream to soft peaks; add a pinch of kosher salt and whip until stiff. Refrigerate until serving time. Remember that this will begin melting right as it hits the warm soup, so plan the service accordingly. The idea is to have the visual effect of the cream melting into and melding with the soup. Also the taste and texture it gives to the soup is wonderful. It's essential.

SALADS AT THE LODGE

Salads at the Lodge are the second component in our dining experience and need to complement the flavors they follow and anticipate the entrée to come. With this in mind, we try not to overwhelm guests with too much vegetable, but, admittedly, the salads are substantial. Their recipes are also among the most requested. In fact, when we were asking guests for their requests for this book, many just said "All salads and dressings" or "Soups and salads." We are often blessed with Mario's fresh greens in the spring and early summer, and we seek out local sources for interesting lettuces as much as we can. The dressings are the key though. Our basic acid-to-oil formula is one part acid to two parts oil, with very few exceptions. We use very good vinegars and fresh juices, and good olive, nut and vegetable oils. The other constant is a touch of sugar, just enough to soften the acidity and round out the natural sweetness of the oils. Many of our dressings are slightly sweet and are often paired with lettuces and toppings that are sharp, spicy and/or salty, sometimes fruity. This blend of sweet, spicy and salty is a common one in our food at the Lodge.

I suggest a mix of greens for all these salads, and sometimes am specific about which to use. Often a blend of spicy arugula and sweet red leaf is best paired with a sweeter dressing; a sharper, more tart dressing is best with romaine, spinach, and butter lettuce. Many dressings and other components are interchangeable, so do mix 'n match. Dressings double easily and keep well.

Vinaigrettes are paired with the salads that follow. For croutons, see page 147. Here are some other basics.

Pickled Red Onions

1 large or 2 small red onions, thinly sliced
   (3/8 inch thick)
1/2 cup warm water
1/2 cup rice wine vinegar or cider vinegar
4 teaspoons sugar
1/2 teaspoon salt
Pinch cayenne
1/2 teaspoon tarragon or oregano

Combine the water, vinegar, sugar, salt, cayenne and herb in a one-quart stainless steel or glass bowl. Place the sliced onions in a colander and run some very hot tap water over them for about 30 seconds. Shake off excess water and immediately transfer to the bowl with the vinegar mixture. Press the onions down a bit, although the liquid may not entirely cover them. Cover with

plastic wrap and store in refrigerator for two hours, until they turn bright pink violet. They can be stored this way for two days; after that they become mushy. Drain well before using.

Toasted Nuts

All nuts benefit from a light toasting; once this is done, they can be stored in the fridge for quite a while. So always do more than you need. This is the time to use that kitchen timer! Once the oils in the nuts heat up, they go very quickly from toasty to burned.

Simple Toasted Nuts

1 cup chopped nuts (pecans, walnuts, pine nuts,

  almonds or hazelnuts)

About 1 teaspoon extra virgin olive oil, to lightly coat

  the nuts

1/2 teaspoon salt

  Toss all together and toast on a small sheet pan in a 325° oven for 8 to 10 minutes. Check at 8 minutes.

Sweet and Spicy Nuts or Seeds

1 cup chopped nuts (pecans, walnuts, almonds,

  or pumpkin seeds)

about 1 teaspoon olive oil

1/2 teaspoon sugar

1/2 teaspoon salt

pinch of cayenne

  Toss all together and toast on a small sheet pan in a 325° oven for 8 to 10 minutes.

Candied Nuts

2 cups sugar

2 cups water

1 + 1/4 cups walnuts, pecans, or other nuts

  Make a basic simple syrup of the sugar and water: Combine in a one-quart saucepan and bring just to a boil, then remove from heat and cool. Meanwhile, spread the walnuts on a sheet pan sprayed with cooking spray and salt lightly. Toast in a 325° oven for 6 minutes. Remove from the oven, add about 3 tablespoons syrup to the nuts, and stir well to moisten evenly. Return the pan to the oven and bake for 8 minutes more, until they look kind of glazed. Remove from the oven to a rack and cool completely. They will set and crisp on the pan and you need to scrape from the pan with a metal spatula. Set aside at room temperature. Save the sryup for another use.

Buttermilk Dressing

This dressing is our version of ranch dressing, wonderful with fresh veggies as a dip and great as a quick summer sauce for grilled fish.

1/3 cup buttermilk

1/3 cup. mayonnaise

1/2 cup sour cream

1/4 cup lemon juice

3/4 teaspoon dill weed (dried)

1/2 teaspoon salt

1/8 teaspoon fresh pepper

1/2 teaspoon sugar

touch of Tabasco

  Whisk all together in bowl. Thin with a little water if too thick. Store in refrigerator. Makes about 1 + 1/2 cups.

Greens, Beets, Pecans, and Maytag Blue

FOR EIGHT

A great salad any time of the year but especially in the spring when we get the baby gold, red and striped beets. Baby beets can be steamed and peeled, and cut in wedges or even served whole if rather small. Larger, older beets need to be cooked, peeled and cut into julienne strips on the mandoline, or in a food processor with julienne blade.

4 quarts mixed salad greens, washed and spun dry

2 to 2 + 1/2 cups julienned, cooked beets,

    about 5 to 6 medium beets

1 cup crumbled Maytag Blue, Point Reyes,

    or other good domestic blue cheese

1 cup chopped pecans, tossed with 1 teaspoon extra

    virgin olive oil, salted lightly and toasted

    at 325° for 10 minutes

Place greens in a large bowl. Drizzle about a half cup of dressing around and over the greens. Turn greens lightly with your hands to mix evenly. Taste and add more if needed. Divide among 8 cool salad plates (not ice cold). Sprinkle about a quarter cup beets per salad on top of the greens. Sprinkle the crumbled Blue cheese, then the toasted pecans. Serve immediately.

Orange Walnut Vinaigrette

3 tablespoons orange juice

1 teaspooon orange zest

3 tablespooons sherry vinegar

1 tablespoon sugar

1 tablespoon minced yellow onions

1 teaspoon dry mustard

1/3 cup walnut oil

1/3 cup olive oil

1 teaspoon salt

Combine all in a 2-cup glass measure. Blend till smooth with a stick blender. Makes one cup.

FOR POPPYSEED VINAIGRETTE

half of 1 beaten egg

2 tablespoon sugar

1/2 teaspoon dry mustard powder

3 tablespoons raspberry vinegar

3 tablespoons rice wine vinegar

1 tablespoon chopped yellow onion

1/3 cup walnut oil

1/3 cup canola oil

1/2 teaspoon kosher salt

1/2 teaspoon poppyseeds

FOR CELERY SEED VINAIGRETTE

1/3 cup raspberry or cider vinegar

2 tablespoons sugar

1/2 teaspoon dry mustard powder

1 tablespoon chopped yellow onion

1/2 teaspoon kosher

1/3 cup walnut oil

1/3 cup canola oil

1/2 teaspoon celery seed

Mixed Greens with Roasted Asparagus, Egg, and Pickled Red Onions

One of our favorite early season salads featuring asparagus. The bright greens and asparagus with the lovely yellow and white egg strewn across it and the violet pink onions remind me of Easter! All those eggs!

4 quarts mixed salad greens, washed, spun dry

    (a good mix of leaf lettuces, spinach,

    arugula, frisée, or your favorites)

32 medium sized asparagus spears,

    trimmed to 4-inch lengths

4 eggs, hard-boiled, cooled, peeled, and grated

    (use the large holes of a hand grater)

Pickled Red Onions (page 130)

Orange Tarragon Vinaigrette

Preheat the oven to 400°. Bring 4 quarts water to a boil. Add one tablespoon salt. Tie the trimmed asparagus spears together in two bunches with the tips all level (we usually use the rubber bands that come with the original bunches). Lower the bunches into the boiling water minding the tips and blanch for 1 to 2 minutes, until they just turn bright green. Remove immediately with tongs; place upright in a colander/strainer and run very cold water over them to stop the cooking. (You can also use a bowl filled with cold water and some ice and transfer the bundles to this cold water bath.)

Drain the asparagus; spread out on a sheet pan in a single layer and pat dry. Brush very lightly with extra virgin olive oil and sprinkle with salt and pepper. Roast in a hot oven for 5 to 8 minutes, or until very lightly browning and sizzling a bit. Remove from the oven and set aside in a relatively warm spot until serving. (We like to pop these back in the oven just before we assemble the salads.)

Drain the Pickled Red Onions. Place the greens in a large bowl. Pour about a half cup of dressing around and over the greens. Turn and mix the greens gently with your hands to distribute the dressing evenly. Taste and add more if needed.

Divide among 8 plates. Arrange 4 spears on top of each salad, then a strip of grated egg, then a bundle of the Pickled Red Onions. Serve at once.

Orange Tarragon Vinaigrette

3 tablespoons rice wine vinegar

3 tablespoons orange juice

1 teaspoon orange zest

1/2 teaspoon dried tarragon, or 1 teaspoon fresh

4 teaspoons sugar

1 green onion, chopped

3 tablespoons plain yogurt

3 tablespoons walnut oil

1/3 cup canola oil

1/2 teaspoon kosher salt

1/2 teaspoon white pepper

Combine all in a two-cup glass measure. Blend till smooth with an immersion stick blender. Makes one cup.

Roasted Asparagus Salad with Fresh Goat Cheese

FOR EIGHT

I often make my own fresh goat cheese, using milk from Holly Stone in Flagstaff, who has La Mancha Dairy Goats. I also like Laura Chenel Chevre and Montchevre out of Canada. All good grocers carry goat cheese now, and Trader Joe's and Costco have these brands.

4 quarts mixed salad greens, washed, spun dry
> (a good mix of leaf lettuces, spinach,
> arugula, frisée, or your favorites)

32 medium-sized asparagus spears,
> trimmed to 4-inch lengths

1 cup soft fresh goat cheese

1 cup pine nuts, toasted and lightly salted (salt nuts
> just as they come out of the oven so the salt will
> adhere to the oils the nuts exude in the roasting
> process)

Prepare asparagus as in the recipe for Mixed Greens with Roasted Asparagus, Egg, and Pickled Red Onions (page 134) through the initial roasting. Set aside in a warm spot. Just before serving, re-warm the asparagus in a medium oven. Dress the greens with about half the vinaigrette and divide among 8 salad plates.

Lemon Chive Vinaigrette

1/3 cup lemon juice

 2 tablespoons chopped chives

1 medium clove garlic, minced

1/2 teaspoon dry mustard

1/2 teaspoon Dijon mustard

2 teaspoons sugar

1/2 teaspoon kosher salt

1/4 to 1/2 teaspoon freshly ground pepper

1 teaspoon capers

1/3 cup olive oil

1/3 cup extra virgin olive oil

> Combine all in a 2-cup glass measure. Blend till smooth with an immersion stick blender. Makes one cup.

Minted Green Salad with Feta and Toasted Walnuts

FOR EIGHT

This is a perfect spring and summer salad that came to us through the "dream state" of Shirley Ward, also known as Nettie Clark, the first cook I worked with when I started here in 1981. Shirley had cooked here with Susan Garland during the filming of *Kingdom of the Spiders*. Shirley brought many ideas to us throughout the years and really helped me get clear and be true to what we're doing here.

4 quarts mixed salad greens, washed and spun dry

1 cup crumbled feta cheese

1 large English cucumber, split lengthwise, seeded (scoop out the seeds by sliding a spoon down the center of the halved cucumber) sliced into 1/8-inch half-moons

1 cup chopped walnuts, tossed with 1 teaspoon extra virgin olive oil, 1/4 teaspoon kosher salt and 1/4 teaspoon sugar, toasted at 325° for 10 minutes.

1 small to medium red onion, sliced into very thin (1/16-inch) rings. (This is best done with a mandoline, but a very sharp knife, handled with care, can be used. Separate the rings to "fluff" them.)

Mint Vinaigrette

Place the greens in a bowl. Pour about half a cup of dressing over the greens, turn and mix gently with your hands to distribute. Divide among 8 salad plates. Sprinkle with feta, then cukes, then walnuts, then mound a little fluffy bundle of red onion on top. Serve immediately.

Mint Vinaigrette

1/3 cup rice vinegar

1 teaspoon dry mustard

1 teaspoon minced garlic

2 tablespoons sugar

1 tablespoon beaten egg

1/3 cup olive oil

1/3 cup canola oil

1/2 teaspoon kosher salt

pinch of white pepper

1 tablespoon chopped fresh mint leaves

Combine all in a 2-cup glass measure. Blend till smooth with an immersion stick blender.

Makes one cup.

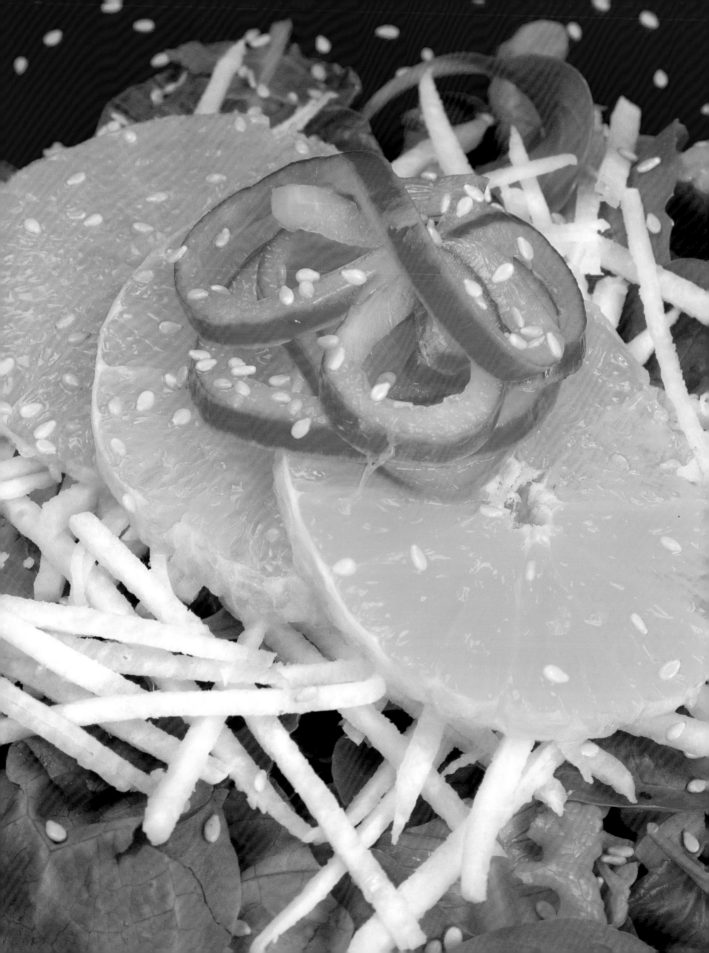

Mixed Greens with Jicama, Orange, and Pickled Red Onions

FOR EIGHT

A refreshing salad to serve with a heartier Southwestern meal.

4 quarts mixed salad greens

2 to 2 + 1/2 cups peeled and julienned jicama
   (1 large jicama)

4 medium oranges, peeled and sliced into 1/8-inch
   rounds

Pickled Red Onions (page 130)

Sesame Seed Vinaigrette

Place the greens in a bowl, pour about a half cup of dressing over, and mix gently with your hands. Divide among 8 salad plates. Sprinkle a crisscross bed of jicama on top. Arrange atop 4 overlapping rounds of orange, mound a small bundle on onions on top. Sprinkle the remaining sesame seeds over all. Serve immediately.

Sesame Seed Vinaigrette

2 tablespoons raspberry vinegar

3 tablespoons rice wine vinegar

1 tablespoon chopped yellow onion

1 tablespoon sugar

1 scant teaspoon dry mustard

1/3 teaspoon kosher salt

1/3 teaspoon worcestershire sauce

dash Tabasco

3 tablespoons toasted sesame seeds (1 tablespoon in
   the dressing, 2 tablespoons for garnish)

1/3 cup canola oil

1/3 cup walnut oil

Combine all in a 2-cup glass measure. Blend till smooth with a hand-held stick blender. Makes one cup.

{ It's easier than you think to make a good vinaigrette! }

Spicy Slaw, Mixed Greens, and Toasted Pumpkin Seeds in Cilantro Citrus Vinaigrette

FOR EIGHT

Another salad to serve with a Southwestern or Mexican style meal; this is a fairly substantial salad in itself, with all the veggies, so plan this with a lighter entrée like fish. This makes a very satisfying supper with a bowl of Sopa de Posole or Albondigas.

4 quarts mixed greens, washed and spun dry

2 cups peeled and julienned jicama

    (a mandoline is best for this)

2 cups finely shredded green cabbage

    (again best with the mandoline)

1 cup finely shredded red cabbage

1/2 cup shredded carrot

1/2 cup julienned red bell pepper

2 jalapeños, seeded and minced

Cilantro Citrus Vinaigrette

1 cup Toasted Pumpkin Seeds

One hour before serving, combine jicama, cabbages, carrot, peppers and chiles. Drizzle about half a cup of dressing over slaw; toss to mix well.

Cover and refrigerate till serving.

Dress greens and divide into eight portions. Top each serving with about three-fourths cup of slaw. Sprinkle with Toasted Pumpkin Seeds and serve.

Cilantro Citrus Vinaigrette

1 green onion, chopped

1/2 teaspoons minced jalapeño,

    seeds and membranes removed

1 tablespoon sugar

2 tablespoons chopped cilantro

1 teaspoon orange zest

3 tablespoons orange juice

3 tablespoons rice wine vinegar

2 teaspoons soy sauce

1/3 cup canola oil

1/3 cup extra virgin olive oil

Combine all in a 2-cup glass measure. Blend till smooth with a hand-held stick blender. Makes one cup.

Toasted Pumpkin Seeds

1 cup raw pumpkin seeds

1 teaspoon olive oil

1/8 teaspoon kosher salt

1/8 teaspoon sugar

Toss all together and toast at 325° for 5 to 8 minutes, till they pop!

Mixed Greens with Crispy Goat Cheese and Tart Cherries

FOR EIGHT

This elegant little salad has all the elements we love in a salad, crispy and creamy cheese, sweet and sharp onion, and tart sweet fruit, all enhanced by a fabulous vinaigrette.

4 quarts mixed greens, (spinach, arugula and frisée, washed, spun dry)

8 ounces plain goat cheese (we use Laura Chenel, or Montchevre)

1/2 cup all purpose flour

1/4 teaspoon salt

1/4 teaspoon black pepper

2 eggs, well beaten with 2 teaspoons of water

1 cup Panko (see note at end of recipe) or fine, dry, plain breadcrumbs

1 medium sweet onion, sliced very thinly

1 cup dried tart cherries (not sweet Bing cherries)

Champagne Mustard Vinaigrette

At least 2 hours before serving, prepare the goat cheese. These can be done up to 6 hours ahead. With a very sharp, thin knife, or with dental floss, cut the goat cheese log into 8 rounds. Place the flour in a small bowl, add the salt and pepper. Place beaten eggs in another small bowl, and the Panko in a third small bowl or on a small plate. Gently grab one slice of cheese with the left hand, dust with flour with the right hand. Dip the floured cheese into the egg mixture with the left, shaking off the excess. Then into the bowl of Panko, again dusting each slice with the dry right hand. Place the breaded rounds on a parchment-lined sheet pan. Set the pan on a level spot in the freezer for at least one hour.

Preheat the oven to 450°. At serving time, remove the pan from the freezer. Very lightly dab the nearly frozen cheeses with a little extra virgin olive oil, and place them on the upper shelf of the oven. Set the timer for 10 minutes and check. They should be light golden and just beginning to "droop" a little. If not, bake a few minutes more. Timing varies with how long the cheeses were frozen, how cold the freezer, how hot your oven really is, etc. When golden brown, remove from the oven and set aside in a warm spot while you assemble the salads.

Toss the greens lightly with dressing; divide among 8 salad plates. Sprinkle with tart cherries. Place a small bundle of sweet onions in the center and a warm cheese on top. Serve right away.

Panko is very fine light Japanese breadcrumbs. Most good grocers carry it now in the Asian section. Sometimes we add finely ground toasted pecans to the breadcrumb mix for another level of flavor.

Champagne Mustard Vinaigrette

3 tablespoons champagne

3 tablespoons champagne vinegar

1 tablespoon sugar

1 + 1/2 teaspoon Dijon mustard

half of 1 beaten egg

1 tablespoon heavy cream

1/2 teaspoon kosher salt

1/4 teaspoon freshly ground pepper

1/3 cup olive oil

1/3 cup extra virgin olive oil

Combine all in a 2-cup glass measure. Blend till smooth with a hand-held blender.

Mixed Greens with Pickled Red Onions and Toasted Cashews in Lime Mint Vinaigrette

FOR EIGHT

This salad has a vaguely Asian feel about it; I like to serve it with Baby Back Ribs with Asian Barbecue Sauce. We prefer English or "hothouse" cukes because their skin is tender and edible, and they have fewer seeds. The farmers' markets in your area are sure to have some good varieties in season.

4 quarts mixed greens (red leaf, spinach, arugula)

1 large English cucumber, split lengthwise, seeded, and sliced into 1/8-inch half moons

1 cup chopped cashews, tossed with 1 teaspoon soy and toasted at 325˚ for 10 minutes, until set and dry

Lime Mint Vinaigrette

Pickled Red Onions (page 130)

Dress the greens with a half cup dressing, mixing gently with your hands. Divide among 8 chilled plates. Sprinkle with toasted cashews. Spread cucumber slices randomly. Place a small bundle of red onions on top. Serve immediately.

Lime Mint Vinaigrette

3 tablespoons rice vinegar

3 tablespoons lime juice

1 teaspoon dry mustard

1 teaspoon peeled and minced garlic

2 tablespoons sugar

half of 1 beaten egg

1/3 cup olive oil

1/3 cup canola oil

1/2 teaspoon kosher salt

pinch of white pepper

1 tablespoon chopped fresh mint leaves

Combine all in a 2-cup glass measure. Blend until smooth with a hand-held blender.

Greens with Bacon and Egg in Curry Vinaigrette

FOR EIGHT

Curry Vinaigrette was one of the originals in the recipe box when I came to work at Garland's, sort of a 70s-style thing when we began to branch out from Thousand Island and Blue Cheese. We have re-worked it over the years to lighten it up for current tastes. This dressing is also great with roasted asparagus, or a cucumber salad, or croutons, red onions and golden raisins or cherries.

4 quarts mixed greens (red leaf, romaine, spinach)

12 ounces medium sliced bacon (not thick sliced)

4 to 5 eggs, hard boiled, cooled, peeled, and grated

1 cup chopped cashews, tossed with 1 teaspoon soy sauce and toasted at 325° for 10 minutes, till browned

8 green onions, trimmed and sliced thinly on the diagonal into 1/8-inch rings

edible flowers for garnishing (such as nasturtiums, marigolds, Sweet William, pansies)

Curry Vinaigrette

Stack the strips of bacon in 2 piles. Cut very narrow crosswise strips, about 1/4 inch wide. Transfer the raw bacon to a heavy skillet over medium high heat. Fry the bacon slowly, breaking up the pieces as they soften so they will cook evenly and completely, until crisp. Remove with a slotted spoon to a plate or bowl lined with several paper towels. When this has cooled a bit, transfer to another paper towel-lined bowl and set aside at room temperature until serving time.

Grate the cooled and peeled eggs on the large holes of a hand grater. We use a 4-sided box grater.

Toss the greens with about a half cup of the dressing and divide among 8 salad plates. Sprinkle with the bacon, then some cashews, the eggs, and finally with green onions. Garnish with a flower. Serve immediately.

Curry Vinaigrette

1/4 cup rice wine vinegar

1 tablespoon lemon juice

1 teaspoon soy sauce

2 tablespoons honey

1/2 teaspoon dry mustard

1 tablespoon peanut butter

1/2 teaspoon curry powder

1/8 teaspoon pepper

1/2 teaspoon kosher salt

2/3 cup canola oil

Combine in a 2-cup glass measure. Blend all until smooth with a hand-held blender.

Mixed Greens with Parmesan, Croutons, Bacon, and Red Onions in Herb Vinaigrette

Another classic salad for us at the Lodge, good any time of the year.

4 quarts mixed greens (crisp romaine, spinach)

2 cups shredded Parmesan (not grated or ground)

12 ounces regular cut bacon, sliced thin
   and cooked crisp

5 cups croutons

1 large red onion, very thinly sliced in rings
   and separated

Herbed Croutons

Herb Vinaigrette

Herbed Croutons

half a loaf French, Italian, or sourdough bread cut into
   3/4-inch cubes, enough for 5 cups

1/3 cup extra virgin olive oil

1/2 cup butter (1/4 pound)

3 cloves garlic, peeled and crushed

1/2 teaspoon salt

pinch each dried basil, oregano, cayenne, celery seed

> Heat the oven to 325°. Spread bread cubes in a sheet pan and bake for 10 minutes while preparing the seasoning. Melt the olive oil and butter in a small saucepan. Add the garlic, salt, oregano, basil, cayenne, and celery seed. Take the lightly toasted croutons from the oven (they should still be soft) and put them into a 2-quart bowl. Pour the seasoning oil over, turning and tossing to mix. Spread the croutons again on the pan, return to the oven, and bake until crisp, but not hard, 10 to 15 minutes more. Cool on the pan, then transfer back to the bowl. Hold at room temperature until serving.

Place the greens in a bowl, add the croutons, dress with half the vinaigrette, mixing well but gently. Divide among 8 salad plates. Sprinkle the Parmesan over, then the bacon. Mound a small bundle of red onion on top. Serve immediately.

Herb Vinaigrette

4 tablespoons lemon juice

2 tablespoons balsamic vinegar

1 clove garlic, peeled and minced

1 tablespoon plain yogurt

2 teaspoons Dijon mustard

1/2 teaspoon sugar

1/8 teaspoon dried sage

1/8 teaspoon dried thyme

1/8 teaspoon dried basil

1/8 teaspoon dried oregano

pinch cinnamon

1/3 cup olive oil

1/3 cup extra virgin olive oil

> Combine all in a 2-cup glass measure. Blend till smooth with a hand-held blender
>
> Thin with a little water if needed. Makes about one cup.

Shaved Parmesan, Toasted Pine Nuts, and Golden Raisins with Greens in Balsamic Vinaigrette

FOR EIGHT

An all purpose salad, good any time of the year. This dressing is always in my fridge.

4 quarts mixed greens (crisp romaine, spinach, arugula)

4 to 5 ounce wedge of Parmesan Reggiano

1 cup pine nuts, lightly salted and toasted at 325°
 for 8 minutes

1 large red onion, very thinly sliced into rings,
 separated

1 cup golden raisins or tart cherries

Balsamic Vinaigrette

Using a mandoline or a very sharp paring knife, shave very thin strips off a flat edge of the Parmesan. Shave enough for 4 to 5 variously sized pieces for each salad. Transfer them to a plate or tray large enough that they can lie flat, not piled too much. You won't use the whole wedge; it just needs to be large enough to hang on to!

Toss the greens with about a half cup of dressing, then divide among 8 salad plates. Sprinkle the golden raisins or cherries, then the pine nuts, then place 4 to 5 shavings over the greens. Mound a small fluffy bundle of red onions on top. Serve immediately.

Feel free to use all extra virgin olive oil in this dressing. We have both pure and extra virgin in our kitchen because I like to use pure for sautéing and soups, and use extra virgin in sauces and salads where the flavor is more pronounced. Sometimes I just want a softer olive flavor. There is the cost difference, of course.

Balsamic Vinaigrette

1/4 cup balsamic vinegar

1 tablespoons lemon juice

1 tablespoons water

1 clove garlic, peeled and minced

1/2 teaspoon kosher salt

1/8 teaspoon freshly ground pepper

1 tablespoon sugar

2 teaspoons Dijon mustard

1/3 cup olive oil

1/3 cup extra virgin olive oil

Combine in a 2-cup glass measure. Blend until smooth with a hand-hand blender. Hold at room temperature until serving time. Store any extra in the fridge; it will keep for several weeks.

{ Pack up a jar of your best homemade vinaigrette and tie a fresh herb sprig to the bottle for a great hostess gift. }

Jicama, Pineapple, Avocado and Jalapeños with Greens in Orange Chile Mint Vinaigrette

FOR EIGHT

This is a classic Mexican salad combination, often served without the lettuce and just a simple lime dressing. This vinaigrette is an offshoot of a basic rice vinegar dressing from our cook Shirley, again from the dream state! This is perfect with the Pork in Oaxacan Mole Verde.

4 quarts mixed salad greens (red leaf, butter, spinach)

4 cups peeled and julienned jicama (best done on a mandoline)

4 cups diced fresh pineapple, about 1/2-inch cubes

3 cups diced avocado, dressed with 2 tablespoons of the vinaigrette

1/2 cup finely minced seeded jalapeños (see note)

Orange Chile Mint Vinaigrette

Toss the greens gently with 1/2 cup dressing and divide among 8 salad plates. Scatter jicama over the greens. Distribute some of the pineapple among the jicama strips. Place a small mound of avocado on top. Sprinkle the minced jalapeños over all. Serve immediately.

An easy way to sprinkle the jalapeños is to dry them first. Place the minced peppers in the center of a double layer of paper towels. Gather the towel up in a bundle and squeeze out some of the excess moisture. Transfer back to a small bowl until serving time. Much easier to fling over the salad now.

Orange Chile Mint Vinaigrette

1/3 cup rice wine vinegar

half of 1 beaten egg

3 tablespoons sugar

1/2 teaspoon salt

1/8 teaspoon ground red chile

1/2 teaspoon orange zest

1/3 cup canola oil

1/3 cup walnut oil

1 tablespoon chopped fresh mint leaves

Combine all in a 2-cup glass measure. Blend till smooth with a hand-held blender.

Makes about one cup.

Baby Tomatoes, Bacon, and Feta with Croutons and Greens in Lemon Oil Vinaigrette

FOR EIGHT

This salad was inspired by a famous salad from Canlis Restaurant in Seattle. They make a wonderful Caesar variation there with a lemon mint dressing.

4 quarts mixed salad greens, well washed, spun dry (use some crisp greens here, such as romaine and escarole)

5 cups croutons

12 ounces regular cut bacon

2 pints (32 to 40) mixed baby pear, cherry or grape tomatoes, mixed colors if possible

1 to 1 + 1/2 cups finely crumbled feta cheese

Lemon Oil Vinaigrette

Herbed Croutons (page 141)

> Stack the strips of bacon in two piles. Cut very narrow crosswise strips, about 1/4 inch wide. Transfer the raw bacon to a heavy skillet over medium high heat. Fry the bacon slowly, breaking up the pieces as they soften so they will cook evenly and completely, until crisp. Remove with a slotted spoon to a plate or bowl lined with several paper towels. When this has cooled a bit, transfer to another paper towel-lined bowl and set aside at room temperature until serving time.

Place the greens in a bowl. Add the croutons. Pour about half of the dressing over and around; toss the greens gently. Taste the greens; add more dressing if needed. Divide the greens and croutons among 8 salad plates. Sprinkle some of the feta over evenly, then some of the bacon. Top each salad with 4 to 5 assorted baby tomatoes, nestled into the cheese, bacon and greens. Serve immediately.

MIXED GREENS WITH BABY TOMATOES IN BUTTERMILK DRESSING Toss 4 quarts mixed greens with Buttermilk Dressing (page 131). Divide among 8 plates and sprinkle with cucumber crescents. Tuck baby tomatoes among the greens. Garnish with nasturtiums or other colorful edible flowers.

Lemon Oil Vinaigrette

1/3 cup lemon juice

1 medium clove garlic, minced

half of 1 beaten egg

1 teaspoons sugar

1/2 teaspoon kosher salt

1/4 teaspoon freshly ground pepper

2 scant tablespoons grated Parmesan

1/2 teaspoon Worchestershire sauce

2 teaspoons chopped fresh mint

2/3 cup extra virgin olive oil

> Combine all in a 2-cup glass measure. Blend till smooth with a hand-held blender.

Warm Figs, Gorgonzola, and Greens with Fig Balsamic Vinaigrette

FOR EIGHT

A truly wonderful late summer salad. This makes a great dinner with a good lentil chowder and some crusty sourdough bread. A Pinot Noir would be nice, too.

4 quarts mixed greens, washed, spun dry (use red and green leaf and spicy arugula or frisee)

16 figs, ripe but still firm

1 to 1 + 1/4 cups crumbled Gorgonzola

1 cup chopped pecans, tossed with 1/2 teaspoon sugar, 1/2 teaspoon sugar, 1/2 teaspoon salt and a pinch of cayenne, toasted at 325˚ for 8 to10 minutes

Fig Balsamic Vinaigrette

Split each fig vertically, down the center, leaving the halves attached at the base. Lay each fig out on a parchment-lined sheet pan. Lightly brush each fig with extra virgin olive oil and sprinkle with a touch of kosher salt and fresh ground pepper. Set aside, lightly covered, until serving time.

Thirty minutes prior to serving, preheat the oven to 400˚. Ten minutes before serving, bake the figs for 6 minutes, just until they begin to sizzle and brown at the edges. Remove from the oven while you set up the salads.

Dress the greens with half the vinaigrette and divide among 8 salad plates. Sprinkle the Gorgonzola over the greens and place two warm split figs on each salad. Sprinkle the spiced pecans over all and serve immediately.

Fig Balsamic Vinaigrette

4 tablespoons Fig Balsamic Vinegar

2 tablespoons orange juice

1 clove garlic, peeled and minced

1 teaspoon Dijon mustard

1/2 teaspoon kosher salt

1/3 cup extra virgin olive oil

1/3 cup olive oil

1 teaspoon sugar

Combine all in a 2-cup glass measure. Blend till smooth with a hand-held blender.

MIXED GREENS WITH BEETS, FETA, AND WALNUTS

Omit the figs, Gorgonzola, and pecans. Instead, add two to two and a half cups julienned cooked beets (about 5 to 6 medium beets), 1 cup crumbled feta cheese, and 1 cup chopped walnuts tossed with 1 teaspoon extra virgin olive oil, 1/4 teaspoon salt, 1/4 teaspoon sugar and toasted at 325˚ for 8 to 10 minutes.

Fig Balsamic Vinegar

1 quart balsamic vinegar

6 dried figs, chopped

2 teaspoons orange zest

1 teaspoon lemon zest

1 tablespoon sugar

1 inch piece of vanilla bean

Combine the figs, zests, sugar and vanilla in a food processor and pulse till finely chopped. Transfer to a 2-quart container (not metal) and stir in the balsamic. Cover and steep for 2 weeks. Strain well.

Point Reyes Blue Cheese with Apples, Greens, and Walnuts in Apple Cider Vinaigrette

FOR EIGHT

The very best fall and winter salad.

4 quarts mixed salad greens, washed, spun dry

(red leaf, oak leaf, arugula and spinach)

3 medium apples (preferably red and green mixed;

good choices are MacIntosh, Golden Delicious,

Fujis, Jonathans, or Winesaps)

1 cup finely crumbled Point Reyes Blue Cheese

(or another good domestic blue)

Apple Cider Vinaigrette

1 + 1/4 cups chopped Candied Walnuts

Pour about third of a cup of vinaigrette into a one-quart bowl. Wash, quarter and core one apple at a time, and slice into quarter-inch wedges directly into the bowl of vinaigrette. Gently stir the slices from time to time so they do not discolor. Cover and refrigerate until serving.

Dress the greens lightly; divide among 8 plates. Sprinkle the blue cheese over the lettuce, lay out 5 apple slice in spoke fashion and sprinkle candied walnuts over all. Serve immediately.

Whenever possible, do try to use tree-ripened organic apples. In order to do this, you need to buy apples in the fall and winter and seek out the farmer's markets.

Apple Cider Vinaigrette

1/3 cup apple cider

3 tablespoons cider vinegar

1 tablespoon minced onion

1 + 1/2 teaspoon dry mustard

2 to 3 tablespoons sugar

1/2 teaspoon kosher salt

1/8 teaspoon pepper

1/2 cup hazelnut or walnut oil

1/2 cup canola oil

Combine all in a 2-cup glass measure. Blend till smooth with a hand-held blender.

Candied Walnuts

2 cups water

2 cups sugar

1 + 1/4 cups walnuts

Make a basic simple syrup of the sugar and water: Combine in a one-quart saucepan; bring just to the boil, then remove from heat and cool. Meanwhile, spread the walnuts on a sheet pan sprayed with cooking spray and salt lightly. Toast in a 325° oven for 6 minutes. Remove from the oven, add about 3 tablespoons syrup to the nuts, and stir well to moisten evenly. Return the pan to the oven and bake for 8 minutes more, until they look glazed. Remove from the oven to a rack, and cool completely. They will set and crisp on the pan and you need to scrape from the pan with a metal spatula. Set aside at room temperature.

{ Support your local farmers! Local fresh food is worth every penny! }

Mixed Greens with Pears, Roquefort, and Pecans in Celery Seed Vinaigrette

FOR EIGHT

A wonderful autumn salad and a great old time Lodge dressing.

4 quarts mixed greens, washed, spun dry

    (red leaf and spinach, watercress)

4 large ripe yet firm pears (red Bartletts, d'Anjou)

1 cup crumbled Roquefort cheese

1 cup chopped pecans, tossed with 1 teaspoon extra

    virgin olive oil, 1/2 teaspoon kosher salt, and

    toasted at 325˚ for 8 to10 minutes

Celery Seed Vinaigrette

Pour a third of a cup of vinaigrette into a one-quart bowl. Quarter and core one pear at a time, and slice each quarter lengthwise into quarter-inch wedges. Slice directly into the bowl with the vinaigrette, stirring the wedges gently so that they don't discolor. Cover and refrigerate till serving.

Place the greens in a large bowl, dress, and divide among 8 salad plates. Sprinkle Roquefort around; lay out 5 wedges of pear, and sprinkle pecans over the top. Serve immediately.

Celery Seed Vinaigrette

1/3 cup raspberry white wine or cider vinegar

2 tablespoon sugar

1/2 teaspoon dry mustard

1 tablespoon chopped yellow onion

1/2 teaspoon kosher salt

1/3 cup walnut oil

1/3 cup canola oil

1/2 teaspoon celery seed

Combine all in a 2-cup glass measure. Blend till smooth with a hand-held blender.

Roasted Portobellos, Red Onions, Pomegranates, and Pine Nuts with Greens in Moutarde Vinaigrette

FOR EIGHT

A great salad for fall and early winter, when the pomegranates are happening. This is a hearty salad, with the meaty portobellos, so serve this with a lighter entrée such as Scaloppine of Chicken, Roasted Quail, or Breast of Duckling. Also great with a sturdy chowder or stew and crusty bread for a casual supper.

4 quarts mixed greens, washed, spun dry (spinach, romaine, arugula, frisée)

6 medium portobello mushrooms

1 large pomegranate, peeled and membranes removed

1 medium red onion, sliced very thinly into rounds

1 cup pine nuts, toasted at 325° for 8 minutes, lightly salted just out of the oven

Moutarde Vinaigrette

Heat the oven to 350°. Pull the stems off the mushrooms and place both caps and stems on a lightly oiled sheet pan. Brush all the pieces with extra virgin olive oil and season with kosher salt and fresh ground pepper. Roast for 10 to 15 minutes, till browning very slightly, and becoming juicy and fragrant. Do not let them dry out! Remove from the oven and set aside to cool a bit. When cool enough to handle, cut into half-inch slices. Place in a small bowl and hold, covered, in a warm spot till serving time.

Place the greens in a large bowl; toss lightly with about a half cup of dressing, divide among 8 warm plates. Spread some red onion rings over the greens, then top with 5 to 6 slices of warm mushroom. Sprinkle some pomegranate seeds around the mushrooms and some pine nuts over all. Serve at once.

Moutarde Vinaigrette

1/3 cup lemon juice

2 teaspoons sugar

1 tablespoon Dijon mustard

1 tablespoon whole grain mustard

1 tablespoon Parmesan cheese

1/2 teaspoon Worcestershire sauce

1/3 cup olive oil

1/3 cup extra virgin olive oil

1 to 2 teaspoons of water, to thin, as needed

Combine all in a 2-cup glass measure. Blend till smooth with a hand-held stick blender. Hold at room temperature till serving time. Makes one cup.

MAIN DISHES & SIDES

Early dinner classics at the Lodge included Apple Glazed Stuffed Pork Chops, Chicken Supreme (chicken breasts on chipped beef with a mushroom soup glaze), and Salmon with Tut's Sauce. Dickie Warlick (a.k.a. Tut), harkened from Portland and poached a mean salmon filet. His sauce was a weird but incredibly delicious combination of odd ingredients. We give the recipe in the following pages although the dish does not appear on our menu today.

Many of our main dishes can be made ahead and so are great for entertaining. But all get loving attention. Deceptively simple roast chicken is an example. Seeing them lined up in hotel pans, one is reminded of other elaborate feminine rituals of "getting ready."

These chickens are not just plopped in the pan and baked. They are

rinsed, then patted dry, dusted inside and out with a special herb rub and finally refrigerated uncovered overnight. This assures complete seasoning and moist, tender meat. They are roasted, then cooled, then carved, before "the girls" are finally brought to temperature, lightly drizzled with sauce, and ready to be presented.

Putting together a menu is like inviting guests to the shared table. Every course contributes its own subtlety or vivaciousness, and the opportunities for pacing and pairing are sometimes the inspiration of the moment, taking into account personality, seasonality, contrasts, complements, and—that little mysterious "something more."

Invariably the printed menus announce birthdays and anniversaries celebrated here each evening. We are honored to be part of these special occasions.

A Sampling of Seasonal Menus

Orange Cinnamon Swirl Bread
Asparagus Pea Soup
Mixed Greens with Pears,
    Gorgonzola and Candied
    Walnuts in Champagne
    Vinaigrette
Alaskan Halibut with Cucumber
    Fennel Relish and Horseradish
    Crème Frâiche
Beluga Lentil Pilaf
Sautéed Rainbow Chard
Strawberry Rhubarb Shortcakes
    with Warm Vanilla Cream
Recommended Wine: Pinot Grigio

~

Rosemary Raisin Bread
Asparagus Leek Chowder
Mixed Greens with Beets, Point
    Reyes Blue Cheese, and Pecans
    in Lemon Chive Vinaigrette
Roasted Loin of Pork with Pinot
    Demi-glace and Rhubarb
    Compote
Sweet Potato Gratin
Broccolini and Baby Carrots
Warm Chocolate Baby Souffle Cake
Recommended Wine: Pinot Noir

~

Sweet Nutty Bread
Asparagus Corn Chowder
Mixed Garden Greens with
    Cucumbers, Gorgonzola,
    Candied Pecans, and Sweet
    Onions in Lemon Herb
    Vinaigrette
Grilled Breast of Duckliing with
    Tart Cherry Bourbon Sauce
Cheddar Sage Polenta
Green Beans and Sweet Peppers
Apricot Berry Tart
Recommended Wine: Shiraz

Oat Sesame Bread
Coconut Crabmeat Chowder
Mixed Greens with Cucumber,
    Cabbage, Cashews, and Pickled
    Red Onions in Mint Vinaigrette
Grilled Alaskan Halibut in Tomato
    Coriander Lime Broth
Lemon Jasmine Rice Timbale
Broccolini and Baby Carrots
Bittersweet Chocolate Tart
Recommended Wine: Dry Reisling

~

Olive Oil Brioche
Summer White Bean Soup
Mixed Greens with Beets, Feta, and
    Sweet Onions in Orange
    Tarragon Vinaigrette
Alaskan Halibut with Sweet Corn
    Relish and Dill Horseradish
    Cream
Couscous Pilaf
Baby Carrots and Sugar Snaps
Berry and Apricot Pie
Recommended Wine: Sauvignon
    Blanc

~

Red Chile Bread
Tomatillo Bisque
Mixed Garden Greens with Jicama,
    Pineapple, and Avocado in
    Cumin Citrus Vinaigrette
Grilled Filet of Beef with Ancho
    Chile Sauce, Mole Style
Fideo con Cotija
Green Bean, Sweet Peppers, and
    Corn
Cinnamon Orange Pots de Crème
Recommended Wine: Rojo

Black Pepper Focaccia
Leek and Lemon Mint Soup
Mixed Organic Garden Greens with
    Boucheron, Pine Nuts, and Red
    Onions in Fig Balsalmic
    Vinaigrette
Scaloppine of Chicken with Roasted
    Tomato, Olive, and Feta
Fresh Black Pepper Fettucine
Squash and Sweet Peppers
Espresso Panna Cotta
Recommended Wine: Pinot Meunier

~

Honey Corn Sourdough Bread
Butternut Squash and Parsnip Soup
Mixed Greens with Figs, Humbolt
    Fog Goat Cheese, and Candied
    Walnuts in Warm Champagne
    Vinaigrette
Roast Pork Loin with Apple Cider
    Demi-glace and Apple
    Horseradish Cream
Mashed Yukon with Scallions
Braised Swiss Chard
Lemon Pots de Crème
Recommended Wine: Grenache

~

Onion Black Pepper Sourdough
    Bread
Sherried Mushroom Leek Soup
Mixed Greens with Apples, Point
    Reyes Blue Cheese and Pecans
    in Apple Cider Vinaigrette
Grilled Breast of Duckling with
    Grapes and Pinot Demi-glace
Wild Rice and Quinoa Pilaf
Baby Carrots and Red Chard
Garland's Sugar Pumpkin Pie
Recommended Wine: Pinot Noir

FAVORED FISH & MARINADES

We generally have fish or shellfish on our menu twice a week. This was originally based on the delivery schedule of our fish purveyor out of Phoenix. Mike Aviano and Mark Boyce of East Coast Seafood have been providing our seafood for nearly 25 years now. I first met them when I was working for C. Steele, a Scottsdale catering firm, and they had just opened a shop on 16th Street in downtown Phoenix.

Mike and Mark now provide fresh seafood to all the AJ's, Basha's, and Wild Oats grocery stores, as well as most of the better restaurants in the state. Fortunately, throughout their continued growth, they have continued to take excellent care of us, in spite of our small size! When you only offer one entree, it has to be of excellent quality; caring purveyors are an important part of any restaurant's success, and they have been one important key to ours.

This brings me to the types of fish we use and why. We basically stay with the more popular and available fish such as Alaskan halibut, striped bass, white sea bass, salmon and Arctic char. In the early part of the month we try to get American red or Hawaiian snapper, when available. Very occasionally, I can get them to find some Ling cod or sturgeon from the Pacific Northwest.

All these fishes work very well with our serve-up, which requires a brief initial grilling or searing, after which the fish is held for 30 to 40 minutes before being "finished" in a hot oven. This method lends itself to the fish varieties mentioned above. We do not do tuna, sea scallops or sole, which need to come directly off the pan and onto your plate, which we cannot do properly when serving 45 to 50 dinners all at once. Our method should work very well at home and for entertaining.

Prior to grilling, we always marinate our fish for at least 30 minutes. Marinating adds subtle flavors to the fish and makes for a succulent end result. The following are some excellent examples.

Citrus Marinade

Our basic all-purpose marinade.

3 cloves garlic

2 tablespoons chopped ginger

3 green onions

2 tablespoons chopped cilantro or parsley

2 tablespoons Dijon mustard

2 tablespoons sugar

1/4 cup soy sauce

1/2 cup orange juice

1/2 cup lemon juice

1 cup olive oil

Combine in a food processor, pulse to blend till smooth. Transfer and store in a glass jar. Use only what you need to barely cover the fish and save the remainder for another day. Marinate 15 to 20 minutes. No longer!

Makes about 3 cups.

Tequila Marinade

3 cloves garlic

3 green onions

1/3 cup each white tequila, lime juice, triple sec,
orange juice, and soy sauce

3/4 cup olive oil

Combine in a food processor and blend till
smooth. Transfer to a glass jar. Use only what
you need to just cover the fish and save the
rest for another use. Marinate filets for 30
minutes. (Good with chicken, too.)

Teriyaki Marinade

This is a good basic, one we used back in the 70s at
The Steak Pub in Jackson Hole! Sometimes the old
stuff is just what we hanker for. Watch this on the
grill, though. It burns more easily than other
marinades.

1/2 cup vegetable oil

2 cups soy sauce

1/2 cup lemon juice

3/4 cup sherry wine vinegar

1/3 cup sugar

3 garlic cloves, minced

1/4 cup chopped peeled ginger

2 green onions, sliced

Combine all in a one-quart saucepan and heat
until just simmering. Cool completely.
Marinate fish or meat about 30 minutes. Save
the remainder for a later use. Makes 4 cups.

Salmon with Tut's Sauce

"TUT" WAS RICHARD MARK WARLICK, WHO COOKED HERE IN THE 1970S. A NATIVE OF PORTLAND, OREGON, HE BROUGHT HIS MOTHER'S BARBECUE SAUCE FOR SALMON, WHICH QUICKLY BECAME A LODGE FAVORITE. THIS EASY SAUCE AFFORDED TUT SOME TIME FOR A QUICK DIP IN THE OLD SWIMMING HOLE ON HOT SUMMER AFTERNOONS. TUT'S SALMON IS NO LONGER ON THE MENU, BUT HERE IT IS AS A TASTE OF HISTORY.

8 six- to seven-ounce salmon filets

Tut's preparation method called for dipping the salmon in seasoned flour, then eggs, and searing it on the griddle. The filets would be brought to temperature at serving time, covered with hot sauce, accompanied by rice and his other labor-saving favorite, "peas and pims," frozen peas, with chopped pimiento for color.

Tut's Sauce

1/2 pound butter

1 clove garlic, minced or pressed

1/4 cup ketchup

1/4 cup soy sauce

2 tablespoons prepared mustard

dash of Worcestershire sauce

1 tablespoon fresh lemon juice

fresh ground black pepper

Combine all the ingredients in a heavy saucepan and bring just to the boil (do not boil).

Salmon with Raspberry Champagne Sauce

FOR EIGHT

An elegant and beautiful presentation for salmon, and equally great with fresh blackberries. Remember to cook your fish until *just* done, to keep it moist and tender.

Citrus Marinade (page 160)

8 six- to seven-ounce salmon filets

Champagne Sauce

fresh raspberries for garnish

Marinate the fish filets for 30 minutes. Pre-heat the grill to medium high. Drain the filets very well, brush the grill very lightly with oil and cook the fish until just barely firm to the touch, 3 to 4 minutes per side. Transfer the cooked filets to a platter and keep warm.

Serve the filets on warm plates with some warm sauce ladled over. Garnish with fresh raspberries.

Champagne Sauce

2 cups fresh or frozen raspberries

3 cups Champagne or dry white wine

2 cup clam juice

1/3 cup rice vinegar

1/3 cup raspberry vinegar

1 teaspoon peeled and minced fresh ginger

2 tablespoons chopped shallots

1 + 1/2 cups heavy cream

lemon juice, to taste

2 to 3 tablespoons of butter

In a heavy 3-quart saucepan, reduce the liquids, berries, ginger and shallots together by half. Add the heavy cream. Reduce again by a third, until thickened. Strain the sauce well and taste; you may need to add a touch of sugar to balance the acidity. Then whisk in the butter to add sheen and help bind the sauce together. Add salt and lemon juice if needed.

Salmon with Ancho Lime Glaze and Tomatillo Salsa

FOR EIGHT

Tomatillo Salsa is great with many kinds of fish and grilled chicken and pork, too. It actually freezes very well so make a big batch when the tomatoes, tomatillos and chiles come on in the summer.

Tequila Marinade (page 163)

Ancho Lime Glaze

Tomatillo Salsa

8 six- to seven-ounce salmon filets

Marinate the fish filets for 30 minutes. Preheat the grill to medium high. Drain the filets very well, brush the grill very lightly with oil and cook the fish until just barely firm to the touch, 3 to 4 minutes per side. Transfer the cooked filets to a platter and keep warm. Brush with the Ancho Lime Glaze before finishing in a hot oven.

Serve on warm plates with a ladle of hot Tomatillo Salsa on top.

Ancho Lime Glaze

2 tablespoons ancho powder, or ancho purée (page 107)

1 tablespoon soy sauce

1/4 cup lemon juice

1/4 cup orange juice

1/4 cup lime juice

1/4 cup honey

Mix all together and heat for 5 minutes on low until slightly thickened.

Tomatillo Salsa

1 pound tomatillos, husked, rinsed, and halved

1 onion, roughly chopped

half of 1 canned chipotle chile

2 tomatoes, quartered

2 cloves garlic, chopped

salt

pepper

olive oil to toss

1 to 2 tablespoons lime juice

2 tablespoons orange juice

2 to 3 roasted green chiles, peeled, seeded, finely chopped

2 tablespoons fresh chopped cilantro

Preheat the oven to 350°. Toss the tomatillos, onion, garlic, chile, and tomatoes with olive oil. Sprinkle with salt and pepper. Roast for 30 minutes. Remove the piece of chipotle chile, then purée roughly. Add the juices, green chiles, and cilantro. Correct for salt, maybe a bit more orange juice. Heat gently just before serving.

Grilled Fish with Spicy Green Tomato Relish and Soy Honey Glaze

FOR EIGHT

Barely cooked Spicy Green Tomato Relish is quick to put together and bursting with flavor. It complements most fish, except the really delicate ones like sole. I've heard it's pretty good with pork tenderloin, too!

8 six- to seven-ounce filets (salmon, snapper, or bass)

Teriyaki Marinade (page 163)

Spicy Green Tomato Relish

Soy Honey Glaze

Marinate the fish filets for 30 minutes. Preheat the grill to medium high. Drain the filets very well, brush the grill very lightly with oil, and cook the fish until just barely firm to the touch, 3 to 4 minutes per side. Transfer the cooked filets to a platter and keep warm. Brush the Soy Honey Glaze on the grilled filets just before they are finished in the oven.

Spicy Green Tomato Relish

1/2 pound tomatillos, husked and rinsed, chopped

1/2 small bunch of cilantro, chopped fine

4 green onions, chopped fine

3 tablespoons rice wine vinegar

3 tablespoons lime juice

2 tablespoons sugar

2 teaspoons prepared horseradish

2 teaspoons wasabi paste or powder

1 teaspoon salt

olive oil

Place the tomatillos in a food processor and pulse until chopped fairly fine, but not puréed. Transfer to a fine-meshed sieve and drain well. Combine the chopped tomatillos with the remaining ingredients in a medium bowl, mixing gently but well. Taste and add more rice vinegar, sugar, horseradish, or salt to your taste. Let it sit for 10 to 15 minutes to allow the flavors to meld and develop. Taste again. At serving time, heat the relish in a double boiler over very low heat till barely warm. Or, just serve it at room temperature over the warm filets.

Soy Honey Glaze

1 cup rice vinegar

1/2 cup soy sauce

1/2 cup honey

2 tablespoons water

2 teaspoons cornstarch

Mix the cornstarch and water. Add to the other ingredients. Cook until thickened and clear.

Grilled Salmon with Sweet Corn Relish and Horseradish Dill Cream

FOR EIGHT

The perfect summer relish, light and very flavorful, and beautiful on the plate. This is great with any kind of fish. We like to serve it with rice on the side, or sometimes Crispy Polenta.

8 six- to seven-ounce filets (salmon or your favorite)

Citrus Marinade (page 160)

Sweet Corn Relish

Horseradish Dill Cream

Marinate the fish filets for 30 minutes. Preheat the grill to medium high. Drain the filets very well, brush the grill very lightly with oil and cook the fish until just barely firm to the touch, 3 to 4 minutes per side. Transfer the cooked filets to a platter and keep warm.

Ladle the Sweet Corn Relish over each serving on warm plates. Drizzle with Horseradish Dill Cream.

Sweet Corn Relish

1/2 cup finely chopped red onion

1/2 cup extra virgin olive oil

3 cups fresh or frozen corn kernels

1/2 cup diced red bell pepper

1/2 cup diced yellow bell pepper

1 teaspoon sugar

1 teaspoon salt, to taste

1/2 cup rice vinegar

2 tablespoons orange juice

1 tablespoon lemon juice

2 tablespoons chopped green onions

1 large jalapeño, seeded and minced

1/4 pound bacon, cut into bits, cooked till crisp,

then drained

In a heavy one-quart saucepan, combine the red onions, olive oil, corn, peppers, sugar, salt, and rice vinegar. Heat over medium high just until the onions turn pink. Turn off the heat. Add the juices, fold in the green onions, jalapeño, and bacon and taste. Add a touch more lemon or sugar if needed, and set aside in a warm spot until serving.

Horseradish Dill Cream

1/2 cup crème fraîche or sour cream

1 to 2 tablespoons well-drained bottled horseradish

1 tablespoon minced fresh dill

touch of salt and pepper

Whisk together well.

Halibut in Roasted Tomato Herb Vinaigrette

FOR EIGHT

Roasted Tomato Herb Vinaigrette is wonderful any time but especially when made with ripe summer tomatoes. We serve this sauce with salmon quite often, and typically pair it with Black Pepper Fettuccine. We serve Scaloppine of Chicken the same way.

Citrus Marinade (page 155)

Roast Tomato Herb Vinaigrette

8 six- to seven-ounce halibut filets

Marinate the fish filets for 30 minutes. Preheat the grill to medium high. Drain the filets very well, brush the grill very lightly with oil and cook the fish until just barely firm to the touch, 3 to 4 minutes per side. Transfer the cooked filets to a platter and keep warm. Serve on warm plates with a ladle of Roasted Tomato Herb Vinaigrette.

Roasted Tomato Herb Vinaigrette

1/2 cup extra virgin olive oil

1/2 cup chopped shallots or onion

8 to 10 medium Roma tomatoes, halved

1/3 cup sherry vinegar

1 to 2 cloves garlic, minced

1 cup dry white wine

1/2 cup orange juice

salt and freshly cracked black pepper

pinch of sugar

2 tablespoons capers

2 tablespoons chopped fresh basil or oregano

Preheat the oven to 375°. Lay the tomato halves cut side down on a lightly oiled sheet pan. Brush with a touch of extra virgin olive oil and roast on the upper rack of the oven for 12 to 15 minutes or till the skin shrinks and begins to brown a little.

Take from the oven and set aside till cool enough to handle. Remove the skins and chop finely. Heat the oil gently in a heavy 2-quart saucepan. Add the shallots and cook for a few minutes.

Pull the skins from the tomatoes and discard. Chop the tomatoes coarsely and add to the pot, along with all their juices. Add the sherry vinegar and the garlic and bring to a simmer for 5 to 10 minutes. Add the wine, orange juice, salt and pepper and simmer again till reduced some and slightly thickened. It should be brothy. Add a pinch of sugar. Stir in the capers and the basil and serve.

Grilled Fish with Cucumber Fennel Relish and Horseradish Cream

FOR EIGHT

Cucumber Fennel Relish is a nice little relish for winter and spring, when fennel is available and tender. We make a similar relish in summer with tomatoes and basil. We use regular sour cream at the Lodge for all our garnishing creams but you could substitute low fat if that's what you have; please, no fat free!

Citrus Marinade (page 160)

8 six- to seven-ounce filets (salmon, halibut, or bass)

Cucumber Fennel Relish

Horseradish Cream

Marinate the fish filets for 30 minutes. Preheat the grill to medium high. Drain the filets very well, brush the grill very lightly with oil and cook the fish until just barely firm to the touch, 3 to 4 minutes per side. Transfer the cooked filets to a platter and keep warm. Stir the cucumber slices into the warm relish and heat for one minute. Stir in the chopped fennel, taste for salt and pepper, and maybe add a touch more lemon juice. Serve the filets on warm plates with some warm Cucumber Fennel Relish ladled over, and Horseradish Cream drizzled across the top.

Cucumber Fennel Relish

2 small fennel bulbs, trimmed, sliced into 1/8-inch rounds, then cut in julienne strips

1/2 medium red onion, quartered, each quarter sliced lengthways into half moon slivers

1/4 cup finely diced yellow bell peppers

1/4 cup finely diced red bell peppers

1 teaspoon salt

1 teaspoon sugar

1/4 teaspoon red pepper flakes

1/4 cup rice wine vinegar

1/4 cup orange juice

1/4 cup lemon juice

1 + 1/4 cup extra virgin olive oil

1 large English cucumber, or hothouse cucumber, halved lengthwise, de-seeded, and sliced in 1/8-inch half moons

1/4 cup chopped fennel fronds

salt and pepper

In a heavy one-quart saucepan, combine the fennel, red onions, peppers, salt, sugar, and red pepper flakes. Add the vinegar, orange juice, and lemon juice. Heat the mixture over medium-low heat just until barely warm. Turn off the heat. Add the extra virgin olive oil and mix well. Set aside until serving time.

Horseradish Cream

1/2 cup sour cream

1 to 2 tablespoons well-drained bottled horseradish, or to taste

a touch of salt and pepper

Whisk together well. Sometimes we add dill or chives to this.

Tequila-Marinated Halibut or Bass with Grapefruit Avocado Relish

FOR EIGHT

The relish with this dish is great for winter and spring, when citrus is at its peak. If you can, get the Texas "Rio Star" ruby grapefruits; they are the best.

Tequila Marinade (page 163)

8 six- to seven-ounce halibut or sea bass filets

Grapefruit Avocado Relish

Marinate the fish filets for 30 minutes. Pre-heat the grill to medium high. Drain the filets very well, brush the grill very lightly with oil and cook the fish until just barely firm to the touch, 3 to 4 minutes per side. Transfer the cooked filets to a platter and keep warm. Add the grapefruit sections, avocado, and cilantro to the warm relish. Taste and correct the seasonings for sugar and salt.

Serve the filets on warm plates with some warm relish ladled over.

Grapefruit Avocado Relish

1/4 cup extra virgin olive oil

1/2 medium red onion, finely diced

1/4 cup red bell pepper, finely diced

1/4 cup yellow bell pepper, finely diced

1 to 2 tablespoons jalapeño or serrano chile, seeded and minced

1/2 cup orange juice

1/2 cup grapefruit juice

1 teaspooon kosher salt

1/4 teaspoon sugar

2 grapefruit, peeled, seeded, sectioned

1 avocado, peeled and cubed

1 tablespoon lime juice

kosher salt

2 to 3 tablespoons chopped fresh cilantro

Heat the olive oil in a heavy one-quart saucepan. Add the onions, peppers, and chile and cook slowly for a few minutes, till they just begin to soften. Add the juices, salt, and sugar and heat till barely warm. Set aside.

Toss the avocado cubes very gently with the lime juice and a little salt. Set aside till just before serving.

{ Fish loves citrus. Try this when grapefruit is bright and juicy early in the year. }

Arctic Char with Lemon-Fennel Olive Relish and Lemon Vinaigrette

FOR EIGHT

Refreshing and delicious Lemon-Fennel Olive Relish is great with most fish but especially salmon and its milder cousin Arctic char. The acidity of the sauce balances the richness of these fishes. We often simply dust small char filets with seasoned flour and sauté them in olive oil; I think this delicate fish is better this way but larger filets can be marinated and grilled.

Citrus Marinade (page 160)

8 six- to seven-ounce Arctic char filets

    (sea bass and salmon work well too)

Lemon-Fennel Olive Relish

Lemon Vinaigrette

Marinate the fish filets for 30 minutes. Preheat the grill to medium high. Drain the filets very well, brush the grill very lightly with oil and cook the fish until just barely firm to the touch, 3 to 4 minutes per side. Transfer the cooked filets to a platter and keep warm.

Arrange the filets on warm plates with some warm Lemon-Fennel Olive Relish ladled over. Drizzle with Lemon Vinaigrette and serve immediately.

Lemon-Fennel Olive Relish

1/4 cup extra virgin olive oil

1/2 cup lemon juice

1/4 cup chopped Italian parsley

1/3 cup minced red onion

1 cup diced fennel

1/2 cup chopped fennel fronds

1 to 2 tablespoons lemon zest

1/3 to 1/2 cup finely chopped Kalamata olives

1 teaspoon sugar

salt and pepper

1/4 cup fresh orange juice

1 teaspoon sherry vinegar

In a heavy one-quart saucepan, combine the olive oil, lemon juice, parsley, shallots, diced fennel and fronds, the zest and olives, sugar, and salt and pepper. Heat the mixture over medium low heat until barely warm. Add the fresh orange juice and sherry vinegar. Correct for salt. Set aside until serving time.

Lemon Vinaigrette

1/3 cup lemon juice

1 tablespoon minced red onion

1/2 teaspoon sugar

1 teaspoon salt

A few grinds of pepper

2/3 cup extra virgin olive oil

Combine all in a blender and process until smooth. Warm just barely in a double boiler before serving.

Citrus-Marinated Sea Bass with Mango, Avocado and Serrano Relish

FOR EIGHT

A perfectly delicious preparation for fish—light, healthy, vibrant with color and flavor. And easy, too! This is a good one for tuna or swordfish.

Citrus Marinade (page 160)

8 six- to seven-ounce halibut or sea bass filets

Mango, Avocado and Serrano Relish

Marinate the fish filets for 30 minutes. Preheat the grill to medium high. Drain the filets very well, brush the grill very lightly with oil and cook the fish until just barely firm to the touch, 3 to 4 minutes per side. Transfer the cooked filets to a platter and keep warm. Add the mango cubes, avocado cubes, serranos and cilantro to the warm relish. Taste and correct the seasonings for sugar and salt.

Serve the filets on warm plates with some warm Mango, Avocado and Serrano Relish ladled over.

Mango, Avocado and Serrano Relish

2 tablespoons extra virgin olive oil

1/2 medium red onion, finely diced

1/4 cup finely diced red bell pepper

1/4 cup finely diced yellow bell pepper

1/2 cup orange juice

1/2 cup lime juice

1 teaspooon kosher salt

1 teaspoon sugar

2 mangos, peeled, cubed

1 avocado, cubed

1 tablespoon lime juice (or orange or lemon)

kosher salt

1 to 2 tablespoons seeded and minced serrano or

    jalapeño chile

2 to 3 tablespoons cilantro, chopped

Optional: add diced jicama or cucumber

Heat the olive oil in a heavy one-quart saucepan. Add the onions and peppers and cook gently for 2 to 3 minutes. Add the juices, salt and sugar and set aside, off the heat but in a warm spot.

Toss the avocado cubes gently with the lime juice and a bit of salt. Set aside with the mangos and the cilantro until serving time.

Herb-Rubbed Roast Chicken with Lemon Herb Vinaigrette or Mushroom Thyme Sauce

FOR EIGHT TO TEN

It took a new convection oven and a few years of working with it to realize we could now roast chicken for fifty people at a time. (Catherine Todd must be smiling down from the Red Rocks of Heaven, Mary notes).

4 three-and-a-half- to four-and-a-half-pound chickens,
    preferably "naturally raised"
Herb Rub
olive oil to brush the chickens
Lemon Herb Vinaigrette or Mushroom Thyme Sauce

On day one: Rinse the chickens inside and out and pat dry. Brush with a very little olive oil, then lightly dust the birds inside and out with the rub. Cover and save extra rub for the following day. Refrigerate overnight, uncovered.

The next afternoon: Preheat the oven to 425° degrees. Take the chickens from the fridge and give them another all-over dusting of rub. Tuck the the wing tips under and tie the legs together with kitchen string. Arrange in an oiled roasting pan with the legs pointing inward towards the center of the pan. Roast in the hot oven for 25 minutes, then reduce the temperature to 350° and roast for 35 to 45 minutes more, till a lovely crispy golden brown. The chicks are done when the drumsticks move freely in their sockets. Take from the oven and set aside to rest for 15 minutes. Carve the drumsticks, and breast and wing off the body of the bird. Serve a drum and thigh, breast and wing per person with warm Lemon Herb Vinaigrette. There will be leftovers, which are delicious the next day, or freeze for a later use.

Herb Rub

2 tablespoons thyme

2 tablespoons sage

2 tablespoons marjoram

2 tablespoons rosemary

zest of 1 orange

zest of 1 lemon

3/4 cup kosher salt

1/4 cup coarse pepper

Lightly toast the dry herbs and zests in a small skillet over medium low heat. Do not burn! Partially grind the herb/zest mixture in a spice mill and mix with the salt and pepper.

Lemon Herb Vinaigrette

This is one of our all purpose sauces. It comes together very quickly and is great with chicken, fish or grilled veggies. I personally like it with steak and lamb too!

1 + 1/2 cups lightly packed fresh Italian parsley,
    basil, mint and/or fennel (see note at end of recipe)

4 cloves garlic, minced

2 green onions, finely chopped

2 cups olive oil

1/2 cup chicken broth

1/4 to 1/3 cup lemon juice

salt

pepper

pinch of sugar

Combine the mix of herbs, garlic, and green onion in a food processor. Pulse 3 or 4 times to blend slightly. Add one cup of oil and blend. Scrape down the sides of the bowl and blend again. Add the broth with the machine running, then add the remaining oil slowly. Add 1/4 cup of juice, one teaspoon of salt, a few grinds of fresh pepper, and a pinch of sugar. Blend and taste. Add more lemon and salt and pepper if needed. This should be a nice light emulsion. Transfer to a small double boiler to warm gently.

Makes about 3 to 4 cups. Keeps two weeks in the fridge, but loses its bright green color when heated.

The main herb in this should be the Italian parsley with smaller portions of basil and/or fennel and mint. It can be made with all parsley. Curly parsley is really not an acceptable substitute. We rarely use it at the Lodge.

Mushroom Thyme Sauce

A really wonderful sauce that Donald Zealand, our dining room manager, requested one day to serve along with mashed potatoes. This seems better for cooler weather to me.

2 teaspoons olive oil

1 medium yellow onion, finely chopped

3 large cloves garlic, minced

2 teaspoons dry thyme

1 teaspoon sage

1 teaspoon salt

1/2 teaspoon coarsely ground black pepper

3 cups dry white wine

4 cups rich chicken stock

1 cup heavy cream

12 ounces fresh crimini mushrooms, sliced

2 tablespoons butter

1 small bundle fresh thyme

2 small sprigs fresh sage

salt and pepper

1 tablespoon lemon juice, to taste

Heat the olive oil in a heavy 3-quart saucepan. Add the onion, garlic, herbs, salt, and pepper and sweat until juicy, about 5 minutes. Raise the heat a bit and sauté until the veggies begin to brown. Add the wine and reduce by half. Add the stock and reduce again by half, add the cream and reduce until the sauce thickens and becomes slightly shiny about 5 minutes. Strain the sauce into a clean saucepan, pressing very well on the solids to work out all the liquid.

Melt the butter in a large skillet over medium high heat. Add the mushrooms and a little salt and pepper and cover to sweat for a minute or two. Uncover and add about 2 tablespoons of thyme leaves. Chop the sage leaves and add. Cook over medium heat until most of the liquid has evaporated. Add the mushrooms to the sauce, along with a touch of lemon juice. Taste and add more if you like, plus more salt and pepper if needed.

Scaloppine of Chicken with with Tomatoes and Olives

This chicken breast preparation is delicious with very flavorful sauces and the bonus of fresh pasta. Find a few of the combinations in our menu section. For a nice variation, try the scaloppine with Lemon Vinaigrette (page 174).

8 Roma tomatoes, halved

1/2 cup extra virgin olive oil, plus extra for brushing

1 medium red onion, cut in 1/4-inch dice

4 cloves garlic, minced

1/2 teaspoon sugar

1/4 cup sherry vinegar

1 cup dry vermouth

1 cup orange juice

2 cups chicken stock

salt

black pepper

1 to 2 tablespoons lemon juice

1/4 cup chopped chives, Italian parsley, basil, or a

    mixture of the two

16 to 24 good quality olives (Kalamatas, Niçoise,

    Greek)

3/4 cup crumbled feta

8 five- to six-ounce chicken breast halves

2 cups flour, mixed with 1 tablespoon each salt, pepper,

    thyme, marjoram

Preheat the oven to 375°. Lay the tomato halves cut side down on a lightly oiled sheet pan. Brush with a touch of extra virgin olive oil and roast on the upper rack of the oven for 12 to 15 minutes or till the skin shrinks and begins to brown a little. Take from the oven and set aside till cool enough to handle. Meanwhile, heat the oil in a heavy 2-quart saucepan. Add the onion and garlic and sauté till translucent. Sprinkle with the sugar and a tiny bit of salt and pepper. Add the vinegar and vermouth and simmer for a few minutes. Pull the skins from the tomato halves and discard. Chop the tomato halves into large chunks (or break up with your hands) and add to the pan, along with any juices. Add the orange juice and the stock and bring to a brisk simmer, reducing by about a third. Taste and add salt and pepper and lemon juice to brighten the flavors. Stir in the chopped herbs and cook for one minute more. Set aside while preparing the breasts.

Trim the breast halves of any extra fat or cartilage, rinse and pat dry. Lay out a 2-foot piece of plastic wrap on the work surface. Place the breasts, smooth side down, on the plastic and cover with another piece of wrap. Pound the breasts with a meat hammer until flattened to half again their size. Dredge each pounded breast in the seasoned flour and set aside on a clean sheet pan.

Heat a large skillet and add one tablespoon olive oil. Brown the breasts, in batches till golden brown and cooked through, 2 to 3 minutes per side. Transfer to a baking pan, about 9 by 13 inches, overlapping slightly. Ladle about 3/4 cup of the sauce over the breasts, cover with foil and bake for 15 minutes.

Serve over fresh pasta, with a little more sauce, a sprinkling of feta and 2 to 3 olives on each serving.

This dish is a great do-ahead, and keeps well for several days. the sauce can be prepared to the point of adding the herbs, then cooled and held until the next day. This way the herbs retain their freshness and color. The chicken can be pre-cooked, cooled and held also.

Marinated Duck Breasts

Duck breasts are more and more available in the better grocery stores these days. My favorite label is the Maple Leaf brand, which are Peking ducks. Another good label is Grimaud, and these are typically Muscovy ducks. The Muscovys are a leaner duck, and I don't care for them as much; they just don't have the tenderness and succulence. In any case, doing just the breast is a simple way to have this rich and elegant meat for dinner.

8 seven- to eight-ounce duck breast halves

Spicy-Sweet Marinade

Sauce options: See pages 182, 183, and 184

Pour Spicy-Sweet Marinade into a glass, plastic, or ceramic dish that will hold the duck breasts. Make 3 or 4 shallow cuts on the skin of the breasts. Do not cut into the meat! Marinate the breasts skin side down 2 hours.

Preheat the oven to 350°. Heat a large heavy skillet, not non-stick, over medium heat. Take the breasts from the marinade and drain well. Save the marinade for another use.

Add 1 to 2 tablespoons olive oil to the skillet to heat, then lay 4 breasts skin side down in the skillet. Take care with this because they may splatter. Sear the breasts for about 3 minutes till they are very browned on the skin side, then flip and cook for one minute. Place the breast on a baking sheet or pan, skin up, and cook remaining 4 breasts the same way. Finish the breast in the oven for 4 to 5 more minutes, till medium rare to medium; they will be spongy-firm to the touch. Take from the oven and set aside for 10 minutes to rest.

Slice the duck breasts on the diagonal into 4 or 5 pieces. Fan them out slightly on warmed plates. Serve as is or with one of the sauces on pages 182, 183, and 184.

Spicy-Sweet Marinade

2 tablespoons minced ginger

2 tablespoons minced garlic

2 tablespoons Dijon mustard

2 tablespoons hoisin sauce

2 tablespoons honey

1 teaspoon red pepper flakes

1/4 cup chopped cilantro

1 cup orange juice

1/4 cup raspberry wine vinegar

1/2 cup soy sauce

1 cup olive oil

Combine the ginger, garlic, mustard, hoisin, honey, pepper flakes, and cilantro in a food processor and pulse to blend until smooth. Add the orange juice, vinegar, soy, and olive oil and blend.

GRILLING BY MOTORCYCLE LIGHT

Michael Urciuoli was a particularly memorable waiter at the Lodge. Arriving astride a huge motorcycle, he brought a resumé that included a year as the first male car-hop in the state of Utah, expertise in acupressure, and photos of his fine wood sculptures. Often accused of hiring the applicants with the most interesting story, Mary signed him on. Michael certainly met "our profile" and worked here for many years, wooing the guests with endless tricks and excellent service.

One summer evening while Amanda was in the middle of grilling 45 beef filets to order, there was a brilliant flash of lightning, a huge clap of thunder and—darkness. Conversation in the candlelit dining room hushed. As staff scrambled for Coleman lanterns, the gas grill continued to cook the precious filets. Ever resourceful, Michael came to the rescue by driving his motorcycle through the back door of the kitchen to shed light on the grill. Another dinner saved!

Roast Duckling with Blackberry Zinfandel Sauce and others

FOR EIGHT

A very simple and totally delicious way to roast duck, resulting in moist and tender meat and wonderful crisp skin. This requires a two-day preparation.

4 four- to four-and-a-half-pound ducklings

    (we use Maple Leaf brand)

2 tablespoons Chinese five spice powder

1/2 cup orange juice

2 cups soy sauce

1 medium yellow onion, quartered

1 large lemon, quartered

1 large orange, quartered

Remove the giblet sacks from the duck cavities and discard. Rinse the ducks inside and out and pat dry. Arrange in a large well-oiled roasting pan. Stuff each duck with one onion quarter and a lemon and orange wedge. Combine the five spice powder, orange juice, and soy sauce, and whisk together well. Brush the ducks very well with the soy baste and refrigerate, uncovered, overnight.

The next day, preheat the oven to 325°. Baste the ducks once more. Roast in the slow oven for 1 hour 45 minutes to 2 hours, till rich dark golden brown, and the legs move easily. Take from the oven and cool. Carve the breast meat, and the drumstick and thigh, from each duck and set together, 2 servings from each duck.

Lay out the 8 servings on a sheet pan to reheat at dinner time. Discard the duck carcasses (or use to make a rich duck stock for another day).

At dinner time, reheat the duck for 8 to 10 minutes at 325°, just till sizzling. Serve on warmed plates, drizzled with the hot sauce of your choice. Following are some of our favorites.

Blackberry Zinfandel Sauce

2 tablespoons olive oil

1 cup chopped yellow onions

4 garlic cloves, minced

1 teaspoon salt

1/2 teaspoon black pepper

1/4 cup thyme leaves and stems, chopped

4 cups blackberries, fresh or frozen but not sweetened

1/4 cup sugar

1 cup orange juice

3 cups Zinfandel

4 cups rich chicken stock

1 pint fresh berries for garnish

Heat the olive oil in a heavy 3-quart saucepan and add the onions, garlic, salt and pepper, and thyme. Cook over medium heat until very soft and beginning to brown. Add the black berries and sugar and cook until they begin to break down. Add the orange juice and wine and reduce by almost half. Add the stock and reduce until beginning to thicken. Strain the sauce into a clean pan, pressing the solids to extract as much liquid as possible. Taste and correct for salt, sweetness and acidity. You may want a touch of lemon. Keep warm till serving time. Ladle over each duck serving, covering completely and garnish with fresh berries.

Roasted Apples with Cider-Black Pepper Demi-glace

A beautiful sauce for fall, and simple.

4 large cooking apples, peeled, cored, and sliced into

    1/3 inch wedges (try Macintoshes, Jonathans,

    Pippens, or Winesaps)

1 /4 pound butter (1 stick), melted

1 tablespoon sugar

2 teaspoons salt

1 to 2 teaspoons freshly cracked black pepper

Cider-Black Pepper Demi-glace

Preheat the oven to 350°. Mix the apples with the melted butter, sugar, salt and pepper. Spread them out in a lightly oiled roasting pan, in one layer if possible. Roast on the upper rack of the oven for 10 minutes. Turn the apples with a spatula, and roast 5 minutes more, or until tender and browned at the edges. Take from the oven and transfer to a bowl and keep warm. Serve 5 or 6 wedges with the duckling, covered with some hot Cider-Black Pepper Demi-glace.

Cider-Black Pepper Demi-glace

1 tablespoon olive oil

2 cups chopped yellow onion

4 cloves garlic, minced

2 tablespoons fresh thyme

    (or 2 teaspoons dried)

2 tablespoons chopped fresh sage

    (or 2 teaspoons dried)

2 tablespoons chopped fresh marjoram

    (or 2 teaspoons dried)

1 tablespoon coarse black pepper

1/2 teaspoon salt

3 cups dry white wine

3 cups apple cider

3 cups rich chicken stock

1 cup Demi-glace base, chicken or beef (page 198)

additional coarse black pepper, salt to taste

Heat the oil in a heavy 3-quart saucepan. Add the onion, garlic, herbs, pepper and salt and cook over medium heat until golden brown. Add the wine and reduce by half. Add the cider and reduce by half. Add the stock and demi base and reduce till thickening to a nice light sauce consistency. Strain the sauce into a clean small saucepan, pressing very well on the solids. Add 1 + 1/2 teaspoons coarse pepper and a bit more salt, if needed. Cover and keep warm till serving.

Makes about 4 cups.

Peach Bourbon Sauce

A great sauce for summer, of course. This sauce is also great with roast pork or grilled chicken.

2 tablespoons olive oil

1 large yellow onion, chopped fine

4 large garlic cloves, minced

2 tablespoons chopped fresh sage leaves

2 tablespoons fresh thyme leaves

2 tablespoons fresh marjoram

1 teaspoon salt

1/2 teaspoon coarsely ground black pepper

2 cups chopped yellow peaches

1/2 cup Bourbon

3 cups dry white wine, like Sauvignon Blanc

4 cups rich chicken stock

2 tablespoons butter

4 medium yellow peaches, peeled and sliced

1 tablespoon sugar

1/2 teaspoon salt

1 tablespoon Bourbon

Heat the olive oil in a heavy 3-quart saucepan. Add the onions, garlic and herbs and cook till juicy, then beginning to brown. Add the salt, pepper and peaches and cook for 1 to 2 minutes. Add the Bourbon and wine and reduce by a third. Add the chicken stock and reduce by a half. Strain the sauce into a clean saucepan, pressing on the solids to extract as much liquid as possible.

In a large heavy skillet, melt the butter till sizzling. Add the sliced peaches and sauté. Sprinkle the sugar and salt over the peaches and raise the heat a bit to slightly caramelize the sugar. Add the Bourbon and cook 1 to 2 minutes more. Add the peaches to the saucepan.

Taste and correct for salt and pepper. Add a touch more sugar, if needed. Serve very warm with roast duckling or grilled duck breasts.

Grape Sauce

A fine sauce for the late summer and early fall, when the grapes come in. We typically use Concord grapes for this, but have also used red or black seedless grapes.

1 + 1/2 cups finely chopped onion

6 large garlic cloves, minced

2 tablespoons thyme leaves

4 cups halved black or red grapes

1 cup orange juice

1 teaspoon salt

1 teaspoon freshly cracked black pepper

3 cups Pinot Noir or Merlot

4 cups rich chicken stock

1/2 cup Demi-glace base (page 198)

1/3 cup grape jelly

lemon juice to taste

extra grapes for garnish

Combine the onion, garlic, thyme, grapes, orange juice, and salt and pepper in a heavy 3-quart saucepan. Cover and bring to a simmer over medium heat. Cook for 10 minutes, till very tender. Uncover and add the wine and reduce slowly by half. Add the stock and Demi-glace and reduce again by half. Strain the sauce into a clean saucepan, pressing the solids to extract the juices.

Whisk in the grape jelly and cook slowly, reducing a little more. Taste and correct for salt and pepper. Add a bit of lemon if too sweet. Serve with roast duck or grilled duck breasts, garnished with grape clusters and fresh thyme.

Roast Pork Tenderloin with Rhubarb Pear Chutney and Pinot Demi-glace

FOR EIGHT, WITH SECONDS

This is a great use of one of my favorite spring vegetables, rhubarb. Yes, is it botanically a vegetable but it's almost always used in desserts. It even has the old-fashioned nickname of "pie plant." Whatever it is, we love it here. Any remaining sauce can be frozen, and chutney will keep in the fridge one month.

4 small pork tenderloins (natural, not enhanced)

Herb Spice Rub for Pork or Lamb

Pinot Demi-glace

Rhubarb Pear Chutney

Brush the tenderloins with a little olive oil and sprinkle the rub all over the meat. Set aside for 30 minutes while you preheat the oven to 350°. Roast on upper rack of the oven for 8 minutes (set your timer). Reduce the temperature to 300° and roast for about 8 to 10 more minutes. Check at 8. The tenders should be firm but should yield to a gentle squeeze, about 140° on an instant read thermometer. Do not overcook!

Remove from the oven and set aside in the kitchen, covered with a clean towel, for 10 minutes. Slice on the diagonal about 1/3 inch thick. Serve on warmed plates with about 1/3 cup of Demi-glace across the meat and about 2 to 3 tablespoons of chutney on top.

Rhubarb Pear Chutney

1 cup minced red onion

1 tablespoon minced ginger root

4 cloves garlic, peeled and pressed

1/4 cup orange juice

1/4 cup cider vinegar

1/3 cup sugar, to taste

2 + 1/2 cups diced rhubarb

2 + 1/2 cups diced peeled pear

1 cinnamon stick

1/4 teaspoon red pepper flakes

1 teaspoon salt, to taste

Combine the onion, ginger, garlic, juice, vinegar, and sugar in a heavy 3-quart saucepan. Cook over medium heat until the sugar dissolves and the onions soften and become pink. Stir in the rhubarb, pear, spices, and salt and cook for one minute only. Remove from the heat but keep in a warm spot to let the flavors develop and soften. Correct for salt and sweetness, adding a touch more if needed, and maybe a little more acid, too. Makes about 4 cups.

Demi-glace... what is this stuff? Classically, it is a reduction of rich veal stock and brown sauce, made with roux, tomato, beef or veal stock, and wine. The version we make is lighter, without flour.
Demi-glace means "half glaze"— so called because it's cooked down to a glaze, or nearly a glaze, that thickens to a gel when chilled. Its origins are in traditional French cuisine.

Pinot Demi-glace

1 tablespoon olive oil

1 cup chopped yellow onions

3 garlic cloves, chopped

2 tablespoons fresh thyme leaves (1 teaspoon dried)

2 tablespoons chopped sage leaves (1 teaspoon dried)

1 teaspoon coarse black pepper

1/2 teaspoon salt

3 cups Pinot Noir

3 cups rich beef or chicken stock

1 cup Demi-glace base (page 198)

1 to 2 teaspoons sugar

Heat the oil in a heavy 3-quart saucepan. Add the onion, garlic, herbs, pepper, and salt and cook over medium until golden brown. Add the wine and reduce by half. Add the stock and reduce by a third. Add the Demi and reduce till thickening a bit and shiny. Strain the sauce into a clean small saucepan, add a touch of sugar to taste, just to smooth it out. Taste for salt and correct. Keep warm till serving time. Makes about 3 cups.

Herb Spice Rub for Pork or Lamb

2 tablespoons each fennel seeds, mustard seeds, oregano, thyme, sage, rosemary

zest of one orange

1/2 cup salt

1/4 cup coarse black pepper

Combine the seeds, herbs, and zest in a small skillet and toast till fragrant. Grind in a spice mill or coffee grinder and mix with the salt and pepper. Makes about 1 + 1/2 cups.

Baby Back Ribs with Ancho Honey Barbecue Sauce

FOR EIGHT, WITH SECONDS

It took me a long time to convince Mary that we should do baby backs at the Lodge; with only one entrée, we always feel it needs to be really the top-end special. So when we started doing them it was on July 4th, I think, and maybe the long holiday weekends for Memorial and Labor day, traditional "barbecue" times. Now, we do them anytime, and have many requests for them. In fact, we have guests who won't eat pork, but will eat these ribs! Here are two versions of our favorite finger food.

5 full slabs baby back ribs

1/2 cup kosher salt

1/4 cup sugar

1 tablespoon paprika

2 teaspoons chile powder

1 tablespoon coarse black pepper

2 teaspoons cumin

1 teaspoon thyme

1 teaspoon sage

1teaspoon oregano

1/2 teaspoon cayenne

> Preheat the oven to 300°. Combine the salt, sugar, and all the spices and herbs, and mix well. Sprinkle both sides of the slabs with the mixture, fairly generously. You will have some left over. Spread the ribs in 2 baking pans so they only overlap a little. Pour about 2 cups of water into each pan, or about 1/2 inch, cover the pans very tightly with foil, and bake in the very slow oven for about 3 hours.

Pull from the oven and remove the foil, setting it aside. Cool the ribs for 10 to 15 minutes, till they can be handled. Baste each slab with some of the sauce, top and bottom, then cut each slab in half. Recover and put back in the oven for 30 minutes. Uncover the ribs for the last 20 minutes before dinner, to glaze them off a bit. Allow enough time to let the ribs cool a little before serving, because you do eat them with your fingers. . .

Serve with a little extra sauce drizzled on top.

Ancho Honey Barbecue Sauce

1 medium onion, chopped

3 garlic cloves, peeled and chopped

4 ancho chiles, stemmed and rinsed

2 canned chipotle chiles in adobo,

　　with some adobo sauce

1 tablespoon cumin seed

1 tablespoon oregano

2 teaspoons sage

1 teaspoon cinnamon

1/2 teaspoon allspice

1 tablespoon salt

2 cups canned pear tomatoes

5 cups of water

1/2 cup honey, plus more if needed

1/2 cup brown sugar

1/2 cup molasses

1/4 cup each cider vinegar, lemon juice, orange juice

> Combine the onion, garlic, and chiles in a heavy-bottomed 3-quart saucepan. Toast the herbs and spices together in a small skillet until very fragrant and add to the pan. Add the salt, tomatoes and water, cover and cook

over medium heat 30 minutes. Remove from the heat and cool a bit then blend until smooth. Strain the sauce back into the rinsed pan, pressing on the solids.

Add the honey, brown sugar, molasses, vinegar, and juices and bring to a simmer. Cook the sauce slowly for about 45 minutes, till thickened some, and the flavors have mellowed. Add more salt if needed, and more honey if it's too spicy.

Makes about 6 cups of sauce. Extra sauce stores several weeks in the fridge, a few months in the freezer.

Baby Back Ribs with Asian Style Barbecue Sauce

FOR EIGHT, WITH SECONDS

1/2 cup Chinese five spice powder

1/4 cup garam masala

1 teaspoon cayenne

2 tablespoons each coarse black pepper, thyme,

   marjoram, sage

1/4 cup sugar

1/2 cup salt

5 full slabs baby back ribs

Preheat the oven to 300°.

Combine spices, herbs, salt and sugar in a small bowl. Sprinkle both sides of the slabs with the mixture, fairly generously. You may have a little left over.

Lay out the ribs in 2 baking pans so they only overlap a little. Pour about 2 cups of water into the edge of the pans, to a depth of about 1/2 inch. Cover the pans tightly with foil, so they are completely sealed, and bake in the very slow oven for about 3 hours. Pull the ribs from the oven and remove the foil, setting it

aside. Cool the ribs for about 10 to 15 minutes, till they can be handled. Brush each slab with some sauce, top and bottom, then cut each slab in half. Recover and put back in the oven for 30 minutes. Uncover the ribs for the last 20 minutes before dinner, to glaze them off a bit. Allow enough time to let the ribs cool a little before serving, so folks can pick them up.

Serve with a little extra sauce drizzled over the top, and some finger towels on the side.

Asian Style Barbecue Sauce

1/4 cup minced ginger

1/4 cup minced garlic

1/3 cup chopped cilantro

1/2 cup chopped green onions

1 cup brown sugar

1/2 cup honey

1 cup rice vinegar

1/3 cup soy sauce

2 cups ketchup

1/2 cup lime juice

1/2 cup orange juice

1/3 cup hoisin sauce

1 tablespoon toasted sesame oil

1/2 teaspoon red pepper flakes

Combine the ginger, garlic, cilantro, green onions, brown sugar and honey in a food processor. Pulse 5 or 6 times to blend. Add the rice vinegar and pulse to blend. Transfer to a heavy 2-quart saucepan and add the remaining ingredients. Heat the sauce over medium low to a very gentle simmer, about 30 to 40 minutes. Makes about 5 cups; extra sauce stores and freezes very well.

Roast Pork Loin with Tart Cherry Bourbon Confit

A lovely preparation for pork roast, good any time of the year, but really special if you can get some fresh tart cherries. Although come to think of it, if I had some fresh tart cherries, I'd be tempted to make a pie instead. The brine will help the pork loin retain some moisture. This is necessary with today's lean pork. Too lean, in my opinion.

1/4 cup molasses

1/2 cup brown sugar

1 cup kosher salt

4 cloves garlic, minced

2 whole cloves

2 bay leaves

10 cups of water, divided

1 center cut pork loin, about 3 to 4 pounds

1/2 cup Herb Spice Rub for Pork (page 187)

Combine the molasses, sugar, salt, garlic, cloves, and bay leaves with 5 cups of warm water to dissolve the salt. Transfer to a container that's large enough to hold the loin; we use an ice chest that we keep just for this use. Pour another 5 cups of cold water into the container and mix. Add a couple of cups of ice if the brine is still too hot. Submerge the loin in the brine and set aside for 3 hours.

Preheat the oven to 375°. Remove from the brine, rinse the loin and pat dry. Sprinkle the loin generously with the herb rub and place in a lightly oiled roasting pan. Roast for 15 minutes at 375° (set the timer), then reduce the temperature to 325° and roast for about 25 minutes more, or until an internal temperature of 145°.

Remove from the oven and set aside, covered with a towel, for 20 minutes.

Carve into 1/3-inch-thick slices. Serve on warmed plates, about 4 slices, covered with some warm Tart Cherry Bourbon Confit.

Tart Cherry Bourbon Confit

1 tablespoon olive oil

2 small red onions, sliced 1/8 inch thick

1 teaspoon thyme

1 tablespoon chopped fresh sage

1 teaspoon coarse black pepper

1/2 teaspoon salt

1 tablespoon sugar

2/3 cup Bourbon

2 cups medium-bodied red wine
     (Pinot, Merlot or Zinfandel)

1 cup tart dry cherries

2 cups rich chicken or beef stock

2 to 3 tablespoons balsamic vinegar

Heat the olive oil in a 3-quart saucepan. Add the onions, herbs, spices and sugar and sauté slowly till very soft and caramelizing. Add the Bourbon, wine, cherries, and stock.

Mix and reduce till beginning to thicken a bit. Then add the balsamic vinegar.

Reduce slowly for 5 minutes. Correct for salt and pepper. Makes about 4 cups. Stores for several weeks in the fridge.

Roast Pork Loin with Apple and Sweet Onion Compote and Cider-Black Pepper Demi-glace

FOR EIGHT

This is the epitome of a fall and winter entrée here at Garland's. Sometimes if I can find them, I like to add some sliced lobster mushrooms to this compote. They grow pretty well in the Flagstaff area and sometimes I get lucky.

1/4 cup molasses

1/2 cup brown sugar

1 cup kosher salt

4 cloves garlic, minced

2 whole cloves

2 bay leaves

10 cups of water, divided

1 center cut pork loin, about 3 to 4 pounds

1/2 cup Herb Spice Rub for Pork (page 187)

Cider-Black Pepper Demi-glace (page 183)

> Combine the molasses, sugar, salt, garlic, cloves, and bay leaves with 5 cups of warm water to dissolve the salt. Transfer to a container large enough to hold the loin; we keep an ice chest just for this use. Pour another 5 cups of cold water into the container and mix. Add a couple of cups of ice if the brine is still too hot. Submerge the loin in the brine and soak for 3 hours.
>
> Preheat the oven to 375°. Remove the loin from the brine, rinse and pat dry. Sprinkle the loin generously with the herb rub and place in a lightly oiled roasting pan. Roast for 15 minutes at 375° (set the timer), then reduce the temperature to 325° and roast for about 25 minutes more, or until an internal temperature of 145° is reached (you can check

with an instant-read thermometer). Remove from the oven and set aside, covered with a towel, for 20 minutes.

> Slice into 1/3-inch pieces. Serve on warmed plates, about 4 slices per serving, with half a cup of Apple and Sweet Onion Compote on top and about 1/3 cup of Cider Black Pepper Demi-glace poured over.

Apple and Sweet Onion Compote

1 tablespoon olive oil

1 tablespoon butter

3 medium sweet onions, sliced lengthwise,
  then into 1/4-inch half-rounds

1/4 medium head of green cabbage,
  sliced in 1/4-inch-thick strips

1 tablespoon fresh thyme leaves

1 tablespoon sugar

1 teaspoon salt

4 large tart apples, peeled, cored
  and sliced into 1/4-inch-thick wedges

1/2 cup chicken stock

a few grinds of fresh black pepper

> Melt the oil and butter in a large skillet or sauté pan on medium high heat. When the butter begins to sizzle, add the sliced onions and cook, tossing occasionally, till they just begin to soften and color a little bit. Add the cabbage, thyme, sugar, and salt, and toss together well. Cover the pan and let the compote sweat for 5 to 8 minutes, till juicy and wilting. Add the apples, mix well, and add half a cup of the stock. Cook the compote, shaking the pan a bit, until the apples just soften and the juices reduce almost completely. Add a few grinds of pepper, a touch of salt if needed, and set aside, keeping warm till serving time.

A Variation on Roast Pork Loin with Demi-glace and Apple Horseradish Cream

1 center cut pork loin, about 3 to 4 pounds

Cider-Black Pepper Demi-glace (page 183)

Apple Horseradish Cream

> Prepare Roast Pork as directed for Roast Pork Loin with Tart Cherry Bourbon Confit (page 191). Or prepare Pork Tenderloins for a really quick but wonderful meal. Of course, these cuts of pork are interchangeable with all of these sauces, and most of them are great with chicken also.

> Slice the roast pork into 1/3-inch pieces. Serve about 4 slices on warmed plates, with some Cider-Black Pepper Demi-glace poured over all. Top each serving with a small scoop of Apple Horseradish Cream and serve immediately.

Apple Horseradish Cream

A simple little cream that comes together very quickly and really complements the pork and cider sauce.

1 + 1/2 cups heavy cream

1/2 teaspoon salt

a few grinds of fresh black pepper

2 tablespoons well-drained prepared extra hot
    horseradish, more if desired

1 large apple (Golden, Macintosh, Rome)

> Whip the cream with the salt until very stiff. Add the pepper and sprinkle horseradish over the cream. Peel and core the apple. Grate the apple on the large holes of a box grater directly into the cream. Fold the apple and horseradish into the cream gently, taste for salt, add a little more horseradish if you like. Cover and chill until serving time. Makes about 2 cups.

Roast Pork Tenderloin with Oaxacan Mole Verde

FOR EIGHT (WITH LEFTOVERS)

Mole Verde (mo-lay ver-day) is a beautiful pale green sauce that has been a favorite recipe for us, evolving from a much more complicated herb-and-seed-heavy version to this rather light vegetable sauce. It's very flavorful, and healthy too. Good with grilled or baked chicken, fish and shrimp. Truly all-purpose, and it even freezes well!

4 small pork tenderloins (natural, not enhanced)

Southwestern Pork Rub

Mole Verde

> Brush the tenderloins with a little olive oil and sprinkle the rub all over the meat. Place the tenders on a lightly oiled baking pan and set aside for 30 minutes. Preheat the oven to 350°. Set the pan on the upper rack and roast the meat 8 minutes (set your timer). Reduce the oven temperature to 300° and roast another 8 to 10 minutes, or until the tenders are firm but still yield to a gentle squeeze, about 140° at the center when measured with an instant-read meat thermometer. Don't overcook this great little piece of meat!

> Take the meat from the oven and set aside, covered with a clean towel, for 10 minutes. Slice on the diagonal about 1/3 inch thick. Serve on warmed plates with about 1/3 cup of hot sauce over the top.

Southwestern Pork Rub

2 tablespoons each oregano, sage, thyme,

    ground red chile, cumin seed

1 tablespoon cinnamon

1 teaspoon nutmeg

1/2 cup salt

2 tablespoons coarse black pepper

    Combine the herbs, chile, cumin, cinnamon, and nutmeg in a small skillet and heat until toasty and fragrant. Whisk together with the salt and black pepper in a small bowl.

Mole Verde

2 tablespoons olive oil

1 medium white or yellow onion, chopped

3 garlic cloves, peeled and chopped

1 pound tomatillos, papery skin removed,

    rinsed and sliced

1/4 cup chopped hot green chiles

    (fresh roasted or frozen, not canned)

1 + 1/2 teaspoons salt

2 teaspoons each oregano, cumin seeds

1/2 cup raw pumpkin seeds

1/2 cup loosely packed chopped cilantro

    (about 1/2 bunch with some stems)

2 to 2 + 1/2 cups chicken stock, enough

    to make a good sauce consistency

fresh lime juice to taste, about 1 to 2 tablespoons

Heat the olive oil in a heavy 3-quart saucepan over medium high and add the onions, garlic, tomatillos, and salt. Stir them up a bit and reduce the heat to medium. Stir in the hot chiles.

Partially cover the pan and cook slowly for 10 minutes or so until very soft and juicy. Meanwhile, combine the oregano and the seeds and toast in a small skillet till very fragrant and beginning to smoke.

Grind the seed mix in a spice grinder if available or a small food processor works, too. If neither is available, don't worry about it, you're going to blend the sauce anyway. Add the seed mix to the pan, along with the cilantro and the 2 cups of chicken broth. Stir the mixture well to slightly cook the cilantro.

Transfer the sauce to a blender, in batches if necessary, and process until very smooth.

Return to the saucepan, adding a little more stock if too thick. Add one tablespoon of lime juice, more if you like, and salt if needed. Set aside till dinner, or cool completely and reheat gently at serving time.

{ Good relishes, rubs, marinades, and sauces are infinitely interchangeable! }

Roast Pork Tenderloin with Roasted Figs and Sweet Onions and Zinfandel Demi-glace

4 small pork tenderloins (natural, not enhanced)

Herb Spice Rub for Pork (page 187)

Zinfandel Demi-glace

Roast the Tenderloins: Brush the tenders with a little olive oil and sprinkle the rub all over the meat. Set aside for 30 minutes while you preheat the oven to 350°. Roast the pork on upper rack of the oven for 8 minutes (set your timer). Reduce the temperature to 300° and roast for about 8 to 10 more minutes. Check at 8. The tenders should be firm but should yield to a gentle squeeze, about 140° degrees on an instant read thermometer. Careful not to overcook!

Remove from the oven and set aside, covered with a clean towel, for 10 minutes. Slice on the diagonal about 1/3 inch thick. Serve on warmed plates with a small bundle of roasted onions and 2 figs on top of the meat. Drizzle 1/3 cup of hot sauce over all.

Roasted Figs and Sweet Onions

16 large brown figs, stems trimmed (brown turkey figs if you can get them, or good quality dried ones)

3 medium sweet onions, sliced lengthwise, then into 1/4 inch half rounds

About 1/4 cup extra virgin olive oil

2 teaspoons fresh thyme leaves

Kosher salt and freshly ground black pepper

Preheat the oven to 325°. Slice the figs top to bottom, leaving them attached at the base. Lay them out on a lightly oiled sheet pan, spreading them open. Brush lightly with some of the olive oil and sprinkle lightly with salt and fresh pepper. On a separate sheet pan, mound the onion slices in the center. Drizzle a couple of tablespoons on the mound, then the thyme leaves and some salt and pepper. Toss the onions to coat with the seasonings and spread them out on the pan. Put both pans in the oven, with the onions on the upper rack. Roast the figs just till they begin to brown and soften, about 15 to 20 minutes. Remove from the oven. Roast the onions till they're very golden and soft, about 35 minutes. Transfer the onions to a medium sized baking pan, piling them in one half of the pan. Transfer the figs to the other half of the pan, cover loosely with foil and set aside.

Zinfandel Demi-glace

1 tablespoon olive oil

1 cup chopped yellow onion

3 cloves garlic, chopped

2 tablespoons fresh thyme (1 teaspoon dried)

2 tablespoons chopped fresh sage (1 teaspoon dried)

1 + 1/2 teaspoons coarse black pepper

1/2 teaspoon salt

1 tablespoon sugar

3 + 1/2 cups Zinfandel (1 bottle)

3 cups rich chicken stock

1 cup Demi-glace base (page 198)

salt to taste

Heat the oil in a heavy 3-quart saucepan. Add the onion, garlic, herbs, spices, and sugar and cook over medium heat until golden brown. Add the wine and reduce by half. Add the stock and reduce by about a third. Add the Demi base and reduce till thickening a bit and shiny. Strain the sauce into a clean pan and correct for salt. Cover and set aside. Makes about 3 cups.

Beef Stock and Demi-glace

This is a good rich all purpose beef stock and is especially nice for reducing to Demi-glace. There is an excellent product by More than Gourmet called Demi-glace Gold that is available at better grocery stores. It's a clean product without salt or additives. It's sort of expensive, though. This recipe will give you a good amount of Demi that you can tuck away (with a relatively small investment other than your time). First make the stock, then reduce it for Demi-glace.

Beef Stock

3 to 4 pounds beef marrow bones

1 pound beef trim or stew meat

2 + 1/2 cups coarsely chopped celery

2 + 1/2 cups coarsely chopped carrots

2 + 1/2 cups coarsely chopped onions

1 cup chopped tomato

3 to 4 sprigs of parsley, stems and leaves

1/4 cup chopped fresh thyme, leaves and stems

1 tablespoon peppercorns

3 cups red wine (any decent full bodied wine)

2 + 1/4 gallons cold water

Salt and pepper

Preheat the oven to 425°. In a lightly oiled heavy roasting pan, spread the bones and meat; roast for 15 to 20 minutes, until well browned. Add the chopped veggies, reduce the oven to 375°, and continue roasting 20 minutes more. Add the tomatoes, parsley, garlic, thyme, and peppercorns and roast 5 to 10 minutes more.

Remove from the oven and transfer bones and veggies to a 20-quart stockpot. Pour off any excess fat. Set roasting pan on the stove top, over a burner at medium heat, and add the red wine. Bring to a boil and scrape up any bits sticking to the pan. Add to the stockpot along with 3 quarts of cold water. Bring to a boil and cook briskly for 30 minutes.

Add 3 more quarts of water; boil again for 30 minutes. Again add 3 quarts of water; reduce heat and simmer 30 minutes more. Strain into a clean, heavy pot.

Bring back to a brisk simmer and reduce to half gallon. Season *very* lightly with kosher salt and pepper. Cool completely. It will keep in the fridge for 5 days, or freeze in one-quart containers.

Demi-glace

This is not a traditional brown sauce reduction, but better for the cooking we do now.

2 quarts stock

Pour into stockpot, place over medium heat, and reduce by half.

Demi-glace can be used in any sauce recipes calling for a rich beef base. A bit of it can be swirled into the pan that you've just seared your steak in, or pork tenderloin or chop; maybe whisk in a bit of Dijon or whole grain mustard or some mashed green peppercorns. Add a splash of wine, cook it down a little, and finish it off with a touch of heavy cream or butter to give it a nice sheen. A very nice little sauce and all because you have this Demi stashed away in your freezer.

Beef Filets with Forest Mushroom Sauce

A classic sauce for fall but this is actually good anytime. This sauce is good with chicken breasts, and also with wide pasta noodles, such as pappardelle.

2 strips of bacon, diced

1 medium yellow onion, chopped

3 cloves garlic, chopped

2 tablespoons chopped fresh thyme leaves
    (2 teaspoons dried)

2 tablespoons chopped fresh sage leaves
    (2 teaspoons dried)

2 teaspoons coarse black pepper

1 cup mixed dried mushrooms soaked in 2 cups hot
    water (Pluck the rehydrated mushrooms out of the
    soaking water gently, without disturbing the water,
    then allow any grit to settle for a few minutes. Pour
    the liquid off carefully, leaving the grit in the bowl.)

4 cups Cabernet Sauvignon
    or other full-bodied red wine

1 tablespoon olive oil

2 cups sliced crimini (Italian brown) mushrooms

1/2 cup Port

1 cup Demi-glace (page 198)

2 cups water

1 cup heavy cream

8 seven-ounce beef tenderloin filets

salt and cracked black pepper

In a heavy-bottomed 3- or 4-quart saucepan, brown the bacon dice over medium heat till crisp. Add the onion, garlic, chopped herbs, and pepper. Sauté the veggies till very well browned. Drain the mushrooms, reserving the soaking liquid. Finely chop half the mushrooms and add to the pan. Trim and slice (if necessary) the other half of the mushrooms and set aside with the sliced criminis. Pour the reserved mushroom liquid over the browning veggies, along with the 4 cups of wine. Bring to a low boil and reduce by one third.

Strain the sauce base into a clean bowl, pressing well on the solids. Discard the solids. Rinse out the saucepan, and over medium heat sauté the reserved mushrooms in the olive oil. Salt the mushrooms a little and cover for one minute, till wilted. Pour the sauce base over and add the Port. Bring back to a slow boil and add the Demi-glace and water. Reduce slightly, by one fourth. Add the heavy cream and reduce till thickening and shiny. Correct for salt and pepper and set aside, keeping warm, while you prepare the filets.

Heat a grill to medium high. Or heat a cast iron skillet or grill pan over a medium high flame. Sprinkle a little salt and pepper on each filet. Lightly oil the grill or pan. Cook the filets to your liking, but generally cook this lean meat on the medium rare side, about 5 to 7 minutes per side. You can always cook it more, never less. . .

Serve on warmed plates with about 1/3 cup of the hot mushroom sauce covering the filet.

Makes about 3 to 4 cups; extra sauce freezes very well.

Beef Filets with Bourbon Peppercorn Sauce and Maytag Blue Cheese Butter

Another classic steak sauce that's hard to beat. In the 1980s we used to do a green peppercorn sauce and stuff the filets with a chunk of Roquefort or Gorgonzola; that was excellent, too.

2 strips of bacon, diced

1/2 medium yellow onion, chopped

3 cloves garlic, peeled and chopped

2 tablespoons chopped thyme (2 teaspoons dried)

2 tablespoons chopped sage (2 teaspoons dried)

2 teaspoons coarse black pepper

1 cup Bourbon

4 cups Merlot or Zinfandel

1 cup Demi-glace (page198)

2 cups water

1/3 cup Port

1/2 cup heavy cream

1 + 1/2 tablespoons mixed peppercorns

8 seven-ounce beef tenderloin filets

salt and fresh black pepper

Maytag Blue Cheese Butter (recipe follows)

In a heavy-bottomed 3- or 4-quart saucepan, brown the bacon till crisp. Add the onion, garlic, herbs, and coarse pepper, stir well, and cook till very well browned. Pour the Bourbon over and simmer off. Add the red wine, Demi-glace, and water and reduce by a third. Add the Port and heavy cream and reduce thickened a bit and shiny. Strain the sauce into a smaller heavy saucepan, pressing on the solids. Add the peppercorns and heat slowly for 5 minutes.

Let sit for 10 minutes, then correct for salt. Set aside, keeping warm, while preparing the steaks.

Heat a grill to medium high. Or heat a cast iron pan or a grill pan over a medium high flame. Lightly salt and pepper the filets. Lightly oil the grill or pan. Cook the filets to your liking, but generally cook this very lean meat on the medium rare side, about 5 to 7 minutes per side.

Serve on warmed plates with about 1/4 cup of hot sauce over the filets and a slice of Blue Cheese Butter on the top, slightly melting—fabulous.

Maytag Blue Cheese Butter

1/2 cup crumbled Maytag blue cheese (4 ounces) or Gorgonzola, Roquefort or other good blue

1/2 cup slightly softened butter (1 stick)

Combine in a small food processor or mixing bowl and blend till smooth. Spread an 8-inch piece of plastic wrap on the counter, scrape the blue butter onto it, and using the wrap, form the butter into a log about 4 inches long. Twist the ends of the wrap to seal and chill the butter till firm, one hour. To speed up the serving of this at dinnertime, pre-slice the butter into 1/4-inch pats and separate them a little; then hold them in the fridge till entrée time.

Makes about 4 cups of sauce and about one cup of butter.

See a photo of this combination, served with Mashed Sweets and Yukon Golds, on page 222.

Beef Filets with Ancho Chile Cream

One of our best entrées. The ancho-rich sauce is so good with the very tender but rather mildly flavored filet. It's also great with breast of chicken. Lightly pound, flour, and sauté, cover with Ancho Chile Cream, and bake for 20 minutes. Yum!

8 seven-ounce beef tenderloin filets

salt and cracked pepper

Ancho Chile Cream

Heat a grill to medium high. Alternatively, heat a cast iron skillet or grill pan over a medium high flame. Sprinkle a little salt and coarse pepper on each steak. Lightly oil the grill or the pan. Cook the filets to your liking, but generally cook this lean meat on the medium rare side, about 5 to 7 minutes per side. Remember that you can always cook it more, but you can't cook it less! Serve on heated plates with about 1/3 cup of the warm Ancho Chile Cream covering the filet.

ANCHO CHILE SAUCE, MOLE STYLE: For a delicious mole style variation of the Ancho Chile Cream, add 1/4 teaspon cinnamon and 1/8 teaspoon anise seed to the cumin seed, oregano, and sage when you toast them. After adding the beef stock and reducing the sauce (as directed in paragraph 3 of the recipe instructions at right), stir in 2 or 3 wedges from a tablet of Ibarra Mexican Chocolate before adding the cream.

Ancho Chile Cream

4 large dried ancho chiles, stemmed and rinsed

1 canned chipotle in adobo, with some sauce

1/2 medium yellow onion, chopped

4 garlic cloves, peeled and chopped

2 teaspoons each whole cumin seeds,

    oregano, sage, salt

1 cup chopped canned pear tomatoes

4 cups water

3 cups rich beef stock or chicken stock

1 cup heavy cream

Combine the anchos, the chipotle, onion, and garlic in a heavy bottomed 3-quart saucepan.

In a small skillet, combine the cumin seeds, oregano, sage, and salt and toast over medium heat until browning and very fragrant. Add to the pot along with the tomatoes and the water. Mix well, cover and bring to a boil; reduce the heat and uncover, simmering for 30 minutes. Let cool for 5 to 10 minutes, then transfer the solids and most of the juice (all if it fits) to a blender and process until very smooth. Strain the chile purée back into the cleaned saucepan, pressing on the solids to extract as much purée as possible.

Add the 3 cups beef stock and return to a low boil. Reduce by about a third, then add the heavy cream. Boil slowly again, reducing until thickened to a nice medium sauce consistency. Correct for salt and set aside, keeping warm, while preparing filets.

Makes about 3 to 4 cups; extra sauce freezes very well. In fact, I always make a double batch.

For a photo of Beef Filets with Ancho Chile Cream, served with Black Beans, see page 212.

Rack of Lamb with Coriander Crust and Lemon Mint Jam Variation: a Fresh Mint Chutney

Rack of lamb is a big favorite at the lodge. It seems to be a dish that many people hated as children, but they discover how great it is when they have it here. I think it's the marinades we use, and all these great little sauces.

8 small New Zealand or Australian lamb racks, frenched

Lemon Mint Jam (page 204)

FOR THE MARINADE

2 tablespoons coriander seeds

2 tablespoons coarse black pepper

6 garlic cloves, chopped

4 green onions

3/4 cup lemon juice

1 + 1/4 cups olive oil

2 tablespoons salt

2 tablespoons sugar

FOR THE CORIANDER CRUST

1/3 cup coriander seeds

1 tablespoon mustard seeds

1/2 cup chopped cilantro

1/2 cup chopped Italian parsley

1/4 cup chopped sage

1/4 cup fine dry breadcrumbs or Panko
   (fine dry Japanese bread crumbs)

1 teaspoon salt

Combine the seeds, garlic, onions, juice, oil, salt, and sugar in a blender and process until smooth. Transfer to a glass or plastic or non-reactive metal dish that can hold the racks. Trim the silverskin and extra fat off the racks (the silverskin is the very thin white membrane covering the meat of the rack). Place the racks meat side down in the marinade. The bones can be sticking out of the marinade. Set aside for 30 minutes to an hour.

Lightly toast the seeds in a small skillet. Crush the seeds in a spice grinder, do not totally grind them, just break them up. Mix with the herbs and breadcrumbs and set aside.

Grill and roast the racks: Preheat the oven to 350°. Heat a grill to medium high. Or heat a cast iron skillet or grill pan over medium high flame. Remove the racks from the marinade and drain them very well. Lightly oil the grill or pan. Lay the racks meat side down on the grill and sear them for 2 minutes. Remove the racks to a roasting or sheet pan, meat side up. Sprinkle and press about 1 to 2 tablespoons of the crust mixture over the lamb meat, covering lightly. Place the pan in the upper rack of the oven and roast for 10 to 15 minutes, depending on your preference. We find that this lean and tender meat is best medium rare to medium.

Serve on warmed plates with one of the following sauces drizzled over the meat, and a little extra on the side.

"Frenching" means trimming the extra meat and fat from between the bones of a rack of lamb or pork.

Lemon Mint Jam

2 cups lemon juice

2 cups water

1 package dry pectin, like SureJell

2 cups finely chopped fresh mint leaves

5 cups sugar

1 teaspoon salt

Combine the lemon juice and water in a heavy 3-quart saucepan. Stir in the dry pectin and the chopped mint. Bring to a full rolling boil, a boil that can't be stirred down. Stir in the sugar and bring back to a full rolling boil. Stir and boil for one minute. Remove from the heat and add the salt. Transfer to a small sauce pan, cover and keep warm until serving time.

This makes about 4 cups. It stores well in the fridge for a few months. We like this with spicy grilled chicken breasts and of course, lamb chops, when I'm not willing to pop for racks!

Fresh Mint Chutney

2 cups fresh mint leaves, loosely packed

3 green onions, chopped

1 tablespoon minced ginger

1/4 cup lemon juice

1 tablespoon sugar, to taste

1 teaspoon salt

1 to 2 jalapeños, seeded, chopped

1/4 to 1/2 cup water

Combine the mint, onions, ginger, lemon juice, sugar, salt, and jalapeños in a food processor. Pulse to blend to a kind of rough purée, then taste and correct for salt, sweetness, heat, and acidity. When it suits your taste, add 1/4 to 1/2 cup water and blend to a loose purée.

Makes about 2 cups. This does not keep well—it loses its fresh color and flavor overnight. That being said, it doesn't go bad by the next day, so you could have it with your leftovers, or maybe use it to put together a quick lamb or chicken salad.

Braised Lamb Shanks
with Lemon Mint Gremolata

The perfect dish for entertaining because it's completely done ahead of time. Though relatively inexpensive, it is not something people often cook at home, so it makes a special dish for company. We like to serve this with pearl couscous. Start the shanks one day ahead (or even two or three).

8 lamb shanks, 14 to 16 ounces each

olive oil

Herb Spice Rub for Lamb (see page 187)

3 medium carrots, scrubbed and chopped coarsely

3 stalks of celery, chopped coarsely

1 large onion, peeled, chopped coarsely

4 large cloves of garlic, chopped

zest of 2 large lemons

1/2 cup mint leaves, loosely packed

4 cups dry white wine, like Sauvignon Blanc (or red)

4 to 6 cups rich chicken stock

Rub the lamb shanks lightly with olive oil and dust them generously with the herb rub. Place them in a plastic storage container, cover and refrigerate overnight.

The next morning, preheat the oven to 325°. Lightly oil a large roasting pan, at least 12 by 18 inches or large enough to hold the shanks in a single layer. Use 2 pans if necessary. In a large sauté pan, heat about 2 tablespoons olive oil over medium high flame. Sauté the chopped veggies and garlic till beginning to brown at the edges. Transfer the veggies to the roasting pan. Brown the shanks in batches, allowing a few minutes on each side to get a good color and a little crust. Transfer to the pan, laying them on the veggies. Sprinkle the lemon zest and mint leaves over the shanks.

Pour the white wine into the warm sauté pan to deglaze and bring to a boil, scraping the pan to loosen all the good brown bits. Pour the wine over the shanks and add enough chicken stock to almost cover. Seal the pan with heavy aluminum foil, making sure the edges are completely tight. Braise in the oven at 325° for 2 + 1/2 to 3 hours, till the meat is very tender. Remove from the oven and allow to rest, uncovered, for 20 minutes.

Transfer the shanks to a sheet pan and cover with a towel. Pour the liquid from the braising pan through a strainer into a 2-quart saucepan, pressing on the solids to get all the juices. Add the remaining stock and bring to a boil, reducing till thickened. Meanwhile, transfer the shanks back to the roasting pan and recover with foil. Keep warm in a very low oven, about 125° for one hour more. When the sauce has reduced to a light consistency, taste and correct for salt and pepper. Cover and keep warm till serving.

Serve on warmed plates with a ladle of sauce and a sprinkle of Lemon Mint Gremolata.

BRAISED SHANKS WITH LEMON, THYME, AND APRICOT: Substitute 1 cup thyme leaves and stems for the mint. Add 1 cup chopped dried apricots, packed. Substitute beef stock for the chicken.

Lemon Mint Gremolata

zest of 2 lemons

1/3 cup finely chopped Italian parsley

1/4 cup finely chopped mint

1/2 teaspoon salt

Toss together in a small bowl. Cover till serving at room temperature.

Pecan-Crusted Rack of Lamb with Serrano Mint Jam or Ancho Honey Mint Glaze

A few Southwestern variations on a rack of lamb. This marinade and the sauces are also great with chicken, duck breasts, or even pork tenderloin.

8 small New Zealand or Australian lamb racks, frenched

Serrano Mint Jam or Ancho Honey Mint Glaze

PECAN CRUST

3/4 cup chopped pecans, toasted 8 to 10 minutes
   at 325°

1/4 cup chopped Italian parsley (make sure the
   parsley is dry before chopping)

1/3 cup fine dry bread crumbs or Panko

1 teaspoon salt

MARINADE

2 tablespoons coriander seed

2 tablespoons cumin seed

2 teaspoons cinnamon

2 tablespoons oregano

2 tablespoons sage

1 tablespoon chipotle powder

1 tablespoon ancho chile powder

2 tablespoon coarse black pepper

1/4 cup chopped cilantro

6 garlic cloves, chopped

2 tablespoons kosher salt

1/2 cup lemon juice

1/2 cup orange juice

Combine all the ingredients for the crust in a food processor (a mini is great for this) and pulse 3 times to finely chop the pecans and blend the whole together. Do not purée! You want a nice fluffy crumb mixture.

Combine the seeds, cinnamon, herbs, and chile powders in a small skillet and toast over medium heat till fragrant. Grind to a medium texture in a spice grinder or the jar of a blender. Add the remaining ingredients and blend until just combined. Transfer to a glass or plastic or non-reactive metal dish that can hold the racks. Trim the silverskin and extra fat off the racks. Place the racks meat side down in the marinade, allowing the bones to stick out. Set aside for 30 minutes to an hour.

Grill and roast the racks as described on page 203. Serve on warm plates with one of the following great sauces:

Serrano Mint Jam

1 cup finely chopped serrano chiles, seeded

1 cup finely chopped jalapeños, seeded

2 cups finely chopped mint leaves

1 cup cider vinegar

1 cup water

1 package dry pectin, like Surejell

5 cups sugar

1 teaspoon salt

Combine the chiles, mint, vinegar, and water in a heavy 3- quart saucepan. Stir in the pectin well. Bring to a full rolling boil, a boil that can't be stirred down. Stir in the sugar and bring back to a full boil. Boil and stir for one minute. Remove from heat and add salt. Transfer to a small saucepan and keep warm until serving. Makes about 5 cups and keeps well for a few months in the fridge.

Ancho Honey Mint Glaze

1 1/2 cups honey

1/2 cup lime juice

1/2 cup mint leaves, chopped fine

1 cup Ancho Purée (page 107)

    or 1/2 cup ancho powder mixed with 1/2 cup water

1/2 cup orange juice

1 teaspoon salt, to taste

> Combine all in a heavy 2-quart saucepan. Bring to a simmer over medium heat and cook gently for 5 minutes. Correct for salt and acidity. This glaze is very intense so it goes a long way. Extra sauce keeps very well in the fridge.

Apple Serrano Mint Chutney

1 cup chopped red onion

1/2 cup chopped red bell pepper

2 teaspoons minced ginger

2 cloves garlic, minced

3/4 cup sugar

1/2 cup apple cider

1/2 cup apple cider vinegar

2 cups diced peeled apples (Macs, Johnnies,

    or Goldens)

2 serrano chiles, seeded, chopped fine.

1/4 cup chopped fresh mint

1 teaspoon salt, to taste

Combine the onion, pepper, ginger, garlic, sugar, cider, and vinegar in a heavy one-quart saucepan. Bring to a bare simmer over medium heat, just to soften the mixture a little. Add the apples, chiles, and mint, and cook gently for 2 minutes, just until the apples begin to soften. Remove from the heat, add one teaspoon salt or to taste, set aside and keep warm until serving time.

Makes about 4 cups. This semi-fresh chutney keeps for a few days in the fridge. It is also delicious with pork, teriyaki grilled chicken, and curried lamb.

LODGE SIDE DISHES

Side dishes at the Lodge truly complete the meal. Not just boring fillers, these are wonderful dishes. Many of them could serve as the basis for a lighter or vegetarian meal. We use any leftover Black Beans with our egg dishes. The Green Chile Cornbread with soup and a salad makes a quick and easy supper. The Fideo con Cotija is really one of our failsafe dinners at home, coming together in about 20 minutes and out of the oven in 20 more. The addition of some leftover roasted or grilled chicken or a quick sauté of shrimp makes it even more complete on the protein scale. Many of these dishes are easily prepared ahead and hold very well, making them perfect for entertaining.

A NOTE ON VEGETABLE SIDES

We tend to keep our veggie sides pretty simple just because there are already a lot of big flavors on the plates, and because we like the flavor of the vegetables themselves, simply enhanced. Here are a few preparation methods you might like to try.

GREEN VEGETABLES: (BROCCOLLINI, BROCCOLI, GREEN BEANS, SUGAR SNAP PEAS)

Blanch trimmed veggies in rapidly boiling, well salted water just until they're bright green and barely tender. Broccoli will take 4 to 5 minutes, sugar snaps maybe 30 seconds. Drain well in a colander then immediately put the colander into a bowl filled with water and ice to stop the cooking and set the color. Drain well when cool and set aside till serving time. At dinner, we simply sauté the veggies with a little olive oil, a little garlic, some lemon zest, and of course, salt and pepper.

with cold water till the ice melts and the greens are cool. It's important to drain the greens very well at this point. For serving, we toss the greens with some minced garlic, salt, and pepper, sometimes a little lemon zest, and sauté in hot olive oil till warmed through.

BABY CARROTS OR CUT CARROTS

This is our indulgent veggie offering and guests love it. Place the trimmed carrots in a saucepan that holds them comfortably. Add water to just the level of the carrots. Dot with about 3 tablespoons of butter, about 1/4 cup of maple syrup or honey, salt and pepper, and 1/2 teaspoon of basil, thyme, dill, tarragon, or curry powder. If you have any of these herbs fresh, add double the amount. Cover tightly and cook over medium heat till just barely tender, about 10 minutes depending on the size and age of the carrots. Uncover and drain off the excess liquid and serve.

SQUASH, SWEET PEPPERS, CORN, SWEET ONIONS, TOMATOES:

We usually like to use the peppers and onions as a base and sweat them in olive oil and seasonings till very juicy, then toss in the trimmed squash, or corn and tomatoes and simply sauté them till just tender. Again, we season all these veggies very simply, using salt, pepper, and olive oil, and a complementary herb to the rest of the meal. Simple and delicious!

SWISS CHARD, KALE AND OTHER SOFT GREENS:

Trim the greens into large bite-sized pieces and blanch in boiling, well salted water. Chard takes less than a minute, kale and the sturdier greens take about 2 to 3. Drain well in a colander and place into an ice bath as above. Sometimes we pour a scoop of ice over the drained greens and rinse

Cheddar Corn Pudding

FOR EIGHT TO TEN

A Lodge favorite, good any time of the year.

3 cups corn kernels (divided use)

2 cups milk

6 eggs

1 + 3/4 cups heavy cream

1/4 cup cornmeal

2 cups grated sharp Cheddar, pepperjack, or Gruyère

2 teaspoons, scant, kosher salt

few dashes hot pepper sauce

1/3 cup sliced green onions

Preheat the oven to 350°. Blend 2 cups of corn kernels with the milk until smooth. In a large mixing bowl, beat the eggs, then add the corn purée, cornmeal, remaining corn kernels, cream, cheese, and seasonings. Add the green onions and pour into an oiled or buttered 9- x 13-inch baking pan. Bake 20 to 25 minutes. Serve immediately.

Try adding a teaspoon of cracked black pepper, dill, or caraway, or cumin plus half a cup of chopped roasted green chiles.

Baked Cheddar Polenta

FOR OR EIGHT TO TEN

Simple and delicious comfort food that comes together very quickly. Pairs well with roast pork, lamb, or chicken.

4 cups water

2 cups milk

1/2 tablespoon kosher salt

1 teaspoon thyme

1 teaspoon sage

1 + 1/4 cups polenta

2 teaspoon coarse ground black pepper

1 cup grated sharp Cheddar cheese

2/3 cup grated Parmesan cheese

Preheat the oven to 350°. Heat the water, milk, salt, thyme, and sage together in a heavy 2-quart saucepan over medium heat. Whisk in the polenta and pepper until smooth and beginning to thicken just a bit. Mix the cheeses, adding half the mixture to the corn mush. Pour into an oiled 9- x13-inch baking dish. Sprinkle the rest of the cheese on top. Bake uncovered 30 to 35 minutes or until set.

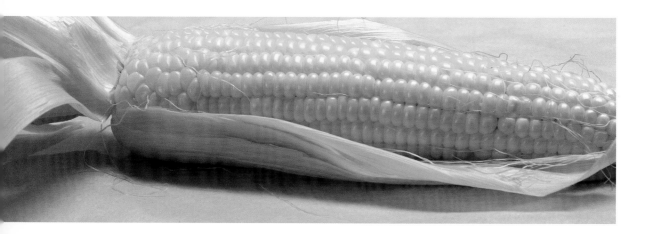

Crispy Polenta

A nice variation on "yuppie mush"! Sage, thyme or chives are nice additions.

2 cups polenta

6 cups water

2 cups milk

2 teaspoons salt

2 large cloves garlic, minced

2 tablespoons each olive oil, butter

2/3 cup Parmesan cheese

1 teaspoon black pepper

1 tablespoon parsley, chopped

> Combine the polenta, water, milk, salt, garlic, oil, and butter in a heavy 2-quart saucepan. Bring to a slow boil, stirring regularly, till it achieves a thick mushy consistency. Stir in the Parmesan, pepper, and parsley. Pour into an oiled shallow pan and set aside in the fridge to cool and set, at least 1 hour. When completely firm, cut into triangles and brown on a griddle with a bit of olive oil. Keep warm till serving.

Cheddar Gratin

One of the best recipes in the book. Curry Sweet Potato variation is outstanding. Thank you, MTK!

5 large Russett potatoes, peeled, sliced 1/8 inch thick using a food processor or a mandoline

1 cup yellow chopped yellow onion

2 garlic cloves, minced

1 teaspoon each salt and cracked black pepper

1 + 1/2 cups grated white Cheddar cheese

2 to 2 + 1/2 cups heavy cream

Preheat the oven to 350°. Mix the potatoes, onion, garlic, salt, and pepper with the cheese in an oiled roasting pan. Cover with cream, then cover the pan tightly with foil. Bake one hour. Uncover and bake 15 more minutes or until golden brown and set.

CURRY SWEET POTATO GRATIN: Substitute 2 sweet potatoes for 2 of the russets and add 2 teaspoons curry powder and one 1 teaspoon thyme.

SPICY SOUTHWESTERN GRATIN: Substitute 2 sweet potatoes for 2 of the Russets and add one teaspoon each ancho powder, cumin, oregano, sage.

Corn and Herb Cakes

Lovely little cakes, great with fish, chicken or pork. We generally use frozen corn for this.

2 + 1/2 cups corn kernels

1 cup milk

2/3 cup flour

2/3 cup cornmeal

1 teaspoon baking powder

3 whole eggs + 3 egg yolks

1/4 pound melted butter

1/4 cup each chopped chives and chopped parsley

1/2 teaspoon salt and 1 teaspoon black pepper

> Process the corn kernels and milk till creamy and chunky. Pour into a large mixing bowl. Mix in the flour and cornmeal. In a separate bowl, whisk the eggs and egg yolks together until smooth and frothy. Add to the corn mixture, then fold in the herbs and seasonings. Ladle batter, about 2 tablespoons per cake, onto a pre-heated griddle. Brown cakes on both sides, then set aside on a sheet pan. Warm through just before serving.

Green Chile Cornbread

A Lodge classic that serves as a meal for many of us throughout the year. Love that creamed corn!

1 cup cornmeal

1 + 1/2 cup flour

2 tablespoons sugar

1 teaspoon salt

1 teaspoon baking soda

2 teaspoons (scant) baking powder

1 + 1/2 cups buttermilk

2 cups creamed corn

2 eggs

1/4 cup canola oil

1 cup hot green chiles, chopped

1 + 1/2 cups jack cheese, grated

1 + 1/2 cups medium Cheddar

> In a large mixing bowl, whisk the dry ingredients together well. Add the buttermilk, creamed corn, eggs, and oil and mix thoroughly.
>
> In an oiled 9- by 13-inch baking dish, layer half the batter, then the chiles and half the cheese, more batter, and then the rest of the cheese on top. Bake at 350° for 45 minutes until just set in the center.

CHEDDAR DILL CORNBREAD: **Add 2 teaspoons each dry dill weed, dill seed, caraway seed and dry mustard to the batter, plus 3 to 4 dashes hot pepper sauce. Skip the green chiles and use 3 cups Cheddar cheese instead of the mixture.**

Black Beans with Cotija

One of my personal favorites; sometimes I'm just hungry for beans and this great salty cheese. This is, of course, wonderful with beef and pork, but we like to serve it with fish, too.

1 tablespoon olive oil

1 cup chopped onion

3 cloves garlic, minced

2 teaspoons each oregano, sage, thyme, cumin

1 teaspoon ancho powder

3 cups dried black beans, sorted and rinsed

kosher salt

1 teaspoon chipotle powder

1/2 cup Cotija cheese, crumbled

> Heat the oil in a 3-quart saucepan and add the onion and garlic. Cook 4 to 5 minutes. Toast the herbs, cumin, and chile powder together in a small skillet till fragrant and add to the onion-garlic mixture. Add the black beans and enough water to cover by about 4 inches.
>
> Cover and cook over medium heat until barely tender, about 1 hour. Add 2 teaspoons of kosher salt and continue cooking gently until fully tender, another hour or more. Drain off excess fluid, leaving the beans moist but not soupy. Let it rest a bit, then correct for salt. Serve with Cotija sprinkled on top.

Cotija is an aged whole-milk Mexican cheese used throughout Mexico in the way we might use Parmesan, as a finishing garnish. It's dry and a little salty-sweet. Cotija's origins are in the Mexican city of the same name in the state of Michoacán. A good Greek or domestic feta is a reasonable substitute, but Cotija is milder and drier.

Fideo con Cotija

This is the "failsafe" quick dinner I most often turn to on busy nights at home. It comes together so quickly and makes such good leftovers—it may be even better the next day!

1 pound angel hair pasta

1 medium onion, chopped

2 garlic cloves, minced

1 23-ounce can Rotel tomatoes (with chiles)

1/4 cup hot green chiles, chopped

2 tablespoons fresh cilantro leaves, chopped

1 cup chicken broth

1/2 teaspoon salt

2/3 cup crumbled Cotija or feta cheese

1/4 cup green onions, chopped

Preheat the oven to 350°. Break the angel hair bundle in half. Sauté in a large skillet in a little olive oil till it browns slightly. Transfer to a metal roasting pan.

Sauté onion and garlic; add the tomatoes, chiles, and cilantro and cook just until heated through. Add to the pasta in the roasting pan, mixing all together well. Place the roasting pan over the burner(s) on top of the stove. Add broth and a little salt. Heat to simmer, then remove immediately. Cover loosely. Bake 20 minutes. Let sit 30 minutes out of the oven. Fluff up the mixture a bit. Sprinkle with cheese and green onions.

If Rotel tomatoes are not available, substitute 2 tablespoons jalapeños, seeded and chopped, plus 2 + 1/2 cups chopped tomatoes and their juices, and a bit of salt. Sauté with the onions and garlic before adding to the browned pasta.

Pearl Couscous Pilaf

A great pasta side that isn't heavy, just delicious.

3 cups pearl couscous

8 cups water

1/2 teaspoon each thyme, oregano, sage

1 cinnamon stick

1 whole clove

2 teaspoons ground cumin

2 teaspoons ground coriander

3/4 teaspoon cayenne

1 tablespoon kosher salt

2 tablespoons olive oil

1/2 cup red bell pepper, finely diced

1/2 cup yellow bell pepper, finely diced

3/4 cup red onion, finely diced

3/4 cup corn kernels

1 clove garlic, minced

1/4 cup extra virgin olive oil

Salt and pepper to taste

Combine the water with all the herbs, spices, salt, and 2 tablespoons olive oil and bring to a boil. Add the couscous. Cook 5 minutes until just tender. Taste. Drain in a large colander, rinse with warm water. Toss lightly with olive oil, and pour back into a heavy saucepan.

Sauté the bell peppers, onion, corn, and garlic together briefly, then toss with the warm couscous and a little extra virgin olive oil just before serving.

Mac and Four Cheeses

A great fall and winter side dish, and a fine dinner for most of us. And kids love it!

1 pound elbow macaroni

1/4 cup butter

1/4 cup flour

2 + 2/3 cups milk

1/2 teaspoon paprika

1/2 teaspoon kosher salt

1/2 teaspoon white pepper

3/4 cup sharp white Cheddar

3/4 cups medium Cheddar

3/4 cups Parmesan

3/4 cups fontina

1 1/2 cups dry bread crumbs

1/4 cup melted butter

Cook the macaroni in boiling salted water until *al dente*. Drain, rinse in cold water, toss in a lightly oiled baking pan. Set aside.

Make a roux: Melt the butter in a heavy 2-quart saucepan. Whisk in the flour and cook over medium heat until light golden and fragrant. Whisk in the milk slowly and cook until thickened and smooth, stirring frequently. Add the paprika, salt, and pepper. Mix the cheeses together and add 2/3 of the cheese to the sauce. Mix well. Combine the sauce with the macaroni. Mix the bread crumbs with the 1/4 cup of melted butter. Sprinkle the remaining cheese on top of the macaroni, then the bread crumbs. Bake at 325° for 20 to 25 minutes, or until heated through and the bread crumbs are toasty.

Creamy Green Chile Rice

This is a Stabo favorite, or maybe it's just that he makes it so well. It comes together easily and keeps well.

3 cups water

2 tablespoons olive oil

1 teaspoon kosher salt

1 teaspoon sage

1 teaspoon oregano

2 cups white Basmati rice

2 cloves garlic, minced

1/2 cup chopped onion

1/4 cup chopped hot green chiles

3/4 cup corn kernels

1 + 1/4 cups Mexican crema (if not available, substitute 1 + 1/4 cups sour cream mixed with 1 teaspoon salt and 1 tablespoon fresh lime juice)

1 tablespoon chopped fresh cilantro (optional)

Bring the water, oil, salt, and herbs to a boil in a heavy 2-quart saucepan. Add the rice, stir, cover, and bring back to a boil. Turn the flame to low and simmer until the moisture is gone, about 15 minutes. Turn off the heat, steam covered for 10 minutes. Fluff and turn into a large bowl to cool a bit

Sauté the onion, chiles, and corn very briefly. Salt to taste. Mix the veggies with the rice, add the crema and cilantro, and turn into an oiled baking pan. Cover with foil and bake at 350° until heated through, about 20 minutes.

{ Just add a salad and many sides make a great dinner on their own. }

Mushroom Wild Rice Pilaf

FOR EIGHT TO TEN

The perfect accompaniment to roast duck, pork, or chicken.

1 + 1/2 cup wild rice

1 tablespoon olive oil

1 teaspoon thyme

1 teaspoon marjoram

1 teaspoon kosher salt

1 teaspoon pepper

1/2 teaspoon cayenne

3 to 4 cups sliced crimini mushrooms

1 cup green onions, chopped

Combine the rice, oil, herbs, and spices with 5 cups of water and simmer for about 45 minutes until the rice is tender and fluffy. Drain off any excess liquid. Sauté the mushrooms in olive oil until starting to soften. Add the green onions and sauté till just tender, then toss with the wild rice.

Where do you go for inspiration in cooking? We go to the market, to interesting cookbooks, and we get a lot of inspiration from the dish itself as we are making it. After all, most dishes are variations on a theme—but even a slight variation can make a lovely flavor ripple. The seasons inspire us too. And we listen to our own palates, responding to what we feel like eating today, this minute.

Pumpkin Lasagna

FOR EIGHT TO TEN

The idea for this came from a class I attended with Guiliano Bugiali, a master of Italian cuisine. It's basically from a traditional Tuscan filled pasta made with cauliflower. I use this as springboard with different vegetables throughout the season.

FOR THE PASTA

2 cups all purpose flour

1 teaspoon kosher salt

2 teaspoons olive oil

2 to 3 eggs

FOR THE BECHAMEL

4 tablespoons butter

1/4 cup flour

3 cups milk

salt and white pepper

nutmeg, freshly ground

FOR THE FILLING

1/4 cup olive oil

1 yellow onion, chopped fine

1 cup finely chopped celery

2 carrots, peeled and chopped fine

2 to 3 cloves garlic, minced

1 small head cauliflower, stemmed and broken
    or cut into flowerets

1/2 to 1 teaspoon pepper flakes

1 + 1/2 teaspoon basil

1 + 1/2 teaspoon kosher salt

2 cups cubed pumpkin or butternut squash

1 + 1/2 to 2 cups stock or water

1 pound ricotta

1/2 cup grated Parmesan

2 eggs

1 teaspoon white pepper

salt to taste

nutmeg, a touch

3 cups Marinara Sauce (Simple Marinara or purchased)

freshly grated Parmesan

Make the pasta: Pulse the flour, salt, and olive oil together in the food processor. Add the eggs one by one to the dry mixture; pulse. Add a bit more egg if needed to bring the dough together. Wrap tightly and set aside for 15 minutes or so before rolling into thin sheets. Place gently in boiling water with a bit of salt and olive oil; cook for one minute or until tender. Rinse in a bowl of cold water with 1 to 2 tablespoons olive oil. Hold, layered with parchment, until ready for final assembly.

Make the bechamel: Melt the butter in a saucepan; whisk in the flour, and cook for a few minutes over medium heat to make a light roux. Add 2 cups of milk, stirring until thickened. Season with salt, white pepper and nutmeg to taste. Set aside with plastic on the surface to avoid developing a "skin."

Make the filling: In a heavy 3-quart saucepan, sweat the onions, celery, garlic, carrots, cauliflower, and seasonings in olive oil. Add one cup of the stock, cover, and cook until the cauliflower begins to break down. Add the pumpkin or squash cubes and the rest of the stock (just enough to not quite cover the veggies). Cook uncovered until the pumpkin is tender and most of the excess liquid is gone. Cool and transfer to a bowl. Add the ricotta, parmesan, eggs, and seasonings.

To assemble: Spray a 9- by 13-inch baking pan with vegetable spray, then lightly cover the bottom of the pan with a thin layer of Marinara Sauce. Layer the pasta sheets, then half the filling, another layer of pasta, the remaining filling, and a top layer of pasta; then a thin layer of bechamel over all. Drizzle four thin lines of marinara the length of the pan. Bake 30 minutes at 350. Set aside to cool for 20 minutes. Cut into 3- by 4-inch rectangles. Serve with a bit more marinara and a sprinkle of freshly grated Parmesan.

Simple Marinara

1/4 cup olive oil

4 to 5 cloves garlic, minced

1 small yellow onion, chopped fine

3 28-ounce cans plum tomatoes,
    drained slightly and pureed

2 tablespoons chopped fresh basil

2 tablespoons chopped fresh Italian parsley

1 tablespoon fresh oregano, or 1 teaspoon dried

1/4 teaspoon red pepper flakes

1 to 2 teaspoons salt, to taste

1 cup dry white wine

Warm the olive oil in a heavy 2- to 3-quart saucepan. Add the garlic and onions and sauté till translucent and very fragrant. Add the tomatoes, all the seasonings and the wine and cook at a slow simmer for 30 to 45 minutes, till thickened and reduced. Correct for salt and pepper and if a bit too sharp, add a pinch of sugar.

Cool completely before refrigerating or freezing. Makes about 6 cups.

Lemon Fettucine

FOR EIGHT TO TEN

This is Donald's favorite. Actually, *all* pastas are his favorite, but as lemon is his other other great passion, this dish is perfection for him!

FOR THE FETTUCINE

2 cups all purpose flour

1 teaspoon kosher salt

2 teaspoons olive oil

3 eggs

FOR THE SAUCE

1/4 cup butter

1/4 cup olive oil

1 + 1/2 cups heavy cream

1 + 1/4 cups chicken broth

1/2 cup (scant) fresh lemon juice

1/4 cup lemon zest

1/4 cup Italian (flat leaf) parsley, coarsely chopped

1 cup shredded Parmesan cheese

salt, pepper to taste

For Black Pepper Fettucine, add 2 teaspoons coarsely ground (not cracked) black pepper to the flour mixture before adding the eggs. We like to serve the Black Pepper version with chicken and with halibut or salmon with Roasted Tomato Vinaigrette. We toss the pasta with olive oil and a little warm chicken broth before putting the whole dish together.

Pulse the flour, salt and olive oil together in the food processor. Add the eggs one by one to the dry mixture; pulse. Add a bit more egg if needed to bring the dough together. Turn the dough out onto a lightly floured work surface (preferably wood) and knead the dough until very smooth and supple. Wrap tightly and set aside for 15 minutes or so before rolling it through the pasta machine. On the final pass, cut into fettucine noodles and lay over a rack to dry.

Melt the butter with the olive oil. Add the cream, broth and juice, bring to a slow boil, reduce till thickened, to about a third of the original volume. Keep warm. Correct for salt, and pepper.

Cook the fettucine until barely tender. Save 3 tablespoons of the pasta water before draining the noodles. Transfer the pasta to a heavy 3-quart saucepan. Add the water, half a cup of Parmesan, freshly ground pepper, warm lemon cream, half the zest. Toss together lightly. Taste for salt and pepper. Mix the rest of the zest and chopped parsley. Garnish with a bit more Parmesan and a fling of the parsley mixture.

Sesame Scallion Rice Noodles

Light yet very flavorful, these noodles go well with some of our slightly Asian entrées, like Green Tomato Relish or Asian Barbeque. They're pretty good on their own too, or with some Teriyaki chicken or shrimp.

1 package rice noodles (rice vermicelli, not rice sticks)

Nuoc Cham Sauce

1/3 cup sesame seeds, toasted

1/2 cup scallions, sliced thinly on the diagonal

> Soak the noodles in warm water for 10 minutes. Then cook in boiling water about 5 minutes until barely tender. Toss with one cup sauce, sesame seeds, and scallions. Keep the rest of the Nuoc Cham Sauce for later use.

Nuoc Cham Sauce

1/4 cup rice vinegar

1/4 cup cider vinegar

juice of 3 limes

1 cup fish sauce

1/4 to 1/3 cup sugar

1 cup cold water

1/2 to 1 teaspoon chile paste (sambal), to taste

1/4 cup shredded carrot

1/4 cup chopped cilantro

> Combine the ingredients in a glass or plastic jar and shake well to blend. Taste and add more vinegar, sugar, or chile paste to your liking. Be mindful of the chile paste; it grows stronger as it infuses the mixture! This lasts awhile in the fridge.

Lavender Coconut Rice Pilaf

A delicate but still very flavorful side that we like to serve with some of our fish dishes, although I have served it with the Asian Barbecue Baby Backs. It's very good alongside curried vegetables or chicken as well. Dried lavender is available at the health food store.

2 tablespoons butter

2 tablespoons vegetable oil

1/2 teaspoon cumin seed

1/2 teaspoon brown mustard seed

2 cups Basmati rice

2 teaspoons salt

1/2 teaspoon thyme

1 heaping teaspoon dried lavender buds

2 cups water

1 + 1/4 cups unsweetened coconut milk

1/2 cup chopped chives or green onions

> In a heavy 2- to 3-quart saucepan, melt the butter with the oil over medium high heat. Add the seeds, rice, salt, and thyme and cook, lowering the heat to medium. Stir the rice until some of it becomes nearly opaque and is just slightly browning a little. Crush the lavender buds with your fingers and add to the rice. (Then rub your fingers behind your ears and on your temples. . .). Add the water and coconut milk, mix well, and cover. Bring just to the boil, uncover, and stir well. Reduce the heat to very low and cover tightly. Check the rice at 12 minutes. If the surface is covered with steam holes and the liquid is absorbed, remove from the heat and set aside, covered, to finish steaming and to cool. After 20 minutes, fluff the rice, add a bit of salt and pepper, mix in the green onions, and serve.

Lavender Garlic Roasted Potatoes

FOR EIGHT TO TEN

Wonderful, fragrant potatoes to go with lamb or pork. Dried lavender buds will work here.

8 to 10 red potatoes, or Yukon golds, or a mixture, cut into 1-inch or so cubes

1/4 cup extra virgin olive oil

3 cloves garlic, minced

1 teaspoon fresh lavender flower buds, crushed

1 teaspoon salt

1 teaspoon black pepper

Heat the olive oil with the garlic, lavender, and seaonings. Toss with the potatoes in a roasting pan. Bake at 375° for 20 minutes, then turn the potatoes with a wide spatula. Bake 10 more minutes until the potatoes are brown and crusty.

Mashed Sweets and Yukon Golds

FOR EIGHT TO TEN

A simply wonderful side for roasted meats and chicken, and excellent with that turkey. This does seem rather autumnal, but we do it in the spring, too.

4 large Yukon Gold potatoes, peeled and cubed (about 4 cups)

2 to 3 sweet potatoes or yams, peeled and cubed (about 4 cups)

1 cup milk

1/4 cup butter

2 tablespoons extra virgin olive oil

4 cloves garlic, minced

salt and coarse black pepper

1/3 cup chopped green onions or chives

2 tablespoons butter, in small bits

Cook the potatoes in plenty of well-salted water until completely tender but not falling apart. Heat the milk, butter, olive oil, and garlic together till very warm. Drain the potatoes very well, then transfer back to the pot and heat over a low flame for a few minutes to dry a bit more.

Whip the potatoes with a hand mixer in the pot, adding the milk mixture slowly until you have a nice fluffy, creamy consistency. Add salt and pepper to taste. Fold in the green onions and dot the top of the potatoes with the butter. Cover and keep warm until serving.

DESSERT

For some of us, dessert is the most important part of the meal, requiring some to choose a lighter starter and entrée (or no entrée) in order to save room. However, at the Lodge we don't really give you that option, having planned your entire meal for you. So it's up to me to try and provide that luscious little sweet finish for you and not overload you with food! I don't know that it always works, for I'm certain not everyone can eat all this food, but it's amazing how many people always finish dessert.

Our desserts reflect the homey, comfortable and seasonal aspects of the Lodge. Fruit pies, tarts and cobblers of the season, along with shortcakes, satisfy the craving we all have for the sweet familiar. A few simple cakes and some fabulous chocolate desserts provide a richer finish to the meal. And, my personal favorites, baked custards or pots de crème.

Our pie crust recipe, Mom's Foolproof, is just that, really easy and consistent. The cake recipes are all simple and can be made a day ahead. And the Bittersweet Chocolate Tart, a classic variation from Joël Robuchon, is superlative, the perfect chocolate dessert. Try a few of your favorites for your family and friends, and everyone will be happily full and satisfied.

R estaurants are theatre. The stage is set in advance. All kinds of things go on behind the scenes that ideally no one is particularly aware of. Waiters "suit up," glasses and silverware are polished, napkins are folded, flowers arranged, candles lit, wine selected. On a perfect evening it becomes a ballet—to the untrained eye, effortless and graceful.

Amanda, with a different personality, could be "The Diva"—or "The Queen of Sauces," as she has been appreciatively dubbed. But because she does not seek the limelight, the food is the main event, and all the staff mere players, creating the space for guests to relax and enjoy, to feel special and cared for.

{ Restaurants are theatre. The stage is set. All kinds of things go on behind the scenes. }

at Garland's Lodge   227

{ "It's not a job . . . it's a lifestyle."   GARY GARLAND

LIVING AND WORKING
AT THE LODGE

Living and working in the same place has particular joys and only a few drawbacks. You certainly can't beat the commute. We are told on a daily basis how lucky we are to live in such a gorgeous spot. We awake to the chatter of birds and roosters crowing (less romantic than it's cracked up to be). We know the bark of each dog who lives on premises. In our subconscious we register the arrival of the earliest employees and the quiet hum of maintenance carts off to work. We often traverse the wooden bridge that spans the thirty-foot wash between our house and the Lodge thirty times a day—a built-in aerobic program. The division of work and play is a bit blurred—same the delineation between staff and family. Our door is always open, and at times often opened.

Without uniforms, badges, or titles to speak of, corporate structure is almost invisible at the Lodge. In a small business, every employee brings more to the table than their labor. Small workspaces and overlapping responsibilities guarantee contact and make cooperation essential. By the end of the season, we know our newcomers well. Many of our employees have been here for a decade. While we are certainly not a commune, we are a community. Family members are staff and staff becomes family.

Bittersweet Chocolate Souffle Cake

FOR EIGHT TO TEN

A simple little cake that comes together quickly, holds well for a day, and is surprisingly light.

8 ounces bittersweet chocolate, chopped

1/4 pound butter

5 eggs, separated

1/2 teaspoon cream of tartar

2/3 cup sugar (set aside 2 tablespoons of sugar to grind with the almonds)

2/3 cup ground almonds

Preheat the oven to 350°. Coat a 10-inch springform pan with cooking spray and then lightly dust with flour. Line the bottom with a circle of parchment. Melt the chocolate and butter together. Set aside to cool.

Beat the egg whites with the cream of tartar till stiff. Transfer to another bowl and set aside. In the mixing bowl used to beat the egg whites, beat the egg yolks and sugar together for 2 to 3 minutes, till thick and pale. Stir in the chocolate and the almonds, then fold the whites in gently and evenly.

Bake until puffed and barely set and the center springs back, approximately 25 to 30 minutes. Cool on a rack. Remove from the springform pan. Slice into 12 individual servings.

Serve with warm Butterscotch Sauce.

Butterscotch Sauce

1 + 1/2 stick butter (6 ounces)

1 cup dark brown sugar

1 cup sugar

1 teaspoon salt

3 tablespoons water

1 cup light corn syrup

1 + 1/2 cup heavy cream

1 teaspoon vanilla extract

1 teaspoon dark rum (optional)

Melt the butter in a heavy saucepan, add both sugars, salt, water, and corn syrup. Bring to a boil over medium high heat until big slow bubbles form across the surface. Remove from heat and slowly stir in the cream. Take care with this, as it may boil up.

Return to heat and simmer until smooth and thickened, about 5 to 8 minutes. Stir in the vanilla and rum, if using.

Makes about 3 + 1/2 cups, more than you are likely to use for the Bittersweet Chocolate Souffle Cake. The recipe can be cut in half, or make it all; it will keep about a month in the fridge. Nice on ice cream during a midnight raid.

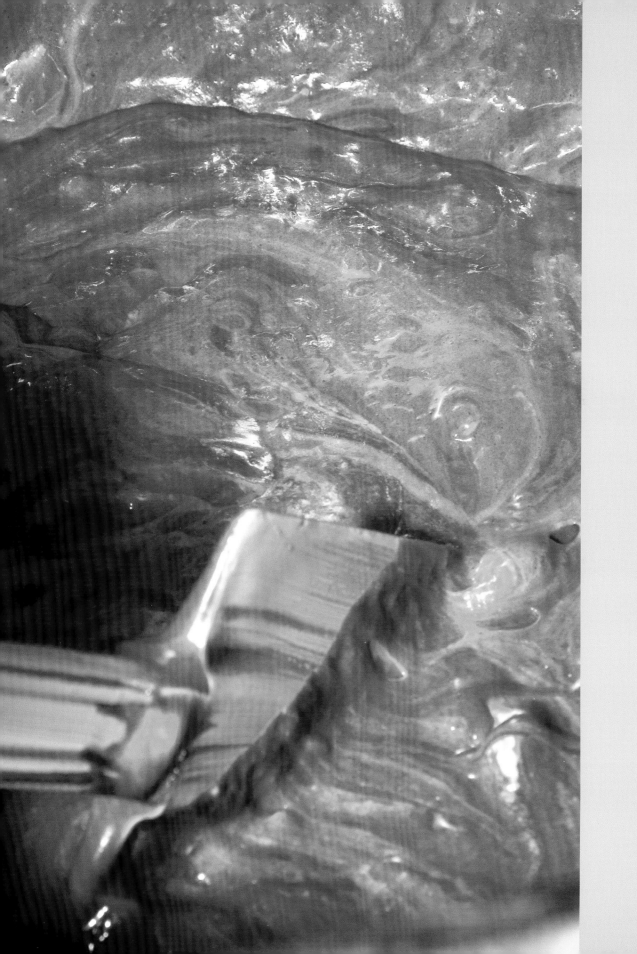

Lemon Pots de Crème

FOR TWELVE

Crème Caramel, Pot de Crème, flan, custard, blancmange, panna cotta, pudding—by any name, these simple, creamy, ethereal desserts are my absolute favorites. They provide a light yet elegant ending to a big meal, are simple to make and need to be made ahead. The perfect finishing touch!

1 cup freshly squeezed lemon juice

1 tablespoon lemon zest

1 + 1/4 cup sugar

12 yolks

5 cups heavy cream

1/2 vanilla bean

> Preheat the oven to 300°. In a heavy saucepan, warm the cream with the vanilla bean.
>
> In a medium bowl whisk the sugar into the juice. Add the zest, then the egg yolks. Whisk in the warm cream. Strain and pour into individual 6-ounce souffle cups.
>
> Bake in a hot water bath covered with foil for 40 to 50 minutes until set. Begin checking at 40 minutes, adding additional cooking time in 5 minute increments. Cool uncovered. Garnish with a swirl of whipped cream and a bit more zest.

Honey Pecan Pots de Crème

FOR TWELVE

4 cups heavy cream

2 cups half and half

1/2 vanilla bean

1/2 to 2/3 cups pecan honey (a yummy product of the Arizona pecan groves. If unavailable, substitute light molasses.)

pinch of salt

12 egg yolks

> Preheat the oven to 325°. Heat the cream together with the vanilla bean until scalded. Whisk in the pecan honey, the salt, and then the egg yolks. Strain and pour into 6-ounce souffle cups. Bake in a water bath covered with foil for 40 to 50 minutes, until set. Cool uncovered, then chill completely in the fridge.
>
> Garnish with a swirl of whipped cream and a tiny sprinkle of candied pecans.

Caramel Pots de Crème

FOR TWELVE

12 egg yolks

1 + 1/2 cups sugar

2 cups half and half

4 cups heavy cream

1 tablespoon vanilla

2 teaspoons dark rum

1/8 teaspoon salt

> Preheat the oven to 325°. Whisk the egg yolks together in a large stainless steel bowl.
>
> Caramelize the sugar in a large heavy saucepan; melt until smooth and deep golden brown. Add both creams. The mixture will bubble up, so take care. Allow to heat until the caramel is melted and smooth. Pour over the yolks, whisking as you pour. Add the vanilla, rum, and salt. Strain back into the pot. Pour into individual 6-ounce serving cups and bake in a hot water bath for 50 minutes.

Blackberry-Peach Cobbler

Himalayan berries (not true "blackberries," but delicious) grow all along Oak Creek, providing a ready supply of fruit for pies and cobblers and jam for anyone energetic enough to pick them. Long sleeves and pant legs recommended!

pastry for pie (page 252)

4 + 1/2 cups of berries, rinsed and stemmed

4 + 1/2 cups peaches, pitted, peeled and sliced

1/4 cup cornstarch

1 + 1/2 cups sugar

2 teaspoons vanilla extract

2 teaspoons orange flower water

4 tablespooons of butter, in bits

Make the pastry for pie. Preheat the oven to 375°.

Mix the cornstarch, sugar and extracts. Toss lightly with the mixed fruit, then pour into a well-buttered 9- by 13-inch baking dish. Dot with a little more butter.

Roll the pastry out into a large rectangle roughly 10 by 14 inches. Cut into 3/4-inch strips. Lay the strips across the fruit in a lattice fashion, trimming and tucking in the edges. Sprinkle the crust with a bit of sugar.

Bake at 375° for 35 to 45 minutes until the crust is golden brown. Spoon into individual serving dishes with a small scoop of vanilla ice cream.

Strawberry Rhubarb Pie

FOR EIGHT TO TEN

This is a "troops' favorite" pie in the spring, matched only by apple in the fall. For me, it is absolutely, hands-down, the very best. The combination of tart rhubarb and sweet berries creates an unbeatable balance.

pastry for pie (page 252)

FOR THE FILLING

3 cups strawberries, sliced

3 cups rhubarb, sliced (about 4 stalks)

1/3 cup cornstarch

1 + 1/4 cup sugar

2 teaspoons vanilla extract

1/4 teaspooon almond extract

2 tablespoons cold butter, in bits

Make the pie pastry. Allow it to chill in the refrigerator while preparing the fruit filling. Preheat the oven to 400°.

Mix the fruit with the cornstarch, sugar, and extract. Roll out one disk of pastry, following the procedure described on page 252, and fit it into a 10-inch pie pan.

Pour the filling into the shell and dot with butter. Roll out the top pastry and cover the fruit. Crimp the edges lightly. Make four one-inch cuts in the top of the crust ("north, south, east, west")—these are vents to release steam—and sprinkle the whole top with a bit more sugar.

Bake at 400° for 10 minutes, then lower the oven temperature to 350° and bake 40 more minutes, or until golden brown.

Lemon Almond Cake

FOR TEN TO TWELVE

One of my favorite cakes of all time. We serve this all year with seasonal fruit. Spring comes with strawberries and rhubarb, summer with peaches and blueberries, and fall with a spiced red wine syrup and dried fruits. All delicious in their time.

1/4 pound butter

2/3 cup olive oil

1 + 1/4 cups sugar

1 pound almond paste, about 1 + 3/4 cups packed

1 tablespoon lemon zest

8 eggs

1 teaspoon vanilla extract

1 teaspoon orange flower water

1 cup flour

1 + 1/2 teaspoons baking powder

1/2 teaspoon salt

1/2 cup lemon juice

1/2 cup sugar

Preheat oven to 350°.

In the bowl of a stand mixer fitted with a paddle, cream together the butter, oil, sugar, and almond paste till fluffy. Add the zest, then the eggs, one by one. Add the extracts.

In a separate bowl, whisk together the flour, baking powder, and salt, then add to the butter-almond mixture. Beat on medium speed for one minute. Pour into 2 buttered and floured 9- by 5-inch loaf pans or 2 buttered and floured 8-inch rounds and bake at 350° for 45 to 50 minutes, or until cake top springs back when pressed with a finger.

Combine the lemon juice and sugar in a small saucepan and heat till sugar dissolves. Cool cakes for 5 minutes in the pans; poke holes with a toothpick or skewer across the entire top of cake, about 3/4 inch apart. Brush the glaze slowly over the cakes. Cool completely, then unmold cake.

This cake keeps very well. Wrap it tightly to keep it in the fridge for a week, double wrap to freeze a few months.

Lemon Shortcakes with Fresh Summer Fruit

One of the essential summer desserts!

FOR THE SHORTCAKE

3 cups unbleached all purpose flour

1 + 1/2 tablespoons baking powder

1 /4 teaspoon salt

1/2 cup sugar

1 tablespoon lemon zest

3 tablespoons shortening

3 tablespoons butter

1 + 1/2 cups heavy cream

FOR THE FRUIT

6 to 7 cups mixed summer fruits: strawberries
and rhubarb, peaches and blackberries,
apricots and blueberries

1 cup sugar, plus 1 to 2 tablespoons, to taste

1 teaspoon vanilla

1 teaspoon orange flower water (optional,
but a nice addition)

FOR THE WHIPPED CREAM

1 cup heavy cream

1 to 2 tablespoons of sugar

dash of vanilla

Preheat the oven to 375°.

Combine the flour, baking powder, salt, sugar, and lemon zest in a medium bowl. Cut in the shortening and butter, then mix in the heavy cream with a wooden spoon until just combined. Turn out onto a lightly floured work surface and knead together gently, 3 or 4 times.

Pat and lightly roll out the dough till about one inch thick. Cut into 12 rounds or squares. Place on a sheet pan lined with parchment. Brush with cream, then sprinkle with sugar. Bake until golden brown, about 10 to 12 minutes. Split when cool.

Lightly mix the fruit, sugar, and extracts, taking care not to break up your berries. Set aside to cool at room temperature for 1 to 2 hours.

Whip the cream. Add the sugar and vanilla, leaving the whipped cream a bit soft.

For each serving, place the bottom half of a shortcake into a bowl, top with fruit, then the top half of the shortcake, and finally a nice dollop of softly whipped cream.

Bittersweet Chocolate Tart

FOR TWELVE

This is the very best chocolate tart ever, originally conceived by Joël Robuchon and widely imitated by the rest of us! Use the best chocolate you can find, but 56% cocoa solids maximum (see note about chocolate, page 242).

FOR THE CRUST

3 cups all purpose unbleached flour

1 teaspoon salt

2 tablespoons sugar

12 tablespoons unsalted butter, cut in bits

    (6 ounces or 1 + 1/2 sticks)

10 tablespoons vegetable shortening

    (6 ounces; see shortening note on page 255)

1/4 cup cold water

1 tablespoon cider vinegar

FOR THE FILLING

1 + 1/2 cups heavy cream

3/4 cup milk

9 ounces bittersweet chocolate, chopped

2 eggs, beaten lightly

1 scant teaspoon vanilla and a pinch of salt

1 cup heavy cream, whipped and sweetened

    slightly, for garnish

Combine dry ingredients in a medium bowl, whisk lightly to blend. Add butter and shortening, toss lightly to just coat the pieces, then cut in with pastry cutter until mixture appears like a very coarse meal. Some fat pieces will look like small beans. Mix water and vinegar together, then sprinkle about 3 tablespoons over the mixture and toss together to blend. Add another tablespoon, toss together to form a ball. You may need more water to have this come together into a cohesive ball, just add it a tablespoon at a time. Your dough should hold together when pressed, and it's better not to have it *too* dry. Form into 2 balls, flatten the balls into fattish discs, wrap and chill, at least 2 hours. This is necessary to rest and relax the gluten in the flour and completely chill all the fats in the mixture. Roll out one piece of pastry and line a 10-inch removable-bottom tart pan as directed on page 253. Chill 5 minutes. Line the shell with foil and fill with dried beans, uncooked rice, or pie weights (the crust is very buttery and will puff). Bake at 375° for 12 minutes, then remove the foil and beans and bake 5 to 8 minutes more, till golden brown. Remove from oven.

Heat the cream and milk together until very hot, but not boiling. Add the chocolate; stir until smooth. Add the eggs, mix well. Add the vanilla and salt. Pour into the baked tart shell. Bake at 350° for 12 to 15 minutes until set but still a bit "jiggly." It will set more as it cools. Garnish with whipped cream and shaved chocolate or cocoa if you like. Serve at room temperature.

Chocolate Profiteroles

FOR EIGHT TO TEN, WITH EXTRAS

A delicious variation on the classic vanilla cream puff, filled with the ice cream of your choice.

1 + 1/4 cups water

1/4 pound butter, in bits

1 + 1/4 ounces bittersweet or semisweet chocolate

1 /4 teaspoon salt

1 scant teaspoon sugar

1 cup flour

3 tablespoons cocoa powder (Dutch process, such as Droste's, if available)

5 eggs

Ganache (page 244)

Line 2 sheet pans with parchment paper. Preheat the oven to 425°.

Combine the water, butter, chocolate, salt, and sugar in a saucepan and bring to a boil, then immediately remove the pan from the heat. Add the flour and cocoa all at once, mixing well with a wooden spoon. Place the pan back over medium heat and stir until the batter is very smooth and shiny.

Transfer the batter to a stand mixer fitted with a paddle and run the machine on low speed for one minute. Add the eggs one by one on medium speed, incorporating each egg completely before adding the next.

Spoon into a pastry bag with a large plain tip. Form 12 evenly sized dollops of batter on each sheet pan. With a dampened finger, pat down the tips of the dollops. Bake at 425° for 15 minutes, then lower the heat to 350° and bake 20 minutes more, until firm and dry.

Cool completely. Slice off tops of profiteroles and remove "doughy" centers. Fill each with a scoop of ice cream and freeze. Allow to thaw a bit before serving. Serve 2 to 3 profiteroles per person, with hot Ganache ladled over.

Warm Chocolate Cake

FOR TWELVE

One of our favorite chocolate desserts, rich yet light in texture and totally pure in flavor. This is good with raspberry sauce or créme Anglaise, also.

12 ounces bittersweet chocolate, chopped

1/4 cup Frangelico, Amaretto, or brandy

1/4 cup strong coffee

5 eggs

1/3 cup sugar

1/4 cup flour

1 cup heavy cream, beaten fairly stiff

Pre-heat the oven to 350°. Butter and flour a 10-inch cake pan. Line with parchment.

Melt the chocolate with the liqueur or brandy and coffee. Transfer to a medium/large bowl and set aside to cool until lukewarm. In a stand mixer bowl over boiling water, whisk the eggs and sugar together until they are just warm. Then beat in the mixer until very pale and tripled in volume. Add a fourth of the egg mixture to the chocolate, then mix all the chocolate back into the egg. Fold in the flour, then fold in the stiffly beaten whipped cream.

Pour into the prepared cake pan. Place the cake pan in a larger pan. Pour water into the larger pan until it reaches about halfway up the sides of the cake pan. Bake 40 to 50 minutes until puffed and firm, but still moist. Remove the pan from the water bath and cool on a rack. Unmold to a plate or cardboard cake form and peel off the parchment paper. Then turn top side up. Before serving, slice into 12 pieces, but keep together. Reheat just before serving for 5 to 6 minutes to warm. Serve on a drizzle of caramel or raspberry or vanilla cream. A bit of whipped cream and some chocolate shavings are a nice finish.

Caramel Sauce

1 cup sugar

1 quart heavy cream

In a heavy 3-quart saucepan, melt the sugar to a golden brown. It will continue to cook and darken, so don't let it get too brown. Add the heavy cream. Be careful as the mixture will bubble up. Stir it down, then simmer it until it is reduced by half. Cool and put into a squirt bottle for drizzling under or over desserts.

The percentage number on a chocolate bar wrapper these days often states the proportion of the bar's weight that actually comes from the cacao bean. The rest is almost entirely sugar. So—the higher the number on the wrapper, the less sweet, more bitter and complex the flavor of the chocolate. Sweetness in a chocolate recipe can come from the sugar in the chocolate or from sugar called for as a separate ingredient. In dessert recipes that depend on an intense chocolate experience for their wow power, look for the very best chocolate you can find. Callebaut, available from kitchen stores and specialty shops, is great. Or Valrhona, or Scharffen Berger. Our range of choices has expanded dramatically in recent years.

{ For wow power, look for the very best chocolate you can find. }

Warm Chocolate Souffles

The perfect make-ahead souffle, light but rich, plus it holds well for serving. We also serve this with Caramel Sauce and Raspberry or Crème Anglaise.

1/4 cup melted butter (for coating cups)

1/4 cup sugar (also for coating cups)

4 ounces of bittersweet chocolate, in chunks

1/4 pound butter, in cubes

1/2 cup heavy cream

1/3 cup unsweetened cocoa powder,

    Dutch process if available

6 eggs, separated, plus the whites of 2 additional eggs

3 tablespoons Frangelico or Amaretto liqueur

1 teaspoon cream of tartar

1/4 cup sugar

8 small chunks of bittersweet chocolate

vanilla ice cream

Brush the inside of eight 6-ounce straight-sided souffle cups with melted butter and dust with a little sugar, coating the insides completely. Place on a sheet pan and set aside. Preheat the oven to 325°.

Melt the chocolate, butter and cream together in a double boiler (or heavy saucepan if you are careful not to burn). Transfer to a large mixing bowl. Sift the cocoa over the chocolate mixture, then whisk in well. Whisk in the 6 egg yolks, then the liqueur.

In a separate bowl, beat the 8 egg whites with the cream of tartar to soft peaks, then gradually add the sugar one tablespoon at a time. Fold egg whites gently into the chocolate mixture. Fill the individual souffle cups. Put a chunk of chocolate in each. The souffles may be held, refrigerated, up to 3 to 4 hours before baking.

Bake at 325° for 30 minutes or until just puffed. Turn out of the the souffle cups onto warm dessert plates, painted with a bit of warm Ganache (page 244) or Caramel Sauce (page 242). Add a tiny scoop of vanilla ice cream and serve immediately.

Ganache

2 cups heavy cream

4 tablespoons butter

1 pound bittersweet chocolate, in chunks

Heat the butter and cream together until very hot, almost boiling. Pour the butter-cream mixture over the chocolate chunks. Let rest a moment to heat through, then stir until fully melted and smooth. Serve warm for a nice glossy sauce.

Gifts from your kitchen. Ummm. . . How about jars of Butterscotch or Caramel Sauce, or Ganache? Or Honey-Rhubarb Sauce to top pancakes and waffles? Pie pastry, wrapped and chilled and tied up with a pretty ribbon, makes a quick hostess gift. Lemon-Almond Cake and Pumpkin Bread are always welcome. Vinaigrettes in a pretty bottle with a cork stopper and a hand-made "hang tag" are fun. Lemon Mint Jam, Serrano Mint Jam, and Ancho Mint Glaze all are good. Or a little container of your very own Demi-glace. Perhaps add an explanatory note with these gifts suggesting uses and whether to refrigerate, and maybe listing ingredients in case your friend may be sensitive to some.

BEN & JERRY'S

30 Community Drive
So. Burlington, VT 05403-6828

Made in the U.S.A.
Plant 50-95

USA
1224843

Lemon Tart

A simple home-style custard tart with wonderfully pure lemon flavor. Nice with a berry compote on the side.

FOR THE CRUST

3 cups all purpose unbleached flour

1 teaspoon salt

2 tablespoons sugar

12 tablespoons unsalted butter, cut in bits

    (6 ounces or 1 + 1/2 sticks)

10 tablespoons vegetable shortening

    (6 ounces; see shortening note, page 255)

1/4 cup cold water

1 tablespoon cider vinegar

FOR THE LEMON CUSTARD FILLING

6 eggs

1 egg yolk

1 cup sugar

zest of 1 lemon

1 cup heavy cream

1/2 cup lemon juice

1 teaspoon vanilla

1 scant teaspoon lemon extract

Combine flour, salt, and sugar in a medium bowl and whisk lightly to blend. Add butter and shortening, toss lightly to just coat the

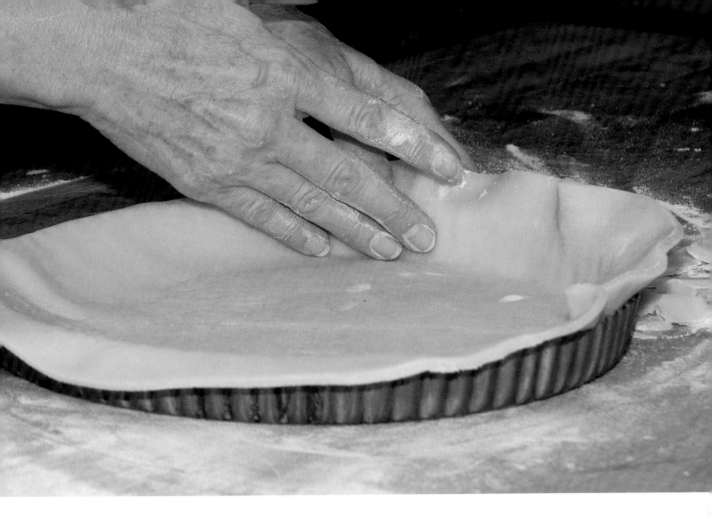

pieces, then cut in with pastry cutter until mixture appears like a very coarse meal. Some fat pieces will look like small beans. Mix water and vinegar together, then sprinkle about 3 tablespoons over the mixture and toss together to blend. Add another tablespoon, toss together to form a ball. You may need more water to have this come together into a cohesive ball, just add it a tablespoon at a time. Your dough should hold together when pressed, and it's better not to have it *too* dry. Form into 2 balls, flatten the balls into fattish discs, wrap, and chill at least 2 hours.

Roll out one piece of pastry and line a 10-inch removable-bottom tart pan as directed on page 253. Chill 5 minutes. Line the shell with foil and fill with dried beans, uncooked rice, or pie weights (the crust is very buttery and will puff). Bake at 375° for 15 minutes, then remove from the oven and remove the foil and beans.

Reduce the oven temperature to 325°.

In a medium bowl, whisk together the 6 eggs, the single yolk, the sugar, and zest of lemon. Blend well. Whisk in the cream, mixing well, then the lemon juice and extracts. Strain the mixture and pour into the warm shell. Bake for 15 to 20 minutes. Do not overbake! Cool on a rack for at least one hour before serving. Garnish with a small fluff of whipped cream and a sprig of mint if you like.

Ginger Shortcakes with Spiced Poached Fruit and Warm Vanilla Cream

FOR TEN TO TWELVE

Warm and delicious for the fall and winter.

FOR THE SHORTCAKE

3 cups unbleached all purpose flour

1 + 1/2 tablespoons baking powder

1 /4 teaspoon salt

1/2 cup sugar

1/4 cup finely chopped candied ginger

3 tablespoons shortening

3 tablespoons butter

1 + 1/2 cups heavy cream

Preheat the oven to 375°.

Combine the flour, baking powder, salt, sugar, and ginger in a medium bowl. Cut in the shortening and butter, then mix in the heavy cream with a wooden spoon until just combined. Turn out onto a lightly floured work surface and knead gently 3 or 4 strokes.

Pat out and or lightly roll out the dough till about an inch thick. Cut into 12 rounds or squares and place on a baking sheet lined with parchment. Brush with cream, then sprinkle with sugar. Bake until golden brown, about 10 to 12 minutes. Split when cool.

Assemble the shortcakes, spooning about a cup of the the warm fruit and juices between the top and bottom of each, then ladle a quarter cup of vanilla cream over the top.

Spiced Poached Fruit

3 cups dried fruit, a mix of currants, dried apricots, figs, prunes, and cranberries

1 cup simple syrup (1/2 cup sugar and 1/2 cup water, heated until the sugar dissolves)

1 cup of dryish white wine

1 large piece of orange peel

1/2 vanilla bean

1 cinnamon stick

1 + 1/2 cups sliced apples

1 + 1/2 cups sliced pears, skin on

2 tablespoons butter

2 tablespoons sugar

Poach the dried fruit in the wine, simple syrup and spices for 15 to 20 minutes to soften and marry the flavors. Sauté the apples and pears in the butter and sugar, then add to the poached fruit.

Warm Vanilla Cream

1 quart heavy cream

1 split vanilla bean

1/2 cup sugar

In a heavy 3-quart saucepan, reduce the cream with the vanilla bean and sugar by a third. Watch carefully and stir down occasionally or the cream will boil up and over. Scrape the soft insides of the bean into the cream and whisk in; remove the husk, rinse, and set aside to dry. (This costly discard can be used to flavor granulated or powdered sugar. Put it in a jar with the sugar, shake, and set aside in the pantry.)

Apple Pie

FOR TEN TO TWELVE

The essential Lodge dessert. Sometimes we add a third of a cup of currants or dried cranberries to this, although often it's best to leave well enough alone.

pastry for double-crust pie (page 252)

1 teaspooon cinnamon

1/2 teaspoon nutmeg

1/3 cup cornstarch

1 +1/4 cups sugar

6 to 7 cups apples, approximately 6 medium large
   apples, peeled, cored, and sliced

2 teaspoons vanilla extract

about 2 tablespoons cold butter, in bits

Make the pie pastry and allow it to chill in the refrigerator while preparing the fruit filling. Preheat the oven to 400°.

Mix the spices, cornstarch, and sugar. Add the apples and vanilla, and toss to combine. Roll out one disk of pastry and fit into a 10-inch pie pan. Pour the filling into the pastry shell and dot with butter. Roll out the top crust, then lay over the fruit. Trim and crimp the edges lightly.

Make 4 one-inch slices in the top crust, sort of "north, south, east and west," to release steam while baking, and sprinkle to top of the pie evenly with a few teaspoonfuls of sugar.

Bake at 400° for 10 minutes, then lower the oven temperature to 350° and bake 40 minutes more, or until golden brown.

ABOUT APPLE VARIETIES

Different apple varieties ripen at different times. Garland's has purposely cultivated an assortment of antique apple varieties that have unique characteristics. The earliest include Gravenstein, Macintosh, and Grimes Golden, then come Pippins and Jonathans. Golden Delicious and Stayman Winesaps ripen later and carry us to the end of the season. If you don't have an apple orchard out your back door, our favorite "store apples" are Granny Smiths and Fujis. Of course we are very proud of our organic, tree ripened fruit, and believe it more flavorful than most commercially available varieties.

MAGIC BEANS?

We use dried beans (from a bin of them dedicated to the purpose) to keep pie pastry from puffing during pre-baking. One day an inexperienced young waitress was watching Amanda fill pie shells with beans. "Is that dessert?" she asked. Amanda said Yes. Later that evening the pie was plated for dessert. The waitress was utterly astonished. "Wow!" she exclaimed. "How did those beans turn into that pie?"

Garland's Apple Tart

This is sort of a basic Dutch apple tart but somehow we started calling it "Garland's" to separate it from the classic double crust apple pie. It's a communication thing between cooks.

FOR THE CRUST

3 cups all purpose unbleached flour

1 teaspoon salt

2 tablespoons sugar

12 tablespoons unsalted butter, cut in bits

   (6 ounces or 1 + 1/2 sticks)

10 tablespoons vegetable shortening

   (6 ounces; see shortening note on page 255)

1/4 cup cold water

1 tablespoon cider vinegar

FOR THE FILLING

1 cups sour cream

3/4 cup sugar

2 tablespoons unbleached flour

1/2 teaspoon salt

2 teaspoons vanilla

1 teaspoon cinnamon

1 egg

4 large cooking apples, peeled and sliced 1/4 inch
   thick (5 medium apples; Grannies, Jonathans,
   Romes, Macintoshs are good choices)

FOR THE STREUSEL

3/4 cup flour

1 cup brown sugar

1/2 cup butter, cold, in cubes

Make the crust: Combine dry ingredients in a medium bowl, whisk lightly to blend. Add butter and shortening, toss lightly to just coat the pieces, then cut in with pastry cutter until mixture appears like a very coarse meal. Some fat pieces will look like small beans.

Mix water and vinegar together, then sprinkle about 3 tablespoons over the mixture, toss together to blend. Add another tablespoon,

toss together to form a ball. You may need more water to have this come together into a cohesive ball, just add it a tablespoon at a time. Your dough should hold together when pressed, and it's better to not have it *too* dry. Form into 2 balls, flatten the balls into fattish discs, wrap and chill, at least 2 hours. This is necessary to rest and relax the gluten in the flour and completely chill all the fats in the mixture.

Make the filling: Whisk sour cream, sugar, flour, salt, vanilla, cinnamon, and egg together until very smooth. Add apple slices to bowl, mix in gently and well, set aside while preparing the tart shell.

Prepare and bake the crust: Preheat oven to 375°. Divide dough into 2 pieces. Roll out one piece on a lightly floured surface to approximately an eighth to a quarter inch in thickness. Trim edges into a large circle. Fold dough in half gently, transfer to a 10-inch shallow fluted removable bottom tart pan. Place over half the pan, then unfold the dough, pressing in the bottom and sides to fit cleanly. With kitchen shears cut the excess edge of the dough, leaving a scant one-third inch above the rim of the pan. Simply fold this down slightly, so it sits on the edge of the pan. Place pan in the freezer for 5 minutes.

Take the other piece of dough, press it gently into a disc, wrap it very well and freeze for another use. Or you can roll it out now, fit it into a pie or tart pan, wrap and freeze for later.

Make the streusel: Combine flour and brown sugar in food processor. Pulse to blend. Add butter cubes, pulse to cut in butter until a coarse meal is formed. Transfer to a small bowl.

Take tart shell from the freezer. Spoon in the apples, spreading them evenly, then scrape in any additional sauce that's left in the bowl.

Bake in the lower third of the oven for 20 to 25 minutes, until the filling is just beginning to set. Pull from the oven and spread streusel over the apples, taking care to cover completely but within the rim of pastry. Place back in the oven, lower the temperature to 350° and continue baking until a lovely deep golden brown, 20 to 30 minutes more.

Cool on a rack for 30 minutes before cutting into 12 wedges. Serve with vanilla ice cream.

This tart can be made with pears with great results and I've also used peaches for a wonderful summer dessert. The pastry freezes very well. It's really best to make a few batches, wrap in discs and freeze.

{ Why do we need so many kinds of apples? Because there are so many kinds of folks. There is merit in variety itself. — Liberty Hyde Bailey, *The Apple Tree* (1922) }

Pumpkin Pie

FOR TEN TO TWELVE

Mario, our gardener, scours seed catalogs in the dead of winter, planting tender seedlings out around the middle of May. Sugar pumpkins are one of the vegetables we have come to prize. Much smaller and more tender fleshed than traditional Jack O'Lantern pumpkins, they make a truly superior pie, and are a festive fall decoration lined up on the kitchen window sill.

pastry for pie (page 252)

4 eggs

1 scant teaspoon vanilla

1/2 cup brown sugar

1/2 cup white sugar

1/2 teaspoon salt

just a pinch black pepper

1 scant teaspoon ginger

1/2 teaspoon cinnamon

1/2 teaspoon nutmeg

1/4 teaspoon cloves

2 medium sugar pumpkins, enough
    to make 2 + 1/2 cups fresh pumpkin purée

2 cups heavy cream

Make the pie pastry and chill, while preparing the filling.

For the pumpkin purée: Cut the sugar pumpkin(s) in half and remove the seeds. Bake flesh side down in a baking pan with a cup of water, tightly covered with foil, about 30 minutes. When cool enough to handle, peel the skin off the halves and purée the pumpkin flesh in a food processor. Measure out 2 + 1/2 cups, saving the remainder for another day.

Line the pie tin with pastry dough, crimping the edges. Chill while you prepare the filling. Preheat the oven to 400°.

Beat the eggs and sugars, then add the pumpkin and spices and finally the cream. Pour into the unbaked pie shell. Bake at 400° for 10 minutes; lower to 350° and bake 30 minutes more until just set. Cool before slicing. Serve with a dollop of lightly sweetened whipped cream

Fall Nut Tart

A wonderful, not-too-sweet tart that's just a perfect addition to the Thanksgiving sideboard.

TART SHELL

3 cups all purpose unbleached flour

1 teaspoon salt

2 tablespoons sugar

12 tablespoons unsalted butter, cut in bits
    (6 ounces or 1 + 1/2 sticks)

10 tablespoons vegetable shortening (6 ounces)

1/4 cup cold water

1 tablespoon cider vinegar

FOR THE FILLING

1/4 pound butter, melted

2 + 1/4 cups mixed nuts: pinons, cashews, slivered
    almonds, chopped hazelnuts, pecans

4 eggs

1/2 cup sugar

1/3 cup maple syrup

1/3 cup corn syrup

1 + 1/2 teaspoons vanilla

1/4 teaspoon salt

1/3 cup heavy cream

1/4 cup bourbon

To make the tart shell: Mix the flour, salt and sugar in a bowl. Cut in the butter and shortening. Combine the water and vinegar and add all at once to the flour mixture. Chill completely before rolling out the dough. See page 253 for more detailed instruction. Roll out, then carefully place in a 10-inch tart pan with a removable bottom. Chill, unbaked, while you prepare the other ingredients. Preheat the oven to 400°.

Melt the butter, then sauté the mixed nuts for a few minutes. In a mixing bowl, whisk the eggs and sugar together. Whisk in the nuts and butter and the other ingredients. Pour into the chilled tart shell. Bake at 400° for 10 minutes. Lower the oven to 350° and bake 20 to 25 minutes more until set. Cool completely before slicing. Garnish with whipped cream or a small scoop of vanilla ice cream.

Regarding shortening... We use shortening in our all purpose pie pastry for the flakiness and handling ability it gives. My preference is to use leaf lard for this with the butter, and I do sometimes when I'm making a double crust pie. However, with so many vegetarians and people with other special dietary needs coming as guests to the Lodge, I think it's safer to use shortening. We now know that shortening, of course, contains unhealthful trans fats, so Crisco has come out with a "no trans fat" version. I've used it at the Lodge and used it for testing for this book. It works just fine.
If you're comfortable using all butter for pastry, by all means use it. It gives an entirely different crust and one that we use often for certain tarts or croustades, but not pies.

Pear Frangipane Tart

FOR TWELVE

A classic French tart, also good made with apples in place of the pears.

FOR THE CRUST

3 cups all purpose unbleached flour

1 teaspoon salt

2 tablespoons sugar

12 tablespoons unsalted butter, cut in bits

    (6 ounces or 1 + 1/2 sticks)

10 tablespoons vegetable shortening (6 ounces)

1/4 cup cold water

1 tablespoon cider vinegar

FOR THE FRANGIPANE CREAM

1 cup butter

1 cup sugar (set aside 1/2 cup to grind

    with the almonds)

2 eggs

2 egg yolks

2 cups finely ground blanched almonds

3/4 cup flour

1 teaspoon vanilla extract

1/4 teaspoon almond extract

3 medium pears, peeled, cored and sliced 1/4 inch thick

1 cup strained apricot jam

Make the tart shell. Mix the dry ingredients in a bowl. Cut in the butter and shortening. Mix the wet ingredients and add all at once to the dry. Chill completely before rolling out the dough. See page 252 for more detailed instruction. Roll out, then carefully place in a 10-inch tart pan with a removable bottom.

Chill, unbaked,while you prepare the other ingredients. Preheat the oven to 400°.

Make the filling: Cream the butter and half a cup of the sugar together, then add the eggs and yolks. Mix well. Grind the almonds with the remaining half cup sugar in the food processor. Add the almonds, flour, and extracts to the butter and eggs; beat together until very light and fluffy.

Spread the filling in the unbaked tart shell. Arrange the sliced pears in a pinwheel, pressing them into the frangipane.

Bake for 12 minutes at 400°, then lower the oven to 350° and bake 25 minutes more, until puffed and very lightly browned. Glaze with the strained apricot jam. Cool before slicing. Heat just slightly if desired before serving with whipped cream.

In spring you may want to substitute sliced strawberries for the pears. Sometimes we cover the top of the cooled tart with a thin layer of Ganache (page 244). Allow to set before slicing. This is really fabulous.

Ibarra Flan

FOR TWELVE

A great little custard and a natural with Filet with Ancho Chile Cream. These unmold best if made the day before and refrigerated overnight, which allows time for the caramel to melt completely .

FOR THE CARAMEL

1 + 1/2 cups sugar

1/4 cup water

1/4 cup corn syrup

1/2 teaspoon lemon juice

2 + 1/2 cups whole milk

2 + 1/2 cups heavy cream

8 ounces bittersweet chocolate

8 egg yolks

4 whole eggs

3 tablespoons sugar

1/4 teaspoon salt

2 teaspoons vanilla extract

1/4 teaspoon almond extract

1/2 teaspoon cinnamon

First make the caramel: combine the sugar, water, corn syrup and lemon juice in a heavy saucepan. Boil until a medium golden brown. Pour into the bottom of ungreased individual soufflé dishes. Set aside to cool.

Preheat the oven to 325°. Heat the milk and heavy cream together. Melt the chocolate in a large double boiler or in the microwave. (If you are using the microwave, be sure to use a microwave-safe bowl and melt in short increments of 30 to 45 seconds, testing after each. When beginning to soften, the chocolate may retain its shape, so stir gently after each stage of melting.) Add one cup of the heated cream, whisk until smooth, and set aside.

Whisk the yolks, eggs, and sugar together. Add the salt, extracts, and cinnamon, the chocolate mixture, and then the rest of the warmed cream, whisking together until smooth.

Strain and pour into the individual dishes. Bake in a water bath, covered with foil, for about 32 minutes, then check for set. Bake 5 to 8 more minutes or just until the centers are barely set. The chocolate makes for a firmer set than other custards.

Acknowledgments and thanks

Boundless thanks to Carol Haralson, our book designer, without whom this book would still be a fantasy. Her design saavy, careful editing, and gentle prodding have been essential.

And to Paula Jansen, our photographer, for her long commutes from Salt Lake, and the energy and joy she brought to the project.

This book is also a gesture of thanks and a tribute to our guests, for their loyalty, support and friendship over the last 30-some years.

Annie Hunter and The Hummingbird House in Sedona generously loaned Vietri dishes, beautiful linens, and miscellaneous props for our photo shoot. Ken Heflin, Jim Bullock, and Samyo Shannon of Show-stoppers constructed the wonderful garland over the front door. Al and Helen Wolfe, Blake Spaulding, and Jen Castle of Hell's Backbone Grill offered invaluable marketing advice.

Special thanks to Judith and Neil Morgan, who "put us on the map" with their wonderful columns and travel articles over the years.

A huge debt of gratitude is owed our present staff: Denise Wright, our calm and competent office manager, who keeps all the reservations in order, a huge job; Cookie Carpenter, cheerfully carrying on the breakfast tradition; Christopher Lane, gifted slam poet and breakfast server; Rogelio Delgado, who has been with us for 12 seasons; Rogelio's brother, Antonio, breakfast dish and kitchen prep for 8 years; and yet another brother, Pablo, who has been here for six years. They are all bright, hard-working, steady, and stalwart. Antonio's wife, Yesi, and Sylvia Lopez conscientiously keep the cabins clean. Mario Valeruz, organic gardener extraordinaire, and Robert Mertis who tends the orchard and presses the cider. Donald Zealand, our dining room manager and "sommelier." His able staff includes the incredibly hard-working Pam Ing-Dobrota, Marcy Ketcham who also doubles as flower gardener and yoga teacher, Mary Nunn and Jenny Greenway. Every team needs pinch

hitters, and Roberto Montes and Stacy Rivera have been ours. Stabo (Steve Hosmer) and Jeff Stevens support Amanda daily in the kitchen. Bill Huber deserves a category all his own. He has washed dishes here for 15 years to sustain his true love, playing and coaching golf and basketball. Special mention to Will Garland for his years at the noble job of Lodge recycling.

Thanks for the gifted hands of our local masseuses and masseurs, Rhonda Peck, Alba Wejebe, Ushii and Caroline Masset, John and Ann Conway and Deena Beckvold, aesthetician, who literally and figuratively go out of their way to make our guests feel good. And to Garielle Drumm, who started yoga classes on the orchard lawn, which inspired our beautiful creekside pavilion.

And then there are the babysitters: Cookie, Michelle, Shannon et al.

And to all those "troops" who came before. . . The Lodge would not be what it is without each and every one of them. Special thanks to Rico Nersesian, whose wonderful sense of taste and years of experience took an already great breakfast menu to new heights. Other noteworthy breakfast chefs included Marcia Kortas, who added so many great dishes, Judy Raymond with her sweet voice, then Linda Bergh, who brought wonderful Southwestern flavors to our menus. "Big Dave" Daniels, "Little Dave" Seabrook, Stephen Benedict, Dan Garland in the earliest days, and now Daniel "Junior."

Susan Garland established the Lodge's reputation for great food, with the help of Mark "Tut" Warlick and Peter Formosa, assistants Jenny DeVaney, Debbie Pritchard, and Shirley Ward, a.k.a. Nettie Clark. Sue Orth and Marianne Banes ably took the helm for a year before Amanda's arrival.

Assistants to Amanda included Shirley Ward, Debbie Lane, Mishabe Mahoney, Kay Daniels Davis, Noel Cox Caniglia, Lynn Nordby, Mike Brosnahan, Christie Helm, Rae Hebert, Jodi Christian, Phil Smith, Guy Ferrantini, Jim Piotter, Martha Clark, Bridget Kearsey, and Lindsey Riibe. Each of them contributed to tne Lodge repertoire.

And to special friends who came as employees, leaving to become lifelong compadres—Mary Fontaine, Nora Daley, Geoffrey Worssam, and Forest Hunter. Rainy

Lautze, Mari Pattison, Michael Urciuoli and Lynn Mikula are still remembered fondly by guests. Lodge gardens bear the imprint of John McArthur, David Adix, and Mitchell Foudray. Breakfast and dinner servers, and other staff too numerous to mention, hold a place in our hearts as well.

Building and remodeling projects required the skills of many: Dave Blauert, architects Max Licher and Mike Bower, Tommy Caniglia, Rob Lautze, Mario Valeruz, Pat "Joker" Lynch, Jock McCoy, Jack McNamara, Greg "Gumball" Faris, Reed Thorne, Randy Plapp, Scott Martin, Morgan Stine, Jim Preston, Bob Carlson, Bob Moulinier, Doug Howland, Ron Olsen, and Bob Wright.

Amanda would especially like to thank Stabo for all his support and friendship through the years and for covering for her while she worked on this project. She also says, "Much gratitude to Drs. Todd Lewis, Jeff Christenson, and Jim Loomis for pulling me through those dark days in December of 2000. Also to Jim and Connie Claybaugh, Pat Loomis, Teresa Caughey, Kristina Price and of course, Mary and Gary. Thanks for keeping me around! To my dear friend, Donald Zealand, thank you for our Border Collies, Maggie and Peggy, and all you do for me. A huge thank you and hugs to my family, Dan and Nora Neveau, Christopher, Matthew, and Danielle; our wonderful kids Kendra Stine Johnson and Ian Stine, who always bring joy to our lives. To my incredible mother, Ginger Renner, whose love, spirit and wisdom are always with me. Last and most importantly to me, my husband Morgan, for his complete support and love through all my endeavors."

Mary would like to thank "the extended Garland family for all their love and support. Also my dad, Robert Lautze, the Lodge's accountant, and his wife Patty, whose annual visits during tax season remind us to count our blessings. Ranking high on the blessings list are my siblings Karen Cleary, Susie Savino, and Steve Lautze, and my 'Arizona brother' Rob Lautze, who put his heart and soul into the orchard. And deepest thanks to Gary and to our sons, Ted and Will Garland, who have kept us grounded in what is truly important."

Index